Teach Yourself VISUALLY™

Knitting Design

Working from a Master Pattern to Fashion Your Own Knits

Visual®

by Sharon Turner

BICENTENNIAL
1807
WILEY
2007
BICENTENNIAL

Wiley Publishing, Inc.

Library of Congress Control Number: 2006926291

ISBN: 978-0-470-06817-5

Printed in the United States of America

10 9 8 7 6 5 4 3

Book production by Wiley Publishing, Inc., Composition Services

Praise for the Teach Yourself VISUALLY Series

I just had to let you and your company know how great I think your books are. I just purchased my third Visual book (my first two are dog-eared now!) and, once again, your product has surpassed my expectations. The expertise, thought, and effort that go into each book are obvious, and I sincerely appreciate your efforts. Keep up the wonderful work!

—*Tracey Moore (Memphis, TN)*

I have several books from the Visual series and have always found them to be valuable resources.

—*Stephen P. Miller (Ballston Spa, NY)*

Thank you for the wonderful books you produce. It wasn't until I was an adult that I discovered how I learn—visually. Although a few publishers out there claim to present the material visually, nothing compares to Visual books. I love the simple layout. Everything is easy to follow. And I understand the material! You really know the way I think and learn. Thanks so much!

—*Stacey Han (Avondale, AZ)*

Like a lot of other people, I understand things best when I see them visually. Your books really make learning easy and life more fun.

—*John T. Frey (Cadillac, MI)*

I am an avid fan of your Visual books. If I need to learn anything, I just buy one of your books and learn the topic in no time. Wonders! I have even trained my friends to give me Visual books as gifts.

—*Illona Bergstrom (Aventura, FL)*

I write to extend my thanks and appreciation for your books. They are clear, easy to follow, and straight to the point. Keep up the good work! I bought several of your books and they are just right! No regrets! I will always buy your books because they are the best.

—*Seward Kollie (Dakar, Senegal)*

Credits

Acquisitions Editor
Pam Mourouzis

Project Editor
Kitty Wilson Jarrett

Technical Editor
Kristi Porter

Editorial Manager
Christina Stambaugh

Publisher
Cindy Kitchel

Vice President and Executive Publisher
Kathy Nebenhaus

Interior Design
Kathie Rickard
Elizabeth Brooks

Cover Design
José Almaguer

Photography
Matt Bowen

Photographic Assistant
Andrew Hanson

Illustrator
Cynthia Frenette

Special Thanks...

To the following companies for providing the yarn for the projects shown in this book:

- elann.com (www.elann.com)
- Muench Yarns (www.muenchyarns.com)
- Cascade Yarns (www.cascadeyarns.com)
- Plymouth Yarn Company (www.plymouthyarn.com)
- Brown Sheep Yarns (www.brownsheep.com)

About the Author

Sharon Turner designs knitwear and publishes a line of knitting patterns under the trademark Monkeysuits. She is the author of *Monkeysuits: Sweaters and More to Knit for Kids* and *Teach Yourself VISUALLY Knitting.* Sharon lives in Brooklyn, New York, with her husband and three daughters.

Acknowledgments

Thank you always to my dear family. For helping with the knitting, many, many thanks go to Kitty Jarrett, Pam Mourouzis, Cindy Kitchel, and Kristen Balouch. Ann Cannon-Brown, of elann.com, and Kirstin Muench, of Muench Yarns, enthusiastically supplied a lot of the beautiful yarns used for the swatches and projects. My compliments and gratitude go out to the models—Alison Andrews, Will Bown, Julie Bubp, Keira Cerda, Andrea Cofield, Katie Doogan, Kaleb Wagoner, and Sarah Wilson—who generously gave their smiles and time. Thanks also to Matt Bowen for the photography and Kristi Porter for her technical expertise. It was truly a pleasure to work again with Pam Mourouzis, Kitty Jarrett, Christina Stambaugh, and Cindy Kitchel, whose wisdom, patience, and willingness to pick up the knitting slack are seemingly infinite. (I can't thank you all enough!)

Table of Contents

chapter 1 Getting Started Designing Knits

chapter 2 Scarves and Shawls

 **Hats**

 **Bags**

chapter 5 Socks

chapter 6 Mittens, Gloves, and Hand Warmers

chapter 7 **Vests**

chapter 8 **Sweaters**

chapter 9 Altering the Master Patterns

chapter 10 Designing Your Own Knits

1

Getting Started Designing Knits

Some knitters like to follow patterns down to the last detail, without making any changes. Many other knitters like to alter patterns: They choose a different yarn than a pattern specifies, omit a collar, use an alternate stitch pattern, or add embellishments. This book provides a wealth of modifiable knitting patterns and helps you understand how to create your own unique knit designs.

Using this book to design your own knits is easy: You simply choose an item and a yarn, and then you select from the various master patterns for scarves, shawls, hats, bags, socks, mittens, gloves, vests, or sweaters. The master patterns include instructions for a wide range of sizes and gauges. Particular yarns are not specified, but yarns for the sample projects are listed, in case you want to replicate them.

A large part of knitting design is math; this book does most of the math for you, allowing you to focus on the fun of choosing colors, stitch patterns, and embellishments. Once you've followed a few of the master patterns through, you'll have a good understanding of how hand-knits are designed and constructed. When you're ready to depart from the master pattern and do your own math and invent your own hand-knits, you can consult Chapter 10 for design guidance. Pretty soon, the only things you'll need to start a knitting project will be a few balls of yarn, a pair of knitting needles, and your imagination.

Using the Master Patterns

Have you ever found a pattern that you liked in size and shaping, but you didn't like the yarn weight or the stitch pattern? Or perhaps on impulse you bought a beautiful yarn, but you have no pattern to suit it. Or maybe you want to experiment with designing your own knits, but you have no idea where to begin. With the help of the master patterns in this book, you can learn to alter an existing pattern, use that beautiful yarn, or create your very own designs.

One Master Pattern, Many Options

You may have seen a cookbook that presents a master recipe, followed by ways to change the recipe to create whole new dishes. In this book, the master pattern functions in the same way. Materials specifications, stitch counts, and, in some cases, shaping instructions appear in the master pattern, and alternate shaping, finishing, edging, and stitch patterns accompany it. You can easily design your own knits by choosing the various options you'd like to put together. For example, you start with the same basic pattern to create a pair of mittens or a pair of gloves. You choose a size, find the appropriate directions for the yarn you're using, and then select from a number of cuff options, stitch patterns, and embellishments to make your mittens or gloves uniquely yours.

The master patterns allow you to learn to create your own unique styles without having to tackle too much complicated math. Each master pattern contains instructions and specifications for *at least* three gauges. The master hat pattern, for example, covers six gauges. Combine that with numerous brim styles, crown-shaping options, and embellishments, and you have an infinite array of options. If you're feeling adventurous, you can go beyond using the various options suggested in the master pattern: You can incorporate color work, cables, or textured stitch patterns into your design by referring to the stitch pattern glossary at the back of the book.

How to Use the Master Patterns

You may have come across some old-fashioned knitting books that use charts and tables instead of long strings of text to present the information you need to knit the items. The master patterns in this book combine the two approaches, using both written steps and tables.

Your first step in using a master pattern is to make some choices. Each pattern in this book includes a wide array of options. For every item, you can choose from many yarn weights, hem treatments, shaping options, and decorative details. After you decide on a pattern—along with shaping and styling preferences—and you are equipped with the appropriate yarn, knitting needles, and other supplies, you need to make and measure a gauge swatch. When your gauge is correct according to the instructions, you can begin.

The instructions for each item are presented in numbered steps, accompanied, where necessary, by tables like the one here. Various hems, brims, ribbings, shaping methods, or stitch patterns are labeled and presented in isolated sections. All you have to do is follow the instructions for your style choice and at the same time follow the information presented in the tables, according to your gauge and size.

Cast On	
Gauge	*No. of Sts to Cast On*
2 sts/in.	28 (32, 36, 40, 44)
3 sts/in.	42 (48, 54, 60, 66)
4 sts/in.	56 (64, 72, 80, 88)
5 sts/in.	70 (80, 90, 100, 110)
6 sts/in.	84 (96, 108, 120, 132)
7 sts/in.	98 (112, 126, 140, 154)

For example, the table above shows how many stitches to cast on to create a hat with a brim that is 14 (16, 18, 20, 22) inches in circumference. Say that you want to design a hat for a toddler who needs a hat about 16 inches around, using yarn that knits to a gauge of 5 stitches per inch. In the table, you'd go to the 5 sts/in. row and then find the number that corresponds to the second-smallest size. You would therefore cast on 80 stitches. Then, you would follow the directions for the brim style and top shaping options you choose.

TIP

Keeping Track of Where You Are

Before you begin knitting, you might want to photocopy the pages of the master pattern you're using and then highlight or circle all the numbers that apply to your size and all the options you intend to use for your design.

Choosing the Right Yarn

The yarn you choose for your project should not only match the pattern in gauge and function but also in feel, or what is known as *hand*. Some yarns knit to a stiff fabric, and other fibers work to a soft drape. Always choose a yarn that you like on its own; you will be spending hours knitting with it, and it's easy to lose interest in a project if you don't like the yarn.

FIBER FOLLOWS FUNCTION

Be sure to select a fiber or fiber blend that is appropriate for the garment's function. For example, you would probably not knit mittens out of cotton since cotton won't keep your hands warm on a cold winter day. Socks and slippers require yarn that maintains elasticity so that they don't immediately stretch out and lose shape. Yarns such as cotton, linen, alpaca, and mohair have little elasticity, so they might not be the best choices for socks.

It is possible to alter and in some cases improve particular characteristics of a fiber by combining it with another fiber. For instance, adding acrylic can improve the body and elasticity of cotton, and alpaca or cashmere can be mixed with wool for added softness. So be sure to consider fiber blends in choosing your yarn.

CHOOSE YARN THAT FEELS RIGHT

In addition to considering a yarn's gauge and the garment's function, you should choose yarn that has the appropriate feel, or *hand*, for your project. A soft shawl with a lot of drape will not work in wool that knits to a stiff and scratchy fabric. If the item is going to touch your skin, be sure it is soft and not itchy. Hand-knit bags sometimes require a firm, tight fabric. You can achieve this by choosing a dense and tightly spun yarn or by using a needle a few sizes smaller than the yarn calls for. Take lots of time to experiment with gauge swatches before making your choice.

THE RIGHT YARN FOR THE STITCH PATTERN

Stitch pattern also affects yarn choice. If you're working an item in seed stitch, intricate cables, lace patterns, or detailed color work, you'll probably want to choose yarn that has crisp and clear stitch definition. All that detail will be lost in an overly fuzzy yarn. However, using a fuzzy yarn is a good opportunity to work in a basic stitch, like garter or stockinette, to let the yarn carry the show. Inelastic yarns—containing nylon or linen, for example—can be difficult to work in textured stitch patterns that use decreases to create bobbles and knots; choose a fiber that has a fair amount of stretch for that purpose. Stitch patterns can also get lost in space-dyed or multicolored yarns, so save such novelty yarns for simpler stitch patterns. Always test your stitch pattern on the yarn you plan to use before jumping into the project.

STANDARD YARN WEIGHTS, GAUGE RANGES, AND RECOMMENDED NEEDLE SIZES

Yarn comes in many thicknesses and is generally labeled— from thinnest to thickest—as fingering, sport, double knitting, worsted weight, bulky, and super bulky. You may come across variations within these categories, as well, such as lace weight, light worsted, Aran weight, heavy worsted, and chunky. These descriptions vary greatly from one manufacturer to the next and from one designer to the next. The table below, based on information from the Craft Yarn Council of America's website, www.yarnstandards.com, gives you a more precise idea of the gauge ranges within which these yarn weights fall, as well as the range of needle and crochet hook sizes recommended for each weight.

Fingering

Sport

Double knitting

Worsted weight

Bulky

Super bulky

Standard Yarn Weight System				
Yarn Weight Category Name	Type of Yarns in Category	Knit Gauge Range* in Stockinette Stitch to 4 Inches	Recommended Needle, in Metric Size Range	Recommended Needle, in U.S. Size Range
Super fine	Sock, fingering, baby	27–32 sts	2.25–3.25 mm	1–3
Fine	Sport, baby	23–26 sts	3.25–3.75 mm	3–5
Light	DK, light worsted	21–24 sts	3.75–4.5 mm	5–7
Medium	Worsted, afghan, Aran	16–20 sts	4.5–5.5 mm	7–9
Bulky	Chunky, craft, rug	12–15 sts	5.5–8 mm	9–11
Super bulky	Bulky, roving	6–11 sts	8 mm and larger	11 and larger

* The gauges listed are guidelines only; this table reflects the most commonly used gauges and needle sizes for specific yarn categories.

Check Your Gauge

After you've chosen the right fiber for your project, you're ready to check your gauge. Before starting any knitting project, you should make a swatch to ensure that you are knitting to the desired gauge. Making a gauge swatch takes only a few minutes, and it can save you from spending hours on an item that ends up too big or too small.

Making a Gauge Swatch

To make a gauge swatch, you need to use the yarn and needle size, and in some cases the stitch pattern, that the pattern calls for. It's not a bad idea to have handy three pairs of needles: the size called for, the next size smaller, and the next size larger. (If you don't use them for this project, you will need them someday for another project.)

1 Cast on the same number of stitches that the pattern says is equal to 4 inches.

2 Work in stockinette stitch (knit on the right side and purl on the wrong side) until the swatch is 4 inches long (measuring from the cast-on edge to the bottom of the needle).

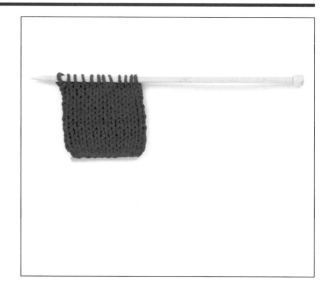

3 Bind off your stitches somewhat loosely, cut the working yarn (leaving about a 6-inch tail), and pull the tail through the last stitch.

Measuring a Gauge Swatch

You can use a ruler, a tape measure, or a stitch and needle gauge tool to measure your swatch. Also, if your gauge swatch is curly and won't lie flat, and if your yarn's care instructions allow, take a warm steam iron to the swatch, pressing only lightly. Let it cool and dry.

① Lay your swatch on a flat surface. Place your measuring device so that the first 2 inches are centered horizontally (and vertically, if you're using the stitch and needle gauge tool) on the swatch.

② Count how many stitches there are in a horizontal 2-inch space and how many rows there are in a vertical 2-inch space.

③ Divide these numbers by 2, and that is the number of stitches and rows you are getting *per inch.*

④ If your pattern lists gauge as a certain number of stitches and rows over 4 inches, multiply your stitch and row counts for 2 inches by 2.

Note: *If your gauge measurement includes a fraction of a stitch, include that in your gauge estimate. For example, if the 2-inch section of your swatch results in 8.5 stitches, your gauge is 4.25 sts/inch, or 17 sts/4 inches.*

FAQ

What should I do if my gauge is different from the one listed in the pattern?

If you are getting more stitches per 4 inches than the pattern calls for, try switching to a needle that is one size larger. If you are getting fewer stitches per 4 inches than the pattern calls for, try switching to a needle that is one size smaller. Make a new gauge swatch and measure again. If necessary, go up or down another needle size, create a new swatch, and measure it again.

It is difficult to match both stitch and row gauge, but it is most important to match the stitch gauge accurately. If the row gauge is slightly off, follow the garment's vertical measurements rather than the specified row counts.

2

Scarves and Shawls

Scarves and shawls, though simple in shape, can encompass many styles. They range from practical warmth-providing garments to decorative accessories. The possibilities are endless: You can showcase a special novelty yarn, experiment with a complicated stitch pattern, or simply knit a plain scarf or shawl in the warmest, softest fiber you can find. You can experiment with edgings, pompoms, tassels, and fringe to create your own unique design.

When making scarves, you don't have to worry about shaping or gauge. Many scarves are knit in reversible patterns—patterns that look good on both the right and wrong sides. Just about any pattern—openwork, textured stitches, cables—will work, though. Try using one of the three stitch patterns show-cased in this chapter or turn to Appendix B for inspiration in design-ing your own scarf.

KNIT END TO END

Most scarves are knit end to end, meaning that you work a small number of stitches for many rows, until the scarf is the desired length. This is a good method for scarves featuring cables and complex openwork because you keep track of stitches over a short row.

KNIT LENGTHWISE

You can knit scarves the long way, casting on a lot of stitches and working back and forth in rows on a long circular needle. This method is good for simple stitch patterns that are easy to keep track of while knitting or for stripes that run the length of the scarf. It is not recommended for lacy yarn-over patterns or complex stitch patterns: If you make a mistake, it can be difficult to count back to the problem over so many stitches per row. To work a scarf this way, you first determine the length of the scarf. You check your gauge in the desired stitch pattern and then multiply the scarf length by the number of stitches per inch you achieved in the gauge swatch. You cast on that many stitches and work until the scarf is the desired width.

Scarf: Master Pattern

The three scarves pictured in this chapter are worked in different stitch patterns, with instructions included for each in three gauges. If your gauge doesn't match exactly to one of the choices here, don't worry. Simply cast on the number of stitches specified for the nearest gauge and knit in the stitch pattern of your choice to the desired length. Your scarf will be slightly narrower or wider than the dimensions given.

You might want to use larger needles than your yarn label specifies to ensure that your scarf is not too stiff and dense to hang comfortably.

Specifications

DIMENSIONS
56 inches long or desired length × varying widths

MATERIALS
Desired yarn, in the amount specified in Table 1

1 pair needles in size needed to obtain desired drape

Tapestry needle

Pompom maker (optional)

2-inch × 3-inch cardboard for tassel (optional)

Crochet hook to suit your yarn thickness (optional)

CONTINUED ON NEXT PAGE

Table 1. Approximate Yardage for Scarf	
Gauge (in Stockinette Stitch)	*Approximate Yardage*
2 sts/in.	125–200 yd.
4 sts/in.	175–300 yd.
6 sts/in.	200–500 yd.

NOTES ON THE SAMPLES

The burgundy tweed twin rib scarf is worked in Brown Sheep *Prairie Silk* (Color #PS400, 72% wool/18% mohair/10% silk, 88 yd./50g ball, 4 sts per inch) on size 9 (5.5mm) needles.

The light pink mesh pattern scarf is worked in Plymouth Yarn *Baby Alpaca DK* (Color #1837, 100% baby alpaca, 125 yd./50g skein, 6 sts per inch) on size 7 (4.5mm) needles.

The raspberry trinity stitch scarf is worked on size 17 (12mm) needles, using one strand each GGH/Muench *Aspen* (Color #15, 50% wool/50% acrylic, 63 yd./50g ball, 2.5 sts per inch) and GGH/Muench *Soft Kid* (Color #73, 70% super kid mohair/25% nylon/5% wool, 151 yd./25g ball, 4.5 sts per inch) held together, resulting in a gauge of 2 sts per inch over stockinette stitch.

Pattern Stitches

TWIN RIB (MULT OF 6 STS)

Twin rib pattern looks the same on both sides, even though the two rows that make up the pattern are different.

1 Row 1 (RS): *K3, p3; rep from * to end of row.

2 Row 2 (WS): *K1, p1; rep from * to end of row.

3 Rep rows 1 and 2 for twin rib.

MESH PATTERN (EVEN NO. OF STS)

Mesh pattern is an easy pattern to work with because you work it the same on both sides. It comes out looking like a neat lace rib. Experiment with different needle sizes until you achieve the desired look.

1 Row 1 (RS): K1, *[yo, sl1, k1, psso; rep from * to last st, k1.

2 Row 2 (WS): Rep row 1.

3 Rep rows 1 and 2 for mesh pattern.

TRINITY STITCH (MULT OF 4 STS PLUS 2)

Trinity stitch, also called bramble stitch, creates a pretty bobble effect. When knit in a tightly spun traditional wool on the needles specified for the yarn, it can look crisp and firm. The sample shown, knit with big needles in one strand of super-bulky yarn and one strand of mohair held together, looks airy and soft.

1 Rows 1 and 3 (RS): Purl.

2 Row 2 (WS): K1, *[k1, p1, k1] into the next st, p3tog; rep from * to last st, k1.

3 Row 4: K1, *p3tog, [k1, p1, k1] into the next st; rep from * to last st, k1.

4 Rep rows 1–4 for trinity stitch.

How to Make the Scarves

CAST ON AND WORK SCARF: ALL SCARVES

1. CO sts according to Table 2.

2. Beg with row 1, work in your chosen stitch pattern until scarf measures approx 56 inches, or length desired. End with last row of pattern.

3. BO sts in patt for twin rib scarf, knitwise for mesh pattern scarf, and purlwise for trinity stitch scarf.

4. Cut yarn, leaving a 6-inch tail. Pull tail through last st and secure.

5. Go to "Finishing: All Scarves," below.

Table 2. Cast On for Scarf			
Gauge (in Stockinette Stitch)	No. of Sts to CO for Twin Rib	No. of Sts to CO for Mesh Pattern	No. of Sts to CO for Trinity Stitch
2 sts/in.	12 sts	10 sts	10 sts
4 sts/in.	24 sts	20 sts	22 sts
6 sts/in.	36 sts	30 sts	30 sts

FINISHING: ALL SCARVES

1. Weave in loose ends.

2. Lightly steam to block, if necessary, and if your yarn's care instructions allow. Take care not to mash ribbing or bobbles.

3. Embellish with fringe, pompoms, tassels, or edging of your choice, if desired. See Appendix A for a few ideas.

You will be amazed by how many different looks you can create by knitting a simple rectangle or triangle. If you want to go for an airy and elegant shawl, try a fine silk blend over a lacy stitch pattern. If you're looking for a more go-anywhere, casual style, try a simpler stitch or stripe pattern in a thicker yarn.

RECTANGULAR SHAWLS

A rectangular shawl is the easiest to make, and while it's a perfect opportunity to use an intricate stitch pattern, it can also look terrific in plain garter stitch. You can knit the rectangle from the hem up to the neck, working many stitches in rows on a long circular needle, or you can work it from side edge to side edge. If you choose the latter method, be sure to use a stitch pattern that looks good sideways.

TRIANGULAR SHAWLS

Most triangular shawls are worked from the pointed tail up to the neck, which means you increase stitches over a long series of rows to generate the shape. The yarn-over increase works beautifully because it forms a decorative line of eyelets along the edges. Be sure to choose a yarn and needle size that work together to produce a fabric with good drape.

This pattern is just a big rectangle, so you can work it in any yarn and in any stitch pattern. Here is a chance to showcase an unusual yarn—a luxurious hand-dyed wool or a novelty yarn like ribbon or tape. With no shaping to keep track of, you have the freedom to explore something out of the ordinary.

The shawl is knit from one side edge to the other. Instructions are given for six gauges in three stitch patterns, but these are just general guidelines. You can play around with needle size and the final size of the shawl to get the look you want.

Specifications

DIMENSIONS

Approximately 52 inches wide × 18 inches from hem to neck

MATERIALS

Desired yarn, in the amount specified in Table 3

Note: *The gauge in Table 3 refers to the yarn's gauge as listed on the manufacturer's ball band. To encourage drape, use needles larger than the yarn label calls for and don't worry about achieving the yarn's recommended gauge.*

1 pair straight needles in size needed to obtain drape

Note: *You may find it easiest to work back and forth on a long circular needle as the shawl gets larger and heavier.*

Tapestry needle

Pompom maker (optional)

2-inch × 3-inch cardboard for tassel (optional)

Crochet hook to suit your yarn thickness (optional)

CONTINUED ON NEXT PAGE

Table 3. Approximate Yardage for Rectangular Shawl	
Gauge (in Stockinette Stitch)	*Approximate Yardage*
2 sts/in.	550–650 yd.
3 sts/in.	650–750 yd.
4 sts/in.	800–1,000 yd.
5 sts/in.	950–1,150 yd.
6 sts/in.	1,000–1,250 yd.
7 sts/in.	1,150–1,350 yd.

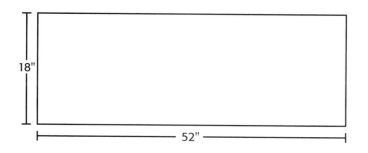

18"

52"

NOTES ON THE SAMPLE

The lavender peacock stitch rectangular shawl is worked in Cascade Yarn *Venezia* (Color #103, 70% merino wool/30% silk, 102 yd./100g ball, 3 sts per inch) on size 11 (8mm) needles.

TIP

Border or No Border?

Many stitch patterns work beautifully without edgings. You can always crochet or knit a border onto the shawl later if you change your mind. If you want to knit a shawl without a knit-in border, it's a good idea to use a stitch pattern that lays flat.

On the other hand, knitting the border right into the shawl allows you more freedom in choosing a stitch pattern—without the bother of added finishing later. Garter stitch, seed stitch, ribbing, and even loop stitch are all good border stitch choices.

GARTER RIB PATTERN (MULT OF 4 STS PLUS 2)

This stitch pattern does not look like most ribbing. It's very easy to do, and it looks the same on both sides.

1 Row 1 (RS): K2, *p2, k2; rep from * to end of row.

2 Row 2 (WS): Rep row 1.

3 Rep rows 1 and 2 for garter rib.

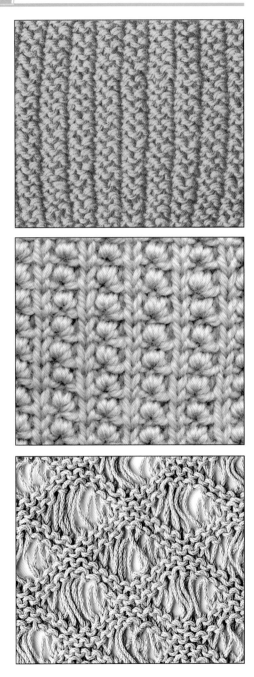

PILLARED KNOT STITCH (MULT OF 4 STS PLUS 1)

This beautiful stitch pattern can get very tight, so if you want your shawl to hang nicely, use a soft yarn on a bigger needle than specified.

1 Row 1 (RS): K1, *[p3tog, without slipping stitches from the left needle, bring yarn to back and knit the same 3 stitches together without slipping stitches from the left needle, bring yarn to the front and purl the 3 stitches together], k1; rep from * to end of row.

2 Row 2 (WS): Purl.

3 Rep rows 1 and 2 for pillared knot stitch.

SEAFOAM PATTERN (MULT OF 10 STS PLUS 6)

This drop stitch pattern works beautifully as a lightweight summer wrap.

1 Row 1 (RS): Knit.

2 Row 2 (WS): Knit.

3 Row 3: K6, *yo twice, k1, yo 3 times, k1, yo 4 times, k1, yo 3 times, k1, yo twice, k6; rep from * to end of row.

4 Rows 4 and 8: Knit across, dropping the yo loops as you go.

5 Rows 5 and 6: Knit.

6 Row 7: K1, *yo twice, k1, yo 3 times, k1, yo 4 times, k1, yo 3 times, k1, yo twice, k6; rep from * across, ending last rep with k1.

7 Rep rows 1–8 for seafoam pattern.

CONTINUED ON NEXT PAGE

Stitch Patterns for the Rectangular Shawl with Knit-in Border

STOCKINETTE DROP STITCH (ANY NO. OF STS)

This pattern is easy and looks very elegant. Use this stitch pattern with a knit-in border.

1. Rows 1 and 5 (RS): Knit.
2. Rows 2 and 6 (WS): Purl.
3. Row 3: K1, *yo twice, k1; rep from * to end of row.
4. Row 4: Purl across, dropping the yo loops as you go.
5. Rep rows 1–6 for stockinette drop stitch.

RIDGE AND EYELET STITCH (EVEN NO. OF STS)

This eyelet pattern forms a simple yet pleasing three-dimensional fabric. The rows between the eyelets are raised, creating a wavy effect.

1. Rows 1 and 5 (RS): K1, *k2tog; rep from * to last st, k1.
2. Row 2 (WS): K2, *yo, k1; rep from * to end of row.
3. Rows 3 and 7: Knit.
4. Rows 4 and 8: Purl.
5. Row 6: K1, *yo, k1; rep from * to last st, k1.
6. Rep rows 1–8 for ridge and eyelet stitch.

PEACOCK STITCH (MULT OF 12 STS)

This easy stitch pattern produces an undulating fabric. Use this stitch pattern with a knit-in border.

1. Row 1 (RS): P2tog twice, [yo, k1] 4 times, *p2tog 4 times, [yo, k1] 4 times; rep from * to last 4 sts, p2tog twice.
2. Rows 2 and 4: Purl.
3. Row 3: Knit.
4. Rep rows 1–4 for peacock stitch.

How to Make the Rectangular Shawl

RECTANGULAR SHAWL WITH NO BORDER: CAST ON

1 CO sts according to Table 4.

2 Beg with row 1, work in chosen stitch pattern until shawl measures approx 52 inches, or width desired. End with any row for garter rib, row 1 for pillared knot, and row 2 or 6 for seafoam pattern.

3 BO sts in patt for garter rib, purlwise for pillared knot stitch, and knitwise for seafoam patt.

4 Cut yarn, leaving a 6-inch tail. Pull tail through last st and secure.

5 Go to "Finish Shawl: All Rectangular Shawls," page 22.

Table 4. Cast On for Rectangular Shawl with No Border			
Gauge (in Stockinette Stitch)	No. of Sts to CO for Garter Rib	No. of Sts to CO for Pillared Knot St	No. of Sts to CO for Seafoam Pattern
2 sts/in.	34 sts	33 sts	36 sts
3 sts/in.	54 sts	53 sts	56 sts
4 sts/in.	74 sts	73 sts	76 sts
5 sts/in.	90 sts	89 sts	86 or 96 sts
6 sts/in.	110 sts	109 sts	106 sts
7 sts/in.	126 sts	125 sts	126 sts

FAQ

How do I use a different stitch for a rectangular shawl with no border?

Just add or subtract a few stitches to come up with a cast-on number that works for your stitch pattern. For instance, for a stitch pattern that is a multiple of 5 sts, change the cast-on number above to the closest multiple of 5.

For example, to make a rectangular shawl using the diagonal check pattern shown at a gauge of 4 stitches per inch, cast on 75 stitches and work as follows:

1 Rows 1 and 4: *P1, k4; rep from * to end of row.

2 Rows 2 and 3: *P3, k2; rep from * to end of row.

3 Rows 5 and 8: *K1, p4; rep from * to end of row.

4 Rows 6 and 7: *K3, p2; rep from * to end of row.

5 Rep rows 1–8 for diagonal check pattern.

CONTINUED ON NEXT PAGE

RECTANGULAR SHAWL WITH KNIT-IN BORDER: CAST ON

You can work any of the three stitch patterns provided on page 20 for this shawl. Or you can substitute a stitch pattern that is a multiple of 2, 3, 4, 6, or 12 sts. Just be aware that the first and last 2 sts of every row are knit to form the garter stitch edging. The first and last two rows of the shawl are also worked in garter stitch.

 1 CO sts according to Table 5.

2 Knit 2 rows.

3 Next row (RS): K2, work row 1 of st patt across to last 2 sts, k2.

4 Next row (WS): K2, work row 2 of st patt across to last 2 sts, k2.

5 Continue working st patt as established, knitting first and last 2 sts of every row for garter stitch for border, until shawl measures approx 52 inches, or width desired. End with row 6 for stockinette drop stitch pattern, any WS row for ridge and eyelet stitch, and row 1 for peacock stitch.

6 Knit 2 rows.

7 BO all sts knitwise.

8 Go to "Finish Shawl: All Rectangular Shawls," below.

FINISH SHAWL: ALL RECTANGULAR SHAWLS

1 Weave in loose ends.

2 Lightly steam to block to measurements, if necessary and if your yarn's care instructions allow. Take care not to mash delicate stitch work.

3 Embellish with fringe, pompoms, tassels, or edging of your choice, if desired. See Appendix A for a few ideas.

Table 5. Cast On for Rectangular Shawl with Knit-in Border	
Gauge	**No. of Sts to CO**
2 sts/in.	40 sts
3 sts/in.	52 sts
4 sts/in.	76 sts
5 sts/in.	88 sts
6 sts/in.	112 sts
7 sts/in.	124 sts

Note: The cast-on numbers in Table 5 include the 2 edging stitches at each end (4 sts total). If you are substituting a different stitch pattern from those provided, be sure to add 4 to the number of sts needed to arrive at the new cast-on number.

FAQ

How do I use a different stitch for a rectangular shawl with a knit-in border?

To apply any stitch pattern to this shawl, you just need to add or subtract the appropriate number of stitches to or from the cast-on number. For example, to use a stitch pattern that is a multiple of 5 sts, you can change the cast-on number indicated above to the closest multiple of 5. To include a 2-stitch border like the one here, add 4 sts to that number. A difference of a few stitches won't make a big difference in the finished size. You can also experiment with the size of and stitch used for the border.

These triangular shawls are knit from the point up, starting with just a few stitches and increasing every other row as you go up to produce the triangle shape. Unlike the rectangular shawl pattern, these shawl patterns involve shaping, so separate instructions are given for each of the three stitch patterns. All three designs can be worked in any gauge because you knit until the shawl is the desired size.

Specifications

DIMENSIONS

Approximately 72 inches wide × 34 inches from point to neck, or desired width and length

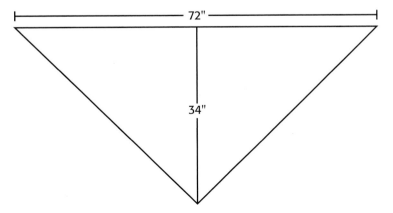

CONTINUED ON NEXT PAGE

MATERIALS

Desired yarn, in the amount specified in Table 6

1 pair straight needles in size needed to obtain drape

Long circular needle in size needed to obtain drape

Note: *You can start the triangular shawl on straight needles, but you will need to switch to a long (at least 29-inch) circular needle as the knitting gets heavy and the straight needle becomes too crowded.*

Stitch markers (for lines of eyelets shawl)

Row counter

Tapestry needle

Pompom maker (optional)

2-inch × 3-inch cardboard for tassel (optional)

Table 6. Approximate Yardage for Triangular Shawl	
Gauge (in Stockinette Stitch)	*Approximate Yardage*
3 sts/in.	400–800 yd.
5 sts/in.	450–950 yd.
7 sts/in.	650–1,250 yd.

Note: *The gauge in Table 6 refers to the yarn's gauge as listed on the manufacturer's ball band. To encourage drape, use needles larger than the yarn calls for and don't worry about achieving the yarn's recommended gauge.*

NOTES ON THE SAMPLE

The green easiest lace triangular shawl is worked in elann.com *Highland Silk* (Color #2117, 80% highland wool/20% silk, 122 yd./50g ball, 5 sts per inch) on size 10 (6mm) needles. This shawl is 72 inches wide × 34 inches from tail to neck.

How to Make the Triangular Shawls

EASIEST LACE SHAWL

This shawl is easy to make. Plus, it's reversible and works well in all gauges. Try using a needle larger than your yarn specifies for a very open lace.

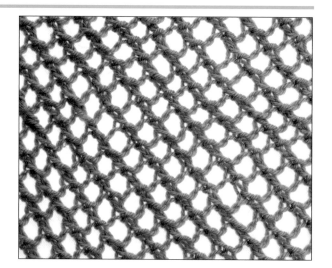

1. CO 2 sts.

2. Knit 2 rows.

3. Row 1 (WS): Knit into the front and back of each st—4 sts.

4. Rows 2, 4, 6, 8, and 10 (RS): Knit.

5. Row 3: K2, yo, k2—5 sts.

6. Row 5: K2, yo, k1, yo, k2—7 sts.

7. Row 7: K2, yo, k1, yo, sl1, k1, psso, yo, k2—9 sts.

8. Row 9: K2, yo, k1, *yo, sl1, k1, psso; rep from * to last 2 sts, yo, k2.

9 Rep rows 9–10, working patt as established, until shawl reaches desired measurements, ending with a WS row.

Note: Keep checking measurements as you go; the dimensions given are approximate, and the final length and width may vary from knitter to knitter.

10 Knit 3 rows.

11 BO all sts knitwise.

12 Go to "Finish Shawl: All Triangular Shawls," page 27.

Note: The yarn-over pattern can cause an asymmetrical slant to one side. You can correct this at the blocking stage or use it to advantage by throwing the longer side over your shoulder or tying the long ends into an elegant knot.

LINES OF EYELETS SHAWL

This shawl uses eyelets to create a graphic pattern that builds as the shawl grows. It's easy to follow once you get all the lines of eyelets in place, after step 19.

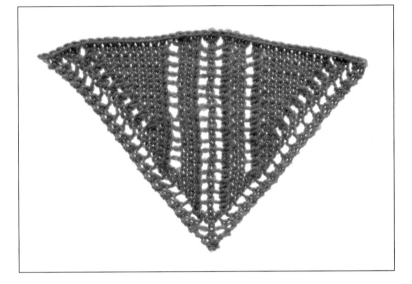

1 CO 3 sts.

2 Knit 4 rows.

3 Row 1 (RS): K1, yo, k1, yo, k1—5 sts.

4 Row 2 (WS): K2, p1, k2.

5 Row 3: K2, yo, k1, yo, k2—7 sts.

6 Row 4: K2, p3, k2.

7 Row 5: K2, yo, k3, yo, k2—9 sts.

8 Rows 6 and 8: K2, p to last 2 sts, k2.

9 Row 7: K2, yo, k2tog, yo, pm, k1 (center axis st), pm, yo, k2tog, yo, k2—11 sts.

10 Row 9: K2, yo, k to 2 sts before marker, k2tog, yo, sl marker, k1 (center axis st), sl marker, yo, k2tog, k to last 2 sts, yo, k2—13 sts.

11 Row 10: K2, p across, slipping markers, to last 2 sts, k2.

12 Rep rows 9 and 10 until you have 19 sts.

13 Next row (RS): K2, yo, k1, k2tog, yo, pm, k2, k2tog, yo, sl marker, k1 (center axis st), sl marker, yo, k2tog, k2, pm, yo, k2tog, k1, yo, k2—21 sts.

14 Next row (WS): Rep previous WS row.

CONTINUED ON NEXT PAGE

⑮ Next row: K2, yo, [k to 2 sts before next marker, k2tog, yo, sl marker] twice, k1 (center axis st), sl marker, yo, k2tog, k to 4th marker, sl marker, yo, k2tog, k to last 2 sts, yo, k2—23 sts.

⑯ Next row (WS): Rep previous WS row.

⑰ Rep last 2 rows until you have 27 sts, ending with a WS row.

⑱ Next row (RS): [K2, yo] twice, k2tog, [k to 2 sts before next marker, k2tog, yo, sl marker] twice, k1 (center axis st), sl marker, yo, k2tog, k to 4th marker, sl marker, yo, k2tog, k to last 6 sts, k2tog, [yo, k2] twice—29 sts.

⑲ Next row (WS): K2, p across, slipping markers, to last 2 sts, k2.

⑳ Rep steps 18 and 19, inc 1 st each end every RS row and working eyelet patt as established, until shawl reaches desired measurements, ending with a WS row.

Note: Keep checking measurements as you go; the dimensions given are approximate, and the final length and width may vary from knitter to knitter.

㉑ Knit 5 rows.

㉒ BO all sts knitwise.

㉓ Go to "Finish Shawl: All Triangular Shawls," on the next page.

REVERSIBLE RICE STITCH SHAWL

This easy shawl looks great on both sides, so it is completely reversible. The rice stitch pattern tends to create a firm fabric, so for a soft drape, try using a needle two or more sizes larger than your yarn specifies.

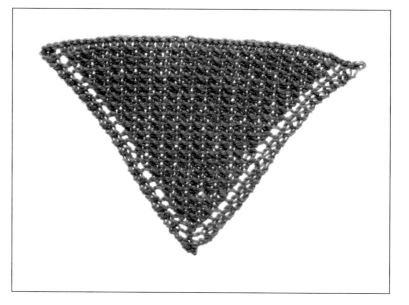

① CO 3 sts.

② Knit 4 rows.

Note: For this pattern, you might want to use a row counter to keep track of the rows.

③ Row 1 (RS): K1, yo, k1 tbl, yo, k1—5 sts.

④ Rows 2, 4, 6, and 8 (WS): Knit.

⑤ Row 3: K2, yo, k1 tbl, yo, k2—7 sts.

⑥ Row 5: K2, yo, p1, k1 tbl, p1, yo, k2—9 sts.

⑦ Row 7: K2, yo, k1 tbl, *p1, k1 tbl; rep from * to last 2 sts, yo, k2—11 sts.

⑧ Row 9: K2, yo, p1, *k1 tbl, p1; rep from * to last 2 sts, yo, k2—13 sts.

⑨ Rep rows 6–9, working patt and yo increases as established, until shawl reaches desired measurements, ending with a RS row.

Note: Keep checking measurements as you go; the dimensions given are approximate, and the final length and width may vary from knitter to knitter.

⑩ Knit 4 rows.

⑪ BO all sts knitwise.

⑫ Go to "Finish Shawl: All Triangular Shawls," below.

FINISH SHAWL: ALL TRIANGULAR SHAWLS

① Weave in loose ends.

② Lightly steam to block, if necessary and if your yarn's care instructions allow. Lace patterns benefit from blocking. Be sure to open the stitch pattern up a bit as you block and take care not to mash delicate stitch patterns.

③ Embellish with fringe, pompoms, tassels, or edging of your choice, if desired. See Appendix A for a few ideas.

TIP

Using Other Stitch Patterns for a Triangular Shawl

You can adapt the triangular shawl to new stitch patterns. You need to perform increases every other row and work new stitches into your pattern as you go along. It's a good idea to make a practice triangle first to ensure that your stitch pattern can be adapted to the shape.

To make a triangular shawl using a two-row stitch pattern that is worked over any number of stitches or over an odd number of stitches, follow the instructions for the easiest lace shawl through row 6. Then follow these steps:

1 Next row (RS): K2, yo, work row 1 of desired stitch pattern up to the last 2 sts, yo, k2.

2 Next row (WS): K2, work row 2 of desired stitch pattern up to the last 2 sts, k2.

3 Rep steps 1 and 2, working the [k2, yo] beg every RS row and the [yo, k2] end every RS row, to desired size.

4 BO loosely.

To make a triangular shawl using a two-row stitch pattern that is worked over an even number of stitches, follow the instructions for the easiest lace shawl through row 4, to 5 stitches. Then follow these steps:

1 Next row (RS): K2, yo, k into front and back of next st, yo, k2—8 sts.

2 Next row (WS): K2, work row 2 (or WS row) of desired stitch pattern to last 2 sts, k2.

3 Next row: K2, yo, work row 1 of desired stitch pattern to last 2 sts, yo, k2.

4 Rep last 2 rows until shawl is desired size, ending with a WS row.

5 BO loosely.

Make a Shawl into a Poncho

It is easy to make either a rectangular or triangular shawl into a poncho. With some creative thinking, you can even finish a shawl so that it functions as either a shawl or a poncho.

How to Make a Shawl into a Poncho

FOLDED RECTANGLE: METHOD 1

If your poncho is approximately the same size as specified in the master pattern, you can fold it and sew it as illustrated here to make it into a poncho.

1. Fold rectangle in half, matching up ends, so that it is approx 18 × 26 inches.

2. Measuring from fold, and leaving 14-inch opening for neck, sew rem 12 inches (or length rem for your rectangle) along top edge, as shown by dotted line.

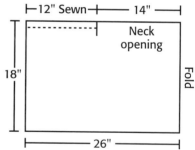

FOLDED RECTANGLE: METHOD 2

This method creates a point in the front and the look of a wrap in the back.

1. Fold rectangle so that the cast-on or bound-off edge meets one of the side edges as indicated in the diagram.

2. Sew where these two edges meet.

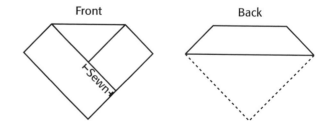

28

FOLDED TRIANGLE

If your poncho is approximately the same size as specified in the master pattern, you can fold it and sew it as illustrated here to make it into a poncho. This will have a point in the front and the back.

1 Fold triangle in half, matching up ends.

> *Note: You can fold over the edge around the neck. This makes it easier to fold the triangle, and it produces a collar.*

2 Sew as indicated by the dotted line in the diagram to close the shawl into a poncho.

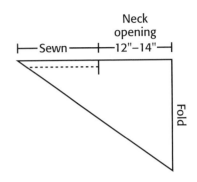

TIE IT UP

If your shawl has an open stitch pattern along the edges and you want to maintain the possibility of it being both a shawl and a poncho, you can tie it closed as described here. This works for both a rectangle and a triangle.

1 Use the same diagrams with fold and stitch lines as guides for folding.

2 Instead of sewing, tie at intervals along the dotted line, using ribbon, crochet chains, or knitted cord.

Note: *If you want to use a stitch pattern that doesn't have openings along the edge and you want the option of tying your shawl closed, you can plan ahead and work eyelets along the sides by working [yo, k2tog] near the beginning and end of rows at even intervals.*

BUTTON IT UP

The yarn-over increases along the edges of the shawls provide built-in buttonholes. If you are using a bulky yarn, you need large buttons; finer yarns require smaller buttons. You probably don't want buttons sewn permanently onto your shawl because they can get caught up in a lacy stitch pattern. Instead, you can make a double-sided button, which works like a cufflink, to hold your shawl closed. You can close your shawl loosely with just one or two double-buttons like the ones shown or space them at even intervals along the edge for a firm closure.

1 Make a double-sided button by tying two buttons together with yarn.

2 Button one side of the double-button to the RS edge where you want to close the shawl and then button the other side of the double-button to the WS of the opposite edge of the shawl so that the edges overlap and close.

Hats

Even though hats look more complicated than scarves, they can be just as simple and even quicker to make. The hats in this book are knit in the round from the brim up on double-pointed needles, eliminating an unsightly back seam and minimizing finishing. You will be surprised by how many different looks you can achieve by using just one master pattern.

Hat patterns are easy to customize: Simply change the brim style, shape the crown a little differently, or add a pompom, tassel, or topknot. The variations that follow are just a few to get you started.

BRIM TREATMENTS

Here are four brim styles that are easy to do but result in completely different styles. The rolled brim is the easiest because it's worked in stockinette stitch. For this master pattern, you can work the ribbed brim in single (1x1) rib, or, if your stitch count is divisible by 4, in double (2x2) rib. You can double the brim length if you prefer to fold it over.

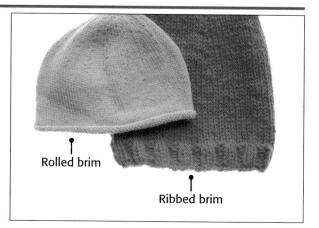

Rolled brim

Ribbed brim

The hemmed brim is folded under at the turning row. The hemmed brim shown here uses a picot hem, which has a tiny scalloped edge, but you can also follow the instructions for a simple purled turning row. Don't be put off by the earflaps—they're knit right on to the brim and are easy to make.

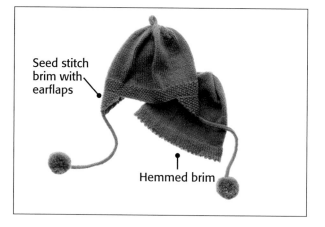

Seed stitch brim with earflaps

Hemmed brim

SHAPING TREATMENTS

After you have completed your brim and knit your hat body to the desired length, you can choose one of several shapings to finish the crown of your hat. The square top is the easiest because it requires no shaping at all. You can leave the top square after finishing, or you can sew the corners together as shown; for a completely different look, attach cords to the corners and tie them together. The rounded top is achieved by working a short series of decrease rounds. The yarn is then cut, and the tail is pulled through the few remaining stitches, cinched tight, and fastened off.

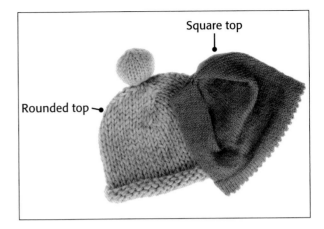

Square top

Rounded top

The pointed top is worked and finished almost like the rounded top, but over many more rounds. To make a long, pointed hat like the stocking cap shown, you work decrease rounds separated by a larger number of non-decrease rounds.

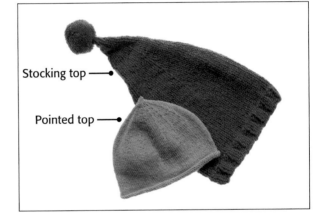

Stocking top

Pointed top

EMBELLISHMENTS

You can decorate your hats all kinds of ways. Try pompoms, tassels, crochet chains, or knitted cords, loops, and balls. Sew a pompom to the top for a traditional look or attach it to the front, off to one side, for a chic style. You can finish the top with a length of knitted cord and then form the cord into a knot or loop, or you can sew a pompom to the end of the cord. Crochet chains also work well as hat ties and pompom or tassel holders. The knitted ball is a fun embellishment—you can make one big one or a cluster of small ones to sew to your hat top.

Hat: Master Pattern

With this one master pattern, you can create countless hat styles, in many shapes, sizes, and stitch patterns. The size range covers the whole family, and the gauges include yarns from sport weight to bulky.

SIZES

XXS (XS, S, M, L)

Brim circumference: 14 (16, 18, 20, 22) inches

MATERIALS

Desired yarn, in the amount specified in Table 1

1 set of double-pointed needles in size needed to obtain gauge

1 set of double-pointed needles one or two sizes smaller than size needed to obtain gauge (for edgings)

Stitch marker to fit your needle size

Tapestry needle

Pompom maker (optional)

Table 1. Approximate Yardage for Hat	
Gauge (in Stockinette Stitch)	Approximate Yardage
2 sts/in.	85–150 yd.
3 sts/in.	100–175 yd.
4 sts/in.	125–225 yd.
5 sts/in.	150–250 yd.
6 sts/in.	175–275 yd.
7 sts/in.	200–325 yd.

NOTES ON THE SAMPLES

The pink rolled-brim hat is worked in Cascade *Lana Grande* (Color #6033, 100% wool, 87 yd./100g ball, 2 sts per inch). It has a round top and is embellished with a knitted ball.

The orange stocking cap is worked in GGH/Muench *Via Mala* (Color #26, 100% wool, 73 yd./50g ball, 3 sts per inch). The brim is worked in 2x2 rib, and the top is embellished with a matching pompom.

The green hat with earflaps is worked in Plymouth Yarn *Galway Worsted* (Color #130, 100% wool, 210 yd./100g skein, 5 sts per inch). The brim and earflaps are worked in seed stitch. The top has round shaping and is embellished with a knitted cord loop. The pompom ties are attached to the earflaps with a knitted cord.

The blue pointed hat with a rolled brim is worked in elann.com *Peruvian Collection Baby Cashmere* (Color #1620, 60% baby alpaca/30% merino wool/10% cashmere, 109 yd./25g ball, 7 sts per inch). A loose pompom is sewn to the front.

The purple hat is knit in Brown Sheep *Naturespun Sport* (Color #N60, 100% wool, 184 yd./50g skein, 6 sts per inch). The brim is hemmed with a picot folding ridge, and the top is square.

CAST ON: ALL STYLES

1 CO sts for your size and gauge, according to Table 2, dividing sts as evenly as possible over 3 or 4 dpns.

Note: *If you want a firm, elastic brim, you might want to CO using needles a size or two smaller than the size you use to work the rest of the hat. For example, a seed stitch brim will likely require needles two sizes smaller, so the brim doesn't end up larger than the body. Ribbed brims can be worked in the same needles as the body, or you can go down a size to ensure lasting elasticity. You can use a needle one size smaller for the rolled brim and for the section of the hemmed brim that gets folded under.*

2 Place marker (pm) and join rnd, taking care not to twist sts.

3 Go to the directions for the desired brim style under "Work the Brim," below.

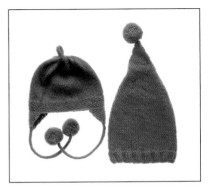

Table 2. Cast On for Hat			
Gauge	**No. of Sts to CO**	**Gauge**	**No. of Sts to CO**
2 sts/in.	28 (32, 36, 40, 44) sts	5 sts/in.	70 (80, 90, 100, 110) sts
3 sts/in.	42 (48, 54, 60, 66) sts	6 sts/in.	84 (96, 108, 120, 132) sts
4 sts/in.	56 (64, 72, 80, 88) sts	7 sts/in.	98 (112, 126, 140, 154) sts

WORK THE BRIM

Here's where you get to start making your hat unique. Choose one of these brims or come up with your own!

Rolled Brim

This brim can be worked over any number of stitches, and it results in a fun and casual style that looks good on hat-wearers of all ages.

1 Knit all rnds, sl marker beg every rnd, until piece measures 1½ inches from CO edge.

2 Go to "Work the Body: All Styles," page 36.

Ribbed Brim

You work this brim over an even number of stitches. If your stitch count is a multiple of 4 sts, you can work it as 2x2 rib, as shown.

1 *K1, p1; rep from * to end of rnd.

2 Rep last rnd, sl marker beg every rnd, until brim measures 1 (1, 1½, 1¼, 2) inches from CO edge.

Note: *If you want a folded ribbed brim, work until brim measures 2½ (2½, 3, 3, 4) inches.*

3 Go to "Work the Body: All Styles," page 36.

CONTINUED ON NEXT PAGE

Hemmed Brim

This brim works best in yarns no thicker than 4 sts per inch.

1 Knit all rnds, sl marker beg every rnd, until piece measures 1 (1¼, 1¼, 1½, 1½) inches from CO edge.

2 Purl next rnd to form folding ridge.

> *Note: For a picot hem like the one shown here, work the folding ridge (step 2) as an eyelet row by repeating (k2tog, yo) around.*

3 Go to "Work the Body: All Styles," below.

Seed Stitch Brim

You work this brim over an even number of stitches. Because seed stitch can create a loose fabric, you should work this brim using needles a size or two smaller than the ones you use for the body.

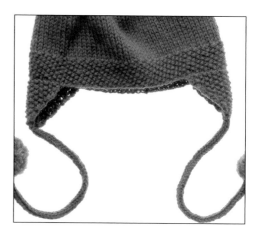

1 *K1, p1; rep from * to end of rnd.

2 *P1, k1; rep from * to end of rnd.

3 Rep last 2 rnds, sl marker beg every rnd, until piece measures 1 (1¼, 1¼, 1½, 1½) inches from CO edge.

4 Go to "Work the Body: All Styles," below.

WORK THE BODY: ALL STYLES

1 Change to larger needles if smaller needles were used for the brim and knit every rnd until piece measures 4 (4½, 5, 6, 7) inches from CO edge or folding ridge. If using a folded ribbed brim, measure from where the brim will fold.

> *Note: If you're making a rounded or short pointed hat, try the hat on the wearer, and if you can barely see the top of wearer's head, it is time to start the top shaping.*

2 Go to the directions for the desired top shaping, under "Work the Top Shaping," on the next page.

WORK THE TOP SHAPING

At this point, you can decide to make the top of your hat rounded, pointed, elongated, or square. Follow the directions for your desired style.

Square Top Shaping

1 Work until piece measures 7 (7½, 8, 9, 10) inches from CO edge or folding ridge. If using the folded ribbed brim, measure from where the brim will fold.

2 Starting at beg of rnd, put first half of sts onto 1 or 2 dpn and put second half of sts onto 1 or 2 dpn. Take a 3rd or 5th dpn and work three-needle bind-off across top. (See page 257.)

3 Go to the finishing instructions for your style, under "Finish the Hat," page 40.

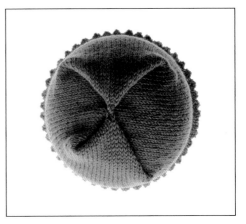

Rounded Top, Pointed Top, and Stocking Cap: Begin Shaping

1 Work 1st dec rnd: *K5 (6, 7, 8, 9), k2tog; rep from * to end of rnd. You should have rem the number of sts specified for your size and gauge in Table 3.

Table 3. Number of Stitches Remaining After First Decrease Round		
Gauge	**No. of Sts Rem**	**No. of Sts to Dec**
2 sts/in.	24 (28, 32, 36, 40) sts	4 sts
3 sts/in.	36 (42, 48, 54, 60) sts	6 sts
4 sts/in.	48 (56, 64, 72, 80) sts	8 sts
5 sts/in.	60 (70, 80, 90, 100) sts	10 sts
6 sts/in.	72 (84, 96, 108, 120) sts	12 sts
7 sts/in.	84 (98, 112, 126, 140) sts	14 sts

CONTINUED ON NEXT PAGE

2 *Without decreasing,* work the number of rnds specified for your size, gauge, and top style in Table 4.

3 Work 2nd dec rnd: *K4 (5, 6, 7, 8), k2tog; rep from * to end of rnd. You should have rem the number of sts specified for your size and gauge in Table 5.

4 Go to the directions for final shaping for your style.

Table 4. Number of Rounds to Work Even After Decrease Round for Tops			
Gauge	**Rounded Top**	**Short Pointed Top**	**Stocking Cap**
2 sts/in.	1 rnd	1 rnd	5 rnd
3 sts/in.	1 rnd	1 rnd	6 rnd
4 sts/in.	2 rnd	2 rnd	7 rnd
5 sts/in.	2 rnd	2 rnd	8 rnd
6 sts/in.	3 rnd	3 rnd	9 rnd
7 sts/in.	3 rnd	3 rnd	10 rnd

Table 5. Number of Stitches Remaining After Second Decrease Round		
Gauge	**No. of Sts Rem**	**No. of Sts to Dec**
2 sts/in.	20 (24, 28, 32, 36) sts	4 sts
3 sts/in.	30 (36, 42, 48, 54) sts	6 sts
4 sts/in.	40 (48, 56, 64, 72) sts	8 sts
5 sts/in.	50 (60, 70, 80, 90) sts	10 sts
6 sts/in.	60 (72, 84, 96, 108) sts	12 sts
7 sts/in.	70 (84, 98, 112, 126) sts	14 sts

Rounded Top: Final Shaping

1 Continue to dec *every* rnd the same number of sts per rnd evenly, as established, until you have rem the number of sts specified for your gauge in Table 6.

2 K2tog to end of rnd.

3 For hats that are 2, 3, or 4 sts per inch: If you are finishing the top with a knitted cord stem, loop, or knot, transfer rem sts to smaller dpn and knit cord to desired length per instructions on page 271; otherwise, skip ahead to step 4.

For hats that are 5, 6, or 7 sts per inch: K2tog to end of rnd before beginning knitted cord or continuing to step 4.

4 Cut yarn, leaving a 10-inch tail. Pull through rem sts and secure.

5 Go to the finishing instructions for your style, under "Finish the Hat," page 40.

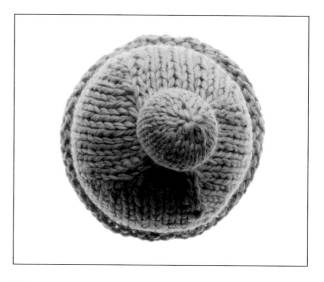

Table 6. Number of Stitches Remaining After Decreasing Every Round, as Established			
Gauge	**No. of Sts Rem**	**Gauge**	**No. of Sts Rem**
2 sts/in.	12 sts	5 sts/in.	20 sts
3 sts/in.	12 sts	6 sts/in.	24 sts
4 sts/in.	16 sts	7 sts/in.	28 sts

Short Pointed Top and Stocking Cap: Final Shaping

① Continue to dec the same number of sts evenly per rnd as established for your gauge, and work the same number of non-decrease rnds between dec rnds as specified for your gauge and style in Table 4, until you have the number of sts specified for your gauge in Table 6.

② Again work the number of non-decrease rnds specified for your gauge and style in Table 4.

③ K2tog to end of rnd.

④ Rep steps 2 and 3. You will have rem the number of sts specified for your gauge in Table 7.

⑤ K2tog to end of rnd.

   Note: *For an odd number of sts, k2tog as many times as possible and k1 rem st.*

⑥ Rep step 5 until you have 1 st rem.

⑦ Cut yarn, leaving a 10-inch tail. Pull through rem st and secure.

⑧ Go to the finishing instructions for your style, under "Finish the Hat," page 40.

Table 7. Number of Stitches Remaining After All Decrease Rounds for Pointed Top	
Gauge	**No. of Sts Rem**
2 sts/in.	2 sts
3 sts/in.	3 sts
4 sts/in.	4 sts
5 sts/in.	5 sts
6 sts/in.	6 sts
7 sts/in.	7 sts

CONTINUED ON NEXT PAGE

FINISH THE HAT

You finish each of the hats a little differently. Go to the instructions for the style you're making.

Finish Hat: All Styles

1 Weave in loose ends.

> **Note:** If you're making the earflap hat, mark the join of the rnd with a safety pin. This will be the center back of the hat.

2 Lightly steam to block, if your yarn's care instructions allow.

3 Embellish as desired. (See Appendix A.)

4 If you are making a hemmed brim hat, go to "Hemmed Brim: Further Finishing," below. If you are making a seed stitch brim with earflaps, go to "Seed Stitch Brim with Earflaps: Further Finishing," on the next page.

Hemmed Brim: Further Finishing

1 Fold brim to the inside along folding ridge and pin in place.

2 Whipstitch CO edge neatly to backs of sts, ensuring that sewing sts don't show on the RS and that hat doesn't pucker.

3 Weave in ends and lightly steam hem to neaten it.

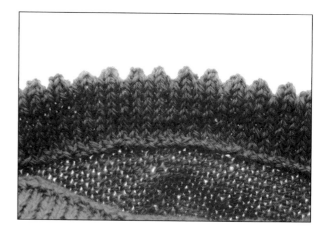

Seed Stitch Brim with Earflaps: Further Finishing

1. Holding hat upright with join of rnd (the back of the hat) facing, pm for left earflap: Beg at the join, measure 1¾ (2, 2¼, 2½, 2¾) inches along brim to the left and mark with a safety pin. Place a second safety pin 3 (4, 4, 4, 5) inches to the left of the first safety pin.

2. With hat upside-down and with RS facing, use smaller needle to pick up and knit the number of sts specified for your size and gauge in Table 8 along CO edge between safety pins for left earflap.

3. Turn and knit this first WS row.

4. Next row (RS)—Beg seed stitch: *K1, p1; rep from * to end of row.

5. Next row (WS): *P1, k1; rep from * to end of row.

6. If you are working at 6 or 7 sts per inch gauge, rep steps 4 and 5.

7. Shape flap—Row 1 (RS): P2tog, *k1, p1; rep from * to last 2 sts, k2tog.

8. Row 2 (WS): *K1, p1; rep from * to end of row.

9. Row 3: K2tog, *p1, k1; rep from * to last 2 sts, p2tog.

10. Row 4: *P1, k1; rep from * to end of row.

11. Rep rows 1–4 until you have the number of stitches shown for your gauge in Table 9.

12. To finish flap without knitted cord tie, cut yarn, leaving a 10-inch tail. Pull tail through rem sts and secure. Skip to step 14 for right earflap.

    Note: *It is not recommended to make the ties if the hat is for an infant.*

13. To work a knitted cord tie on the flap, slip rem sts onto smaller dpn and work knitted cord to length desired (10 inches for child, 12 inches for adult). Attach pompom to end. See Appendix A for knitted cord and pompom instructions.

14. Work right earflap as for left, only place markers at the same measurements to the *right* of the join and pick up sts working from 1st to 2nd safety pin.

Table 8. Number of Stitches to Pick Up for Earflap	
Gauge	**No. of Sts to Pick Up**
2 sts/in.	6 (8, 8, 8, 10) sts
3 sts/in.	8 (12, 12, 12, 14) sts
4 sts/in.	12 (16, 16, 16, 20) sts
5 sts/in.	16 (20, 20, 20, 24) sts
6 sts/in.	18 (24, 24, 24, 30) sts
7 sts/in.	20 (28, 28, 28, 34) sts

Table 9. Number of Stitches Remaining After Shaping Earflap	
Gauge	**No. of Sts Rem After Shaping Earflap**
2 sts/in.	2 sts
3 sts/in.	2 sts
4 sts/in.	4 sts
5 sts/in.	4 sts
6 sts/in.	6 sts
7 sts/in.	6 sts

You can leave the crown of your hat unadorned or you can decorate it. Just a few options are pompoms, tassels, buttons, knots, and loops. For a colorful finish, try using a contrasting color or colors for the finishing touch. See Appendix A for embellishment techniques.

POMPOMS AND TASSELS

You can sew pompoms and tassels tightly to the top singly or in groups. Or, for a more whimsical look, you can attach them with a crocheted chain so they dangle. For babies' and children's hats, attaching two pompoms or tassels like ears can have a cute effect. (For instructions on making pompoms and tassels, see page 268.)

CROCHET CHAINS

You can use crochet chains to attach pompoms and tassels if you want them to swing. You can also crochet ties to earflap hats, kerchiefs, and baby bonnets. Crochet chain loops produce a playful look, and if you use many loops, they can look like a braided pompom. (For instructions on making a crochet chain, see page 272.)

KNITTED CORD

A cute option is to create a topknot, stem, or loop. You do this by knitting the few stitches remaining after shaping as a knitted cord. It's easy to do and requires less finishing than attaching a separate embellishment. You can also knit cords onto earflaps and baby bonnets for firm, durable ties. Just remember to keep the cords on baby apparel short, to avoid danger. (For instructions on making a knitted cord, see page 271.)

KNITTED BALL

Here is a decoration that you don't see very often. Like pompoms, knitted balls can be sewn to hat tops singly or in clusters. If you knit very small balls and cluster them, they can look like berries. A ball is knit separately, filled with polyester stuffing, and then sewn to the top. (For instructions on making a knitted ball, see page 270.)

BUTTONS

When you want to decorate a hat with something other than a pompom or tassel—or if you don't have a lot of yarn left—try sewing a button to that spot. Using a contrasting thread can create an eye-catching touch. Sew buttons in a cluster, as shown, or overlap a small button on a larger button for added detail.

Tutorial: Knitting in the Round on Double-Pointed Needles

All the hats in this chapter are worked in the round on double-pointed needles. This is a good way to make a hat because it requires less finishing and does not create a bulky back seam. You can use a set of four or five needles, depending on how many stitches you are casting on; this lesson describes using four.

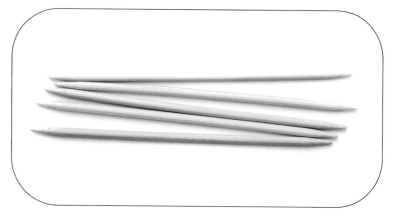

How to Cast On with Double-Pointed Needles

1 CO all the stitches called for onto one dpn. Then slip one-third of the stitches onto a second dpn and one-third onto a third dpn.

Note: If you can't divide the stitches equally in thirds, approximate.

2 Arrange the three needles so that they form a triangle: The needle with the working yarn attached should be the right side of the triangle (a), the center needle should be the base of the triangle (b), and the needle with the first CO stitch should be the left side of the triangle (c).

Note: Make sure the cast-on edge is running around the center of the triangle, untwisted.

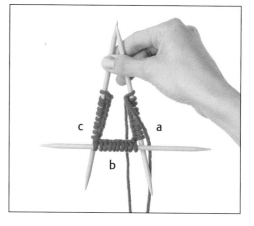

How to Knit on Double-Pointed Needles

① Make sure the needles are facing you, with the needle with the working yarn attached to it on the right. Place a stitch marker after the last CO stitch to mark the end of the round. Hold the needle with the first CO stitch on it in your left hand.

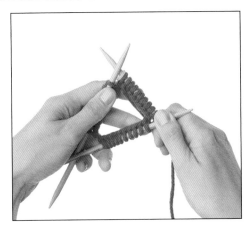

② Using your fourth needle, join the round by knitting the first CO stitch from the left needle, giving the yarn a firm tug (on this first stitch only) so that the join is snug.

Knitting the first stitch joins the round.

③ Knit all the way around until you reach the stitch marker. To begin the second round, slip the marker from the left needle to the right needle and knit the first stitch as in step 2.

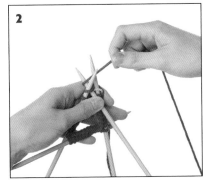

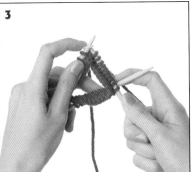

FAQ

I am making a striped hat in the round. Every time I change colors, I get a little stair-step of color at the beginning of the round, so the striping is not seamless. Is there anything I can do about this?

Yes. Here's what you do to significantly reduce the stair-step effect:

1 When you're about to begin the round in the new color, knit the first stitch of the new round using both colors.

2 Knit the rest of the round in the new color.

3 At the beginning of the next round—this is the 2nd round in the new color—knit together as one the two colors that make up the first stitch.

4 Repeat steps 1–3 at each color change.

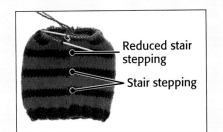

Reduced stair stepping

Stair stepping

chapter 4

Bags

Bags, like scarves and shawls, can be very freeing to knit. Unless you're knitting something like an eyeglass case or mobile phone holder, achieving the exact gauge or fit is not crucial. And there are so many types of bags, each with a unique function, yet wide-ranging in style: practical totes to hold work or knitting projects, dressy evening bags to carry lipstick and keys, tiny bags for mobile phones or MP3 players, fashionable handbags, and the list goes on.

Bags present infinite design possibilities. You can knit them up in all kinds of yarns, in all shapes and sizes. Let your bag's function determine what style to make and what fiber to use.

BAGS MADE FROM RECTANGLES

The easiest bags are made out of rectangles. You just knit a rectangle twice as long as you want your bag to be, fold it in half, and stitch up the side seams. If you want a fold-over flap, you knit it a little longer and include an eyelet buttonhole at the top. If you work a row of eyelets across the top edges, you can turn your rectangular bag into a drawstring bag: Just weave a crochet chain or knitted cord through the eyelets and pull. Or knit a row of eyelets across one top edge and sew buttons to the opposite edge. You can make a fuller rectangular bag that stands up on its own by knitting a gusset.

ROUND BAGS

You can knit a bag in the round similarly to the way you knit a hat in the round. The result can be like a bucket, with a flat bottom, or like a feed bag, with a curved bottom.

WHICH YARN IS BEST?

Knitted bags and handles stretch when you put things in the bag, so yarns that are inelastic but durable, such as cotton, silk, linen, or blends that include these fibers, make excellent choices for these projects. To create a wool bag, try knitting in a tight fabric of stockinette or linen stitch to minimize stretching. You can also add a lining to your bag to eliminate stretching worries and protect your knitting.

FELTED BAGS

You don't have to worry about wool stretching when you felt it. Felting is an excellent option for knitted bags because it produces a stiff and almost impenetrable fabric. The best fibers for felting are wool, mohair, alpaca, and angora. Superwash wool is not a good choice, however, because it has been specially treated to *not* shrink and felt. Wool/mohair blends felt beautifully.

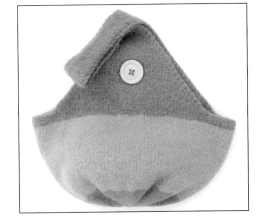

HANDLES

Unless you're making an envelope-type bag or clutch, you will most likely want to attach or knit a handle onto your bag. Again, consider the stretch factor. If you knit loosely in elastic yarn, your handle will stretch as soon as you put something in the bag.

You can knit tubular handles in the round, work the handle and side gussets as one continuous piece, crochet handles, or work decorative ribbed or cabled handles. Take the opportunity to experiment.

Rectangular Bag: Master Pattern

This bag is easy to make, with or without the side panel, which is called a *gusset*. The instructions include three sizes in four gauges: a small bag for carrying a mobile phone or other small items, a medium bag that makes a great short-handled purse, and a large bag that's big enough to carry paperwork. You can make a new size by casting on fewer or more stitches and knitting fewer or more rows.

Specifications

SIZES

S (M, L)

Dimensions without gusset (Width × Height): 4 × 5 (10 × 8, 12 × 14) inches

Dimensions with gusset (Width × Height × Depth): 4 × 5 × 1 (10 × 8 × 4, 12 × 14 × 4) inches

MATERIALS

Desired yarn, in the amount specified in Table 1

1 pair straight needles in size needed to obtain gauge

Stitch holders (for flat version of the gusset handle)

1 set of double-pointed needles in size needed to obtain gauge (for tubular handle)

Tapestry needle

Table 1. Approximate Yardages for Rectangular Bags			
Gauge (in Stockinette Stitch)	Small Bag	Medium Bag	Large Bag
2 sts/in.	20–25 yd.	85–100 yd.	200–300 yd.
3 sts/in.	25–30 yd.	125–150 yd.	250–350 yd.
4 sts/in.	30–40 yd.	150–175 yd.	350–500 yd.

NOTES ON THE SAMPLES

The turquoise gusseted bag is worked in Cascade *Lana Grande* (Color #6024, 100% wool, 87 yd./100g ball, 2 sts per inch). The gussets are worked separately from the tubular handles. This bag is lined with matching fabric and reinforced with thick interfacing. The button loop is a crochet chain.

The large pink and brown rectangular bag is worked in Cascade *Luna* (Colors #705 and #709, 100% cotton, 87 yd./50g hank, 4 sts per inch). The side gussets and handle are worked as one piece, with the gussets in seed stitch and the handle knit as a tube. The stripe pattern is 14 rows A, 14 rows B.

The medium green and purple striped rectangular bag is worked in Brown Sheep *Lamb's Pride Bulky* (Colors #M-184 and #M-100, 85% wool/15% mohair, 125 yd./113g skein, 3 sts per inch). It is a flat bag, lined with matching fabric. The handle is worked in single crochet. The button loop is a crochet chain. The stripe pattern is 8 rows A, 2 rows B.

How to Make the Rectangular Bag

CAST ON: ALL RECTANGULAR STYLES

1 CO sts (in A, if working stripe patt) as specified for your size and gauge in Table 2.

2 Beg with a knit row, work hem in St st for 1 inch, ending with a RS row.

3 Next row (WS): Knit across for hem folding ridge (still using A, if working stripe patt).

4 Go to the appropriate directions under "Work Bag Body," below.

Table 2. Cast On for Flat Rectangular Bag	
Gauge (in Stockinette Stitch)	*No. of Sts to CO*
2 sts/in.	8 (20, 24) sts
3 sts/in.	12 (30, 36) sts
4 sts/in.	16 (40, 48) sts
6 sts/in.	24 (60, 72) sts

WORK BAG BODY

At this point, you choose whether to make your rectangular bag flat or gusseted.

Flat Rectangular Bag Body

You do not make gussets for this style of bag, which is basically a long piece of flat knitting folded in half.

1 Beg with a knit row, work in St st (and beg stripe patt, if desired, still using A) until piece measures 10 (16, 28) inches from folding ridge, ending with WS row (and completing a full A stripe, if working stripe patt).

Note: If you want to make a flap, add the desired length of the flap to the measurement in step 1 and work until that length before working hem.

2 Next row (RS): Purl across for hem folding ridge.

3 Beg with a purl row, work in St st for 1 inch (still using A, if working stripe patt), ending with a RS row.

4 BO purlwise.

5 Go to the finishing instructions for your bag style under "Finish the Rectangular Bag," page 54.

CONTINUED ON NEXT PAGE

Gusseted Rectangular Bag Body

Gussets give this bag extra shape.

1. Beg with a knit row, work in St st (and beg stripe patt, if desired, still using A) until piece measures 5 (8, 14) inches from folding ridge for first side, ending with a RS row.

2. Next row (WS): Knit across row to create ridge along base.

3. Beg with a knit row, work in St st for 1 (4, 4) inches for base, ending with a RS row.

4. Next row (WS): Knit across for ridge along other side of base.

5. Beg with a knit row, work in St st until piece measures 5 (8, 14) inches from last ridge, ending with a RS row.

6. Next row (WS): Knit across for hem folding ridge.

7. Beg with a knit row, work in St st for 1 inch (still using A, if working stripe patt), ending with a RS row.

8. BO purlwise.

9. Go to desired gusset style under "Make Gussets," below.

MAKE GUSSETS

You can make the handle and side gussets as one continuous piece or as two pieces sewn together.

Separate Gussets (Make 2)

You can work the gussets in one color, in stripes, or in another stitch pattern, as long as you achieve the specified gauge.

1. CO sts as specified for your size and gauge in Table 3.

2. Beg with a knit row, work in St st until piece measures 5 (8, 14) inches, ending with a RS row.

3. Next row (WS): Knit across for folding ridge.

4. Beg with a knit row, work in St st for 1 inch, ending with a RS row.

5. BO purlwise.

6. Go to "Gusseted Bag Finishing," page 54.

Table 3. Cast On for Gusset or Gusset/Handle Combination	
Gauge	**No. of Sts to CO**
2 sts/in.	3 (8, 8) sts
3 sts/in.	3 (12, 12) sts
4 sts/in.	4 (16, 16) sts
6 sts/in.	6 (24, 24) sts

Gusset/Handle Combination: Flat Version (Make 2)

You knit two identical pieces and then sew or knit them together at the top of the handle to form this version.

Note: *The flat version of the gusset/handle combination is not recommended for the smallest size at 2 and 3 stitches per inch because there are not enough stitches to work a proper handle. The tubular version works best for those gauges.*

1 CO sts as specified for your size and gauge in Table 3.

2 Beg with a knit row, work in St st until piece measures 5 (8, 14) inches (that is, the length of one side gusset).

3 Work the remainder of the piece—which is the handle—in garter st. AT THE SAME TIME, narrow the handle by k2tog each end every other row until you have half the number of sts you started with.

4 Cont without shaping until the handle section is half the desired total length. Place sts on holder.

5 Go to "Handle/Gusset Combination Bag Finishing," page 54.

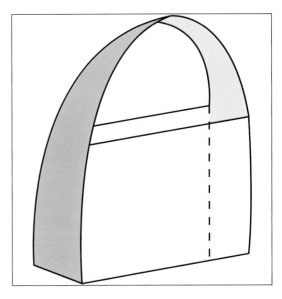

Gusset/Handle Combination: Tubular Version

This gusset/handle combination is worked as one piece.

1 CO sts as specified for your size and gauge in Table 3.

2 Beg with a knit row, work in St st (or desired stitch pattern) until piece measures 5½ (9, 15) inches.

3 Slip stitches to dpn and work handle section as knitted cord to desired length. (See page 271 for knitted cord instructions.)

Note: *If you are working on 8 or more sts, knit cord in the round using 4 dpns.*

4 Slip sts back to single-pointed needle and work back and forth in rows in St st until this gusset side matches the first gusset side.

5 BO in patt st.

6 Go to "Handle/Gusset Combination Bag Finishing," page 54.

CONTINUED ON NEXT PAGE

FINISH THE RECTANGULAR BAG

Flat Bag Finishing

1. Weave in ends, except those that can be used to sew seams.
2. Lightly steam on WS to block and reduce curling, if your yarn's care instructions allow.
3. Fold piece in half with RS facing each other, matching CO edge to BO edge. Pin and sew side seams, including hem.
4. Turn RS out, fold hem to inside along folding ridge, and steam fold and side seams.
5. Pin hem in place and whipstitch all the way around.
6. Weave in any rem ends.
7. Make handle and sew it to corners. (See pages 60–63 for handle suggestions and instructions.)
8. Line the bag, if desired. (See pages 64–65 for lining instructions.)

Gusseted Bag Finishing

1. Weave in ends, except those that can be used to sew seams.
2. Lightly steam all pieces on WS to block and reduce curling, if your yarn's care instructions allow.
3. With RS facing, pin gussets to larger piece, lining up folding ridges, and sew seams, including the hem section.
4. Turn RS out, fold hem to inside, and steam fold and seams.
5. Pin hem in place and whipstitch all the way around.
6. Weave in any rem ends.
7. Make handle and sew it to corners. Or, if using two handles, as in the sample shown, sew them to the front and back panels. (See pages 60–63 for handle suggestions and instructions.)
8. Line the bag, if desired. (See pages 64–65 for lining instructions.)

Handle/Gusset Combination Bag Finishing

1. Weave in ends, except those that can be used to sew seams.
2. Lightly steam all pieces on WS to block and reduce curling, if your yarn's care instructions allow.
3. With RS facing, pin gussets to larger piece, excluding the hems, and sew gusset seams all the way around, starting at folding ridge, working around gusset from ridge to ridge.
4. Turn RS out and fold both hems to inside. Steam folds and seams. Pin and whipstitch hems in place.
5. For flat handle, use three-needle bind-off to join flat handle sts at top. (See page 257 for three-needle bind-off instructions.)
6. Weave in any rem ends.
7. Line the bag, if desired. (See pages 64–65 for lining instructions.)

Here is another way to make a bag. Knit in the round, this style requires less finishing and results in a softer shape. The small bag is tiny—good for a mobile phone or MP3 player. You could dress up the medium bag with beading or knit it in fancy yarn for an evening purse. It's a good idea to work the large bag in a firm yarn and stitch pattern to minimize stretching.

SIZES

S (M, L)

Dimensions (Circumference × Height): 6 × 3½–4½ (16 × 8–9½, 27 × 12–13½) inches

Note: *Heights of the round bags vary due to differing row gauges and styles.*

MATERIALS

Desired yarn, in the amount specified in Table 4

1 set of double-pointed needles in size needed to obtain gauge

1 circular needle in size needed to obtain gauge (for large bag)

Row counter (optional)

Tapestry needle

Table 4. Approximate Yardages for Round Bags			
Gauge (in Stockinette Stitch)	Small Bag	Medium Bag	Large Bag
2 sts/in.	20–25 yd.	85–100 yd.	200–300 yd.
3 sts/in.	25–30 yd.	125–150 yd.	250–350 yd.
4 sts/in.	30–40 yd.	150–175 yd.	350–500 yd.
6 sts/in.	40–60 yd.	175–225 yd.	500–650 yd.

NOTES ON THE SAMPLES

The medium-size violet drawstring round bag is worked in GGH/Muench *Via Mala* (Colors #31 and #34, 100% wool, 73 yd./50g ball, 3 sts per inch). It has a flat bottom and eight eyelets along the top for the crochet chain drawstring. The top edge of the bag and the handle are worked in seed stitch.

The small round pink bag is worked in GGH/Muench *Savanna* (Color #003, 43% alpaca/23% linen/19% wool/15% nylon, 88 yd./50g ball, 4 sts per inch). It has curved shaping for the base and a tiny garter stitch handle. A lazy daisy is embroidered on the front in two colors.

CONTINUED ON NEXT PAGE

How to Make the Round Bag

CAST ON: ALL ROUND STYLES

1 CO sts as specified for your size and gauge in Table 5.

2 Place marker (pm) and join rnd, taking care not to twist sts.

3 Work top edge according to one of the styles listed under "Make Edge," below

4 Go to "Make Bag Body: All Round Styles," on the next page.

Table 5. Cast On for Round Bag	
Gauge	**No. of Sts to CO**
2 sts/in.	12 (32, 54) sts
3 sts/in.	18 (48, 81) sts
4 sts/in.	24 (64, 108) sts
6 sts/in.	36 (96, 162) sts

MAKE EDGE

For an easy, firm edge to your bag, choose garter stitch or seed stitch. The ribbed edge will cinch in a bit, and the hemmed edge will be neat, flat, and more substantial than the others.

Garter Stitch Edge

This edge produces a neat, flat border. When working in the round, you alternate purl and knit rounds for garter stitch.

1 Rnd 1: Purl.

2 Rnd 2: Knit.

3 Rep rnds 1 and 2 until edge measures approx ¼ (1, 1) inch.

Ribbed Edge

If your stitch count is a multiple of 4 sts, you can work this edge as 2x2 rib.

1 Rnd 1: *K1, p1; rep from * to end of rnd.

2 Rep rnd 1 until edge measures approx ¼ (1, 1) inch.

Seed Stitch Edge

This edge may have a larger gauge than the body of the bag because alternating knit and purl stitches every stitch *and* every row tends to create more space between the stitches. If you don't want this effect, try using needles one or two sizes smaller for this edge.

1 Rnd 1: *K1, p1; rep from * to end of rnd.

2 Rnd 2: *P1, k1; rep from * to end of rnd.

3 Rep rnds 1 and 2 until edge measures ¼ (1, 1) inch.

Hemmed Edge

This method forms a tidy edge. Work through step 2 in needles one or two sizes smaller than those used for the body of the bag.

1 Knit all rnds until piece measures ¾ (1, 1) inch.

2 Purl next rnd to form folding ridge.

Note: *For a picot edge, work the folding ridge as an eyelet row by repeating [k2tog, yo] around.*

3 Knit same number of rnds as in step 1.

MAKE BAG BODY: ALL ROUND STYLES

1 Knit every rnd for ½ (1, 2) inches beyond edging.

Note: *If you want a drawstring bag, work as instructed in step 1 for 0 (½, ½) inch and then work 6–12 eyelets, evenly spaced around, by [yo, k2tog]. Then continue knitting every round.*

2 Inc rnd: Inc evenly around the number of sts specified for your size and gauge in the second column of Table 6. You should now have the number of sts specified for your size and gauge in the third column of Table 6.

3 Work without further shaping until piece measures approx 4 (8, 12) inches from CO edge, hemmed edge, or folding ridge for flat-bottom bag or until piece measures approx 3 (7, 11) inches for curved-base bag.

4 Go to desired base shaping under "Shape the Base," below.

Table 6. Increase for Bag Body

Gauge	No. of Sts to Inc Evenly Around	New St Count
2 sts/in.	2 (4, 6) sts	14 (36, 60) sts
3 sts/in.	3 (6, 9) sts	21 (54, 90) sts
4 sts/in.	4 (8, 12) sts	28 (72, 120) sts
6 sts/in.	6 (12, 18) sts	42 (108, 180) sts

SHAPE THE BASE

At this point, you choose whether to give your round bag a curved base or a flat base.

Curved Base Shaping

This base is rounded gradually, like a feed bag or the top of a hat.

1 1st dec rnd: *K5 (7, 8), k2tog; rep from * to end of rnd. You should have rem the number of sts specified for your size and gauge in Table 7.

Table 7. Number of Stitches Remaining After First Decrease Round

Gauge	No. of Sts Rem	No. of Sts to Dec in 1st Dec Rnd
2 sts/in.	12 (32, 54) sts	2 (4, 6) sts
3 sts/in.	18 (48, 81) sts	3 (6, 9) sts
4 sts/in.	24 (64, 108) sts	4 (8, 12) sts
6 sts/in.	36 (96, 162) sts	6 (12, 18) sts

CONTINUED ON NEXT PAGE

2 Knit 1 rnd without shaping.

3 2nd dec rnd: *K4 (6, 7), k2tog; rep from * to end of rnd. You should have rem the number of sts specified for your size and gauge in Table 8.

4 Knit 1 rnd without shaping.

5 3rd dec rnd: Dec the number of sts specified for your size and gauge in Table 9.

6 Rep steps 4 and 5 until you have the number of sts specified for your size and gauge in the third column of Table 9.

7 Next rnd: K2tog to end of rnd, end k1 if necessary.

8 Rep step 7 0 (0, 1) time for 2 and 3 sts per inch and 0 (1, 2) time for 4 and 6 sts per inch.

9 Cut yarn, leaving a long tail. Pull tail through rem sts and secure.

10 Go to "Finish the Round Bag: All Styles," page 59.

Table 8. Number of Stitches Remaining After Second Decrease Round		
Gauge	**No. of Sts Rem**	**No. of Sts to Dec in 2nd Dec Rnd**
2 sts/in.	10 (28, 48) sts	2 (4, 6) sts
3 sts/in.	15 (42, 72) sts	3 (6, 9) sts
4 sts/in.	20 (56, 96) sts	4 (8, 12) sts
6 sts/in.	30 (84, 144) sts	6 (12, 18) sts

Table 9. Decrease Every Other Round for Curved Base		
Gauge	**No. of Sts to Dec per Dec Rnd, Final Dec**	**No. of Sts Rem**
2 sts/in.	2 (4, 6) sts	6 (8, 24) sts
3 sts/in.	3 (6, 9) sts	9 (12, 36) sts
4 sts/in.	4 (8, 12) sts	12 (16, 48) sts
6 sts/in.	6 (12, 18) sts	18 (24, 72) sts

Flat Base Shaping

This base is round but flat, like the base of a bucket.

1 Purl 1 rnd for circular ridge at base.

2 Knit 1 rnd.

3 1st dec rnd: *K5 (7, 8), k2tog; rep from * to end of rnd. You should have rem the number of sts specified for your size and gauge in Table 7 (page 57).

4 2nd dec rnd: *K4 (6, 7), k2tog; rep from * to end of rnd. You should have rem the number of sts specified for your size and gauge in Table 8.

5 Dec the number of sts specified for your size and gauge in Table 10 *every* rnd until you have rem the number of sts specified for your size and gauge in the third column of Table 10.

6 Next rnd: K2tog to end of rnd.

Note: *If you have an uneven number of sts, k2tog as many sts as possible and k1 rem st.*

7 Rep step 6 0 (1, 2) times for 2 sts/inch, 1 (2, 3) times for 3 and 4 sts/inch, and 2 (3, 4) times for 6 sts/inch.

8 Cut yarn, leaving a long tail. Pull tail through rem sts and secure.

9 Go to "Finish the Round Bag: All Styles," below.

Table 10. Decrease Every Round for Flat Base		
Gauge	**No. of Sts to Dec per Dec Rnd**	**No. of Sts Rem**
2 sts/in.	2 (4, 6) sts	2 (4, 6) sts
3 sts/in.	3 (6, 9) sts	3 (6, 9) sts
4 sts/in.	4 (8, 12) sts	4 (8, 12) sts
6 sts/in.	6 (12, 18) sts	6 (12, 18) sts

FINISH THE ROUND BAG: ALL STYLES

1 Weave in ends.

2 Lightly steam on WS to block, if your yarn's care instructions allow.

3 Turn RS out. For hemmed edges, fold hem to inside along folding ridge, steam fold, pin hem in place, and whipstitch all the way around.

4 Make handle and sew it to the corners. (See pages 60–63 for handle suggestions and instructions.) For drawstring version, weave a strand of yarn in and out of eyelets to determine the desired length for the drawstring. Work drawstring as a knitted cord, crocheted chain, or braided yarn, or use ribbon, rawhide, rope, or other cord. See Appendix A for knitted cord (page 271) and crochet chain (page 272) instructions.

Create Handles

You can dress up your bag with unique handles. You can buy premade handles at a craft store, but knitting them is more fun. Be sure to work a handle that is strong enough to support the bag and that will stand up to wear and tear.

How to Make the Handles

GARTER STITCH HANDLE

This is the most basic handle, and it works well for a shoulder bag. Try working it in stripes to liven it up. Instructions are for three widths: ½ (1, 2) inches.

1. CO sts for your size and gauge according to Table 11.

2. Knit every row to desired length.

3. BO knitwise.

4. Go to "Finish and Attach Handles," page 63.

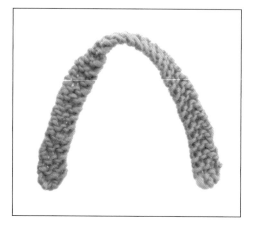

| Table 11. Cast On for Garter Stitch Handle ||
Gauge	No. of Sts to CO
2 sts/in.	— (2, 4) sts
3 sts/in.	2 (3, 6) sts
4 sts/in.	2 (4, 8) sts
6 sts/in.	3 (6, 12) sts

RIBBED HANDLE

This is a flat handle. Instructions are given for three widths: 1 (2, 3) inches.

1. CO sts for your size and gauge according to Table 12.

2. Row 1 (RS): K1, *p1, k1; rep from * to end of row.

   Note: If you want to work this as a seed stitch handle, CO the same number of sts and rep row 1 to desired length.

3. Row 2 (WS): P1, *k1, p1; rep from * to end of row.

4. Rep rows 1 and 2 to desired length.

5. BO in rib.

6. Go to "Finish and Attach Handles," page 63.

| Table 12. Cast On for Ribbed Handle ||
Gauge	No. of Sts to CO
2 sts/in.	3 (5, 7) sts
3 sts/in.	3 (7, 9) sts
4 sts/in.	5 (9, 11) sts
6 sts/in.	5 (11, 17) sts

KNITTED CORD TUBULAR HANDLE

This technique results in a sturdy and attractive handle. Instructions are given for five circumferences: 1 (1½, 2, 3, 4) inches. You need two dpns suitable for your yarn. For a tighter fabric, go down a needle size. For more than 8 sts, knit in the round using 4 dpns.

1 CO sts for your size and gauge according to Table 13.

2 Row 1 (RS): Knit across sts with second dpn but do not turn work.

3 Slide the sts back to the other end of the dpn, ready to work a RS row again. Knit across, pulling working yarn tightly across back to join the tube.

4 Rep step 3 until handle is desired length.

5 BO knitwise.

6 Go to "Finish and Attach Handles," page 63.

Table 13. Cast On for Knitted Cord Tubular Handle	
Gauge	**No. of Sts to CO**
2 sts/in.	2 (3, 4, 6, 8) sts
3 sts/in.	3 (4, 6, 9, 12) sts
4 sts/in.	4 (6, 8, 12, 16) sts
6 sts/in.	6 (9, 12, 18, 24) sts

DROP STITCH HANDLE

This lacy handle includes instructions for three widths: 1 (2, 3) inches.

1 CO sts for your size and gauge according to Table 14.

2 Row 1 (RS): Knit.

3 Row 2 (WS): Knit.

4 Row 3: K1, *yo twice, k1; rep from * to end of row.

5 Row 4: Knit across, dropping the yo loops as you go.

6 Rep rows 1–4 to desired length, ending with row 1 or 2.

7 BO knitwise.

8 Go to "Finish and Attach Handles," page 63.

Table 14. Cast On for Drop Stitch Handle	
Gauge	**No. of Sts to CO**
2 sts/in.	2 (4, 8) sts
3 sts/in.	3 (6, 9) sts
4 sts/in.	4 (8, 12) sts
6 sts/in.	6 (12, 18) sts

CONTINUED ON NEXT PAGE

BASIC CABLE HANDLE

This simple 6-stitch front cross cable makes a wonderful handle. The width is 1 to 3 inches, depending on gauge. To make it, you need a cable needle (cn).

1 CO 6 sts.

2 Rows 1 and 5 (RS): Knit.

3 Rows 2, 4, and 6: Purl.

4 Row 3: Slip first 3 sts to cn and hold at front, k3 from left needle, k3 from cn.

5 Rep rows 1–6 to desired length, ending with row 5.

6 BO purlwise.

7 Go to "Finish and Attach Handles," on the next page.

BRAIDED HANDLE

Here is a fun handle. Instructions are given for a handle that is 1½–2½ inches wide, depending on gauge. You need two stitch holders.

1 CO 9 sts.

2 Row 1 (RS): K1, *p1, k1; rep from * to end of row.

3 Row 2 (WS): P1, *k1, p1; rep from * to end of row.

4 Rep rows 1 and 2 until piece measures approx 2 inches, ending with a WS row.

5 Next row (RS): K1, p1, k1; put rem 6 sts onto holder.

6 Working on first 3 sts only, cont in rib patt until piece is 1–2 inches beyond desired length. Braiding will shorten it. Cut yarn, leaving a 6-inch tail. Put these 3 sts on second holder.

7 Slip center 3 sts to needle and beg with RS row, work in patt through same row, and cut yarn as for first set of sts. Slip these sts onto holder.

8 Slip last 3 sts to needle and work in patt through same row as other two sets of sts.

9 Cut yarn, leaving a 6-inch tail.

10 Lay handle RS up with connected end at top. Braid the sections: Lay right piece over center, lay left piece over center, right over center, and so on, ending with left piece.

11 Slip all sts to needle, ready to beg a WS row.

12 Rejoin yarn and work in patt for approx 2 inches.

13 BO in patt.

14 Go to "Finish and Attach Handles," on the next page.

BRAIDED CABLE HANDLE

This makes a firm and attractive handle. The width of this handle is 1½ to 3 inches, depending on gauge. To make it, you need a cable needle (cn).

1 CO 8 sts.

2 Beg with a knit row, work 2 rows St st.

3 Row 1 (RS): [Slip next 2 sts to cn and hold at back, k2 from left needle, k2 from cn] twice.

4 Rows 2 and 4 (WS): Purl.

5 Row 3: K2, [slip next 2 sts to cn and hold at front, k2 from left needle, k2 from cn], k2.

6 Rep rows 1–4 to desired length, ending with a WS row.

7 Next row (RS): Knit.

8 BO purlwise.

9 Go to "Finish and Attach Handles," below.

CROCHETED HANDLE

Here's an easy handle for crocheters. Use a crochet hook suitable to your yarn.

1 Crochet a chain to the desired handle length.

2 Turn and work one SC into each chain to end.

3 Ch1.

4 Turn and work 1 SC into each SC from row before.

5 Rep steps 3 and 4 to desired width.

6 Cut yarn, leaving a 6-inch tail. Pull tail through last loop and secure.

7 Go to "Finish and Attach Handles," below.

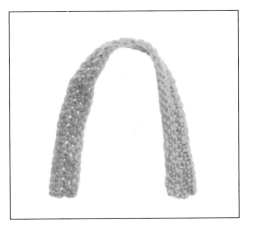

Finish and Attach Handles

1 Weave in ends.

2 Steam to block and neaten the handles, if your yarn's care instructions allow, taking care not to mash ribs or cables.

3 Sew handle ends neatly and firmly to the inside edges of the bag. If you must have the stitches go all the way through the knitting, consider attaching a decorative button on the front to conceal the stitches.

Line a Knitted Bag

Lining your knitted bag is easy. The lining will protect your knitting and enable the bag to safely hold all kinds of items. Choose a lining fabric that complements your yarn colors. These instructions are designed for the rectangular flat and gusseted bags presented earlier in the chapter.

Specifications

SIZES

S (M, L)

Flat rectangular bags (Width × Height): 4 × 5 (10 × 8, 12 × 14) inches

Gusseted rectangular bags (Width × Height × Depth): 4 × 5 × 1 (10 × 8 × 4, 12 × 14 × 4) inches

MATERIALS

Fabric for lining

Interfacing, if a more rigid lining is desired

Note: *You can add an additional lining of thick interfacing between the knit fabric and the lining fabric. Cut the interfacing as you do the lining fabric, hold it together with the corresponding lining pieces, and sew as instructed. You can purchase interfacing in different thicknesses at a fabric store.*

Scissors or pinking shears

Pins

Ruler or tape measure

Sewing machine (optional)

Needle and thread

How to Make the Lining

FLAT RECTANGULAR BAG LINING

1. Cut a piece of lining fabric 5 × 12 (11 × 18, 13 × 30) inches.

2. Fold the fabric with RS facing each other along the width so that it measures 5 × 6 (11 × 9, 13 × 15) inches. Pin the sides tog.

3. Using a sewing machine or a needle and thread, sew side seams, leaving a ½-inch seam allowance on each side.

4. Insert the lining into the bag, wrong sides tog, so that the fold is touching the bottom and the side seams run along the bag's sides.

5. Reach down into the bag and tack the corners in place. Then tack along each side seam twice, about ⅓ and ⅔ of the way up.

   Note: This will keep the lining from pulling the top of the bag down when you put things in it.

6. Fold over the top edge of the lining all the way around so that the folded edge runs neatly along the top edge of the bag, about ½ inch down from the edge. Pin in place.

7. Using a needle and thread, neatly whipstitch the folded top edge of the lining to the bag.

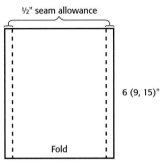

½" seam allowance

6 (9, 15)"

Fold

5 (11, 13)"

GUSSETED RECTANGULAR BAG LINING

1. Cut two pieces of lining fabric 5 × 6 (11 × 9, 13 × 15) inches for the front and back panels.

2. Cut a piece of lining fabric 2 × 17 (5 × 29, 5 × 43) inches for the base and gussets.

3. Pin the long edges of the gusset/base strip around three edges (the gusset sides and base) of the panels, with RS facing each other.

4. Using a sewing machine or a needle and thread, sew seams along pinned edges, leaving ½-inch seam allowance.

5. Insert the lining into the bag with WS together, matching up corners and seams.

6. Reach down into the bag and tack the corners in place. Then tack along each side seam twice, about ⅓ and ⅔ of the way up.

   Note: This will keep the lining from pulling the top of the bag down when you put things in it.

7. Fold over the top edge of the lining all the way around so that the folded edge runs neatly along the top edge of the bag, about ½ inch down from the edge. Pin in place.

8. Using a needle and thread, neatly whipstitch the folded top edge of the lining to the bag.

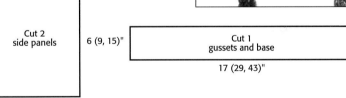

Cut 2
side panels

6 (9, 15)"

5 (11, 13)"

Cut 1
gussets and base

2 (5, 5)

17 (29, 43)"

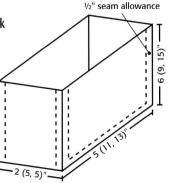

½" seam allowance

6 (9, 15)"

5 (11, 13)"

2 (5, 5)"

The felting process involves exposing a piece of knitting to moisture, heat, and friction in order to shrink it and transform it into a dense, firm, and very strong fabric. Felting requires a carefree attitude because the outcome is not always predictable.

HOW FELTING WORKS

You may have accidentally felted a sweater by washing it in the machine in hot water. When you expose something knit in wool or another animal fiber to wet heat and agitate it, it is likely to shrink and become matted. The fibers open up and become interlocked, creating that dense fabric of felt.

Felting is not an exact science; it's more like a science experiment. Many variables can affect the outcome: water temperature, water hardness, how much agitation occurs, how the fibers were treated before felting, what the fiber blend is, how long the fibers are exposed to heat and moisture, and the amounts of soap and water used. Be prepared for any outcome and be willing to experiment.

THE BEST YARNS FOR FELTING

The best yarns for felting are 100% wool or other animal fibers, such as alpaca, angora, mohair, and llama. You can also try using blends of these fibers. (Superwash wools have been treated so that they will not shrink, so don't use them.) Synthetics are not good felters, but you can try to felt a wool/synthetic blend, as long as it isn't more than 10%–15% synthetic.

Fibers that have been bleached, such as bright whites, and bright colors that have been treated with bleach to take the dye are also not always the best for felting. It is not recommended to use different yarn types in the same piece because they will felt differently. And you need to be careful when felting together multiple colors as they can bleed. No matter what yarn you choose, you should felt a knitted swatch first to get a sense of whether and how it will work.

EQUIPMENT NEEDED FOR FELTING

Felting is easiest and fastest when done in a washing machine. If you don't have a washing machine, you can felt in a bucket or in a bathtub or sink. Don't use a front-loading machine, though, as you must open the machine to check on your item every few minutes.

A zippered mesh laundry bag or pillowcase will protect your washer from the wads of fuzz that come off in the process. You also need bleach-free laundry soap, or mild dish soap if you're felting by hand. A tablespoon is plenty. Because agitation and friction are important factors in felting, a pair of jeans or a canvas sneaker to throw in the machine with your item can be helpful, too.

HOW TO KNIT FOR FELTING

You need to knit the item you want to felt larger than you want it to be—to account for the shrinking—and to knit it at a loose gauge, using needles that are 2mm larger than the size specified for the yarn. For example, if your yarn calls for a size 6 (4mm) needle, you'd knit your item with a size 10 (6mm) needle. A tightly knit fabric can end up too rigid, but only experimentation with swatches will tell.

EXPERIMENT WITH SWATCHES FIRST

Felting is unpredictable; you're taking a risk when you put that handknit item into the washing machine. However, you can get at least some sense of the outcome beforehand by swatching. So before you spend the time knitting a bag that is twice the size you want it to be, test felt a swatch in the same yarn first. Be sure to measure the swatch before and after to get a sense of how much shrinkage occurs when you felt it.

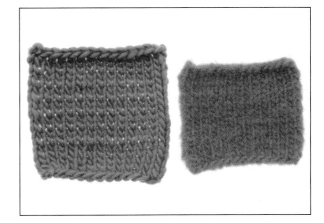

Tutorial: Felted Bag

A knitted bag is a perfect project for experimenting with felting. A bag at any size is useful in some way, so even if your handbag ends up a change purse, you can still use it. This felted bag is easy to knit, and the handles are integrated right into the body, so finishing is a snap.

Specifications

SIZES

One size

Dimensions: Circumference × Height (including handle): Approximately 31 × 25 inches before felting and approximately 22 × 16 inches after felting

Note: *The final size of the bag depends on how much it shrinks during the felting process.*

MATERIALS

1 skein each Brown Sheep's *Lamb's Pride Worsted* (85% wool, 25% mohair, 190 yd./113g skein) in #M-78 Aztec Turquoise (A), and #M-120 Limeade (B)

1 set straight needles in size 10½ (6.5mm) or size needed to achieve gauge

1 circular needle (16–24 inches long) in size 10½ (6.5mm) or size needed to achieve gauge

1 set of double-pointed needles in size 10½ (6.5mm) or size needed to achieve gauge

Row counter

Stitch holder

Tapestry needle

Zippered lingerie bag or zippered pillowcase

Laundry soap

Pair of jeans or canvas sneaker

1 button in size desired

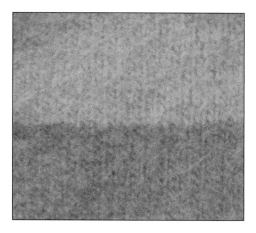

GAUGE

14 stitches and 20 rows to 4 inches over stockinette stitch on size 10½ (6.5mm) needles

M1R (MAKE 1, RIGHT SLANTING, KNIT SIDE)

Use the left needle to pick up the horizontal strand from *back to front* between the last stitch worked on the right needle and the next stitch to be worked on the left needle. Then knit into the front of the picked-up loop.

M1L (MAKE 1, LEFT SLANTING, KNIT SIDE)

Perform as for M1R, only pick up the horizontal strand from *front to back*. Then insert the right needle into the back of the picked-up loop and knit it.

How to Make the Bag

TEST A SWATCH

Remember that felting is not a science. The same yarn on the same needles will felt differently at different temperatures or for different amounts of time. This swatch test should give you a very general idea of what to expect.

1 Using the yarn you have chosen (see pages 66–67 on felting before making your choice) and needles 1.5mm to 2mm larger than your yarn specifies, knit a 6-inch swatch.

2 Treat the swatch as directed in "Felt the Bag," pages 72–73.

3 If you are not pleased with your swatch at this point, experiment with additional swatches for more or less time in the water, or try drying the swatch in the dryer for 10 minutes to see what happens.

4 When you are pleased with the quality of the felting, let it dry and then measure the swatch again.

5 Calculate the percentage the swatch has shrunk. For example, if your 6-inch square swatch becomes a 4½-inch square swatch after felting, it has shrunk 25%. This should give you a sense of how big your bag will come out.

6 Proceed to "Knit the Bag Handles," page 70.

CONTINUED ON NEXT PAGE

KNIT THE BAG HANDLES

1. With straight needle and A, CO 11 sts.

2. Row 1 (RS): Knit.

3. Row 2 (WS): K2, p7, k2.

4. Rep rows 1 and 2 until piece measures 7 inches, ending with a WS row.

5. Next row (RS): K2, m1R, k to last 2 sts, m1L, k2—13 sts.

6. Next row (WS): K2, p to last 2 sts, k2.

7. Rep last 2 rows, inc 1 st as established each end every RS row to 41 sts, ending with a WS row.

8. Cut yarn, leaving a 6-inch tail, and put sts on holder.

9. Rep steps 1–7 for second handle. (Don't cut yarn; leave sts on needle.)

10. Go to "Knit the Bag Body," below.

KNIT THE BAG BODY

1. Still working with yarn A, use circ needle to knit across the 41 sts for the second handle (from straight needle), CO 13 sts, knit across the 41 sts for first handle, CO 13 sts—108 sts.

2. Place marker (pm) and join rnd, taking care not to twist sts. Beg working edge as foll.

3. Rnd 1: P2, k37, p 17, k37, p15.

4. Rnd 2: Knit.

5. Rnd 3: P1, k39, p15, k39, p14.

6. Rnd 4: Knit.

7. Rnd 5: K41, p13, k41, p13.

8. Rnd 6: Knit.

9. Change to B and knit every rnd, knitting as many complete rnds as possible with rem B.

10. Go to "Shape the Base," on the next page.

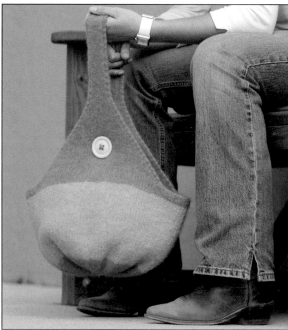

SHAPE THE BASE

Note: Change to dpns when circ needle becomes too large.

① Change to A.

② 1st dec rnd: *K10, k2tog; rep from * to end of rnd—99 sts.

③ Knit 1 rnd without shaping.

④ 2nd dec rnd: *K9, k2tog; rep from * to end of rnd—90 sts.

⑤ Knit 1 rnd without shaping.

⑥ Dec 9 sts evenly around, as established.

⑦ Rep last 2 rnds until 54 sts rem.

⑧ Next rnd: Dec 9 sts evenly, as established, *every* rnd until 18 sts rem.

⑨ Next rnd: K2tog to end of rnd—9 sts.

⑩ Cut yarn, leaving a long tail. Pull tail through rem sts and secure.

⑪ Go to "Finish Before Felting," below.

FINISH BEFORE FELTING

① Weave in ends.

② Join and sew together CO edges of handles firmly, but without overlapping.

③ Go to "Felt the Bag," page 72.

TIP

Fun with Felted Swatches

Before you venture into a large felting project, you should experiment with swatches knit in different animal fibers and even varied stitch patterns. You can use the swatches later as coasters. Embellish them with embroidery after felting for a more finished look.

If a swatch is large enough, you can whipstitch it onto the outside of your felted bag as a pocket. You can also sew six swatches together into a cube to create a stuffed baby toy or paperweight.

CONTINUED ON NEXT PAGE

FELT THE BAG

Although felting is easiest and fastest when done in a washing machine, you can also felt in a bucket or in a bathtub or a sink.

Machine Felting

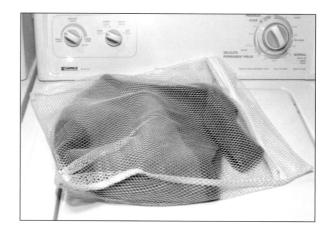

1 Place the knitted bag into a zippered pillowcase or lingerie bag and close.

Note: You'll keep the knitted bag in the zippered bag through the whole process, except to check it during the cycle.

2 Set the washer to the warm or hot wash/cold rinse cycle (small load), start filling the washer, and add approx 1 tablespoon mild dish soap.

3 When the washer is almost done filling, add a pair of jeans or a canvas sneaker and the zippered bag containing your knitted bag.

4 After the machine begins the wash cycle, stop it and check your bag every so often to see how it's doing. (At the very beginning, don't worry if it looks as though it's grown.)

5 Stop when the bag looks felted or when the wash part of the cycle is through, whichever comes first. The knitted bag should have a dense feel, and the stitches should be barely visible, if visible at all. If the bag is felted enough at this point, go to step 7.

6 If the bag is not felted enough after one wash cycle (not including rinse and spin), put it through the wash cycle again, as many times as needed, until it is.

7 Put the bag back into the washer and let it rinse and spin. The cool water locks the fibers and rinses the soap. Spinning removes excess water.

8 Take the bag out of the washer and form it to the desired shape while it is still wet. Stuff it with plastic bags to help shape it, if desired, and set it on a towel to air dry.

9 Go to "Finish After Felting," on the next page.

Hand Felting

1 Fill a bucket, sink, or tub partway with hot or warm water and add 1 tablespoon mild dish soap.

2 Add your bag to the water and agitate it with your hands or a wooden spoon.

Note: When felting by hand, there is no need to put your knitted bag inside a zippered pillowcase or lingerie bag.

3 Keep checking to see if it has felted. Some yarns felt quickly, and others take a couple tries.

4 Stop when the bag looks felted. It should have a dense feel, and the stitches should be barely visible, if visible at all. If the bag is felted enough at this point, go to step 6.

5 If the bag is not felted enough and the water is cooling, squeeze the excess water from the bag and refill the sink or tub with hot water and soap. Agitate the bag in the water again. Do this as many times as needed until it is shrunk and has a dense fabric.

6 Rinse the knitted bag in cool water. Squeeze out the excess water and roll the bag in a towel to get even more water out.

7 Form your knitted bag to the desired shape while it is still wet. Stuff it with plastic bags to help shape it, if desired, and set it on a towel to air dry.

8 Go to "Finish After Felting," below.

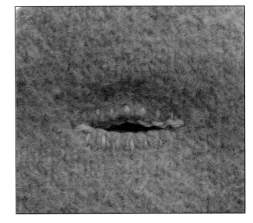

FINISH AFTER FELTING

1 When your bag is completely dry, make a buttonhole by cutting a slit on one side of the bag at the base of the handle strap—about 1½ inches below where the shaping begins—that is about ¼ inch shorter than the diameter of your button.

2 Finish the buttonhole using buttonhole stitch in contrasting yarn. (See page 261 for directions on finishing a buttonhole with buttonhole stitch.)

3 Sew the button on the inside of the opposite handle to correspond with the buttonhole.

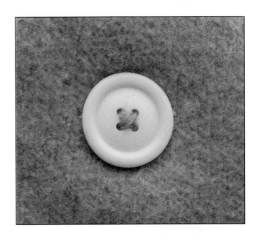

chapter 5

Socks

Most knitters love to make socks. Socks are quick to knit—even when knit in fine yarn—and they're very portable, so you can have them with you all the time. Socks make wonderful gifts. They can be long or short, plain or patterned, thick or thin. Socks don't require a lot of yarn; just a ball or two should do it.

Things to Consider Before Knitting Socks

Before you choose a sock pattern and the yarn to go with it, you should take a moment to consider a few things. Who will wear the socks? What yarns would work best for the socks? What needles are required for that yarn? Will the socks be worn with shoes or as slippers? The answers to these questions should help determine what style sock to knit and what yarn to choose.

TYPES OF SOCKS

Socks can range from highly practical to frivolous, depending on the yarn and stitch pattern used to knit them. Using a sparkly, hairy, or variegated yarn will liven up the plainest sock pattern. You can also adjust the leg length from knee-high to ankle length, depending on your preference. Embroidering initials, flowers, or emblems onto the side of the leg can personalize a very plain pair of socks. Most of the socks in this chapter are fairly practical, though the lacier ones are ornamental, too.

THE BEST YARNS FOR SOCKS

How the socks you are making will be worn should help determine what type of yarn to use. If you are knitting socks to be worn with shoes, choose yarn that is not too thick but very durable. Yarns specifically manufactured and labeled as sock yarns are good for this purpose because these yarns are usually thin and spun with wool that has been reinforced with nylon. If you are making socks for lounging, look for yarns that are soft to the touch and provide warmth. In all cases, choose yarns that have elasticity because the socks will stretch with wear; yarns that have no elasticity will produce socks that stretch out and never regain their original shape.

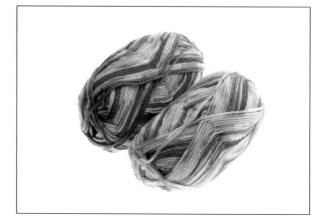

TYPES OF NEEDLES FOR SOCK KNITTING

The socks in this chapter are knit on sets of four double-pointed needles. Some knitters like metal double-pointed needles because the slippery metal enables them to knit faster; others prefer wood or bamboo because the needles don't slide and fall out of the work when it is turned or stored. Plastic double-pointed needles are usually lightweight and less expensive than the other two types.

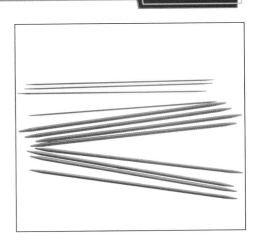

SOCK SIZES

The master sock pattern in this chapter covers the range of sizes shown in Table 1. You measure both the circumference and length of the foot of the wearer to determine which set of instructions to follow. You can adjust the length to suit the wearer.

Table 1. Sock Sizes		
Sock Size	Approximate Foot Circumference (at Widest Point)	Approximate Foot Length (From Tip of Big Toe Diagonally to End of Heel)
XS	5 in.	4 to 6½ in.
S	6 in.	6½ to 7½ in.
M	7 in.	7½ to 8½ in.
L	8 in.	8½ to 10 in.
XL	9 in.	10 to 11½ in.

TIP

Faux Fair Isle Socks

You don't have be an expert knitter to create vibrant socks in eye-catching stripes and color patterns. You can knit any of the sock styles that follow in self-patterning yarn. This is yarn that has been dyed in several colors at measured intervals along the strand. Knitting with self-patterning yarn produces these fun stripes and almost Fair Isle–looking color patterns. The added element of surprise makes knitting with these yarns exciting.

Socks: Master Pattern

You can turn out countless pairs of socks with this master pattern. The sizes range from toddler to men's XL, and the gauges run from 4 stitches per inch to 7 stitches per inch.

Specifications

SIZES

XS (S, M, L, XL)

Approximate foot circumference: 5 (6, 7, 8, 9) inches

Approximate foot length: 4–6½ (6½–7½, 7½–8½, 8½–10, 10–11½) inches

MATERIALS

Desired yarn, in the amount specified in Table 2

1 set of double-pointed needles in size needed to obtain gauge

1 set of double-pointed needles in size one size smaller than size needed to obtain gauge (for hemmed cuff)

Split-ring markers to fit your needle size

Cable needle (for cabled leg styles)

2 stitch holders

Tapestry needle

Table 2. Approximate Yardage for Socks	
Gauge (in Stockinette Stitch)	*Approximate Yardage*
4 sts/in.	100–350 yd.
5 sts/in.	125–400 yd.
6 sts/in.	125–450 yd.
7 sts/in.	150–550 yd.

NOTES ON THE SAMPLES

The gray diagonal rib socks are knit in elann.com *Peruvian Collection Highland Chunky* (Color #0401, 100% wool, 76 yd./50g ball, 4 sts per inch). They have a 2x2 ribbed cuff, a heel stitch flap, and star toe shaping. The diagonal rib is carried onto the instep and up to the beginning of the toe shaping.

The red marl round cable socks are knit in Cascade *220 Quattro* (Color #9433, 100% wool, 220 yd./100g hank, 5 sts per inch). They have a 2x2 ribbed cuff, a heel stitch flap, and wedge toe shaping.

The pink lace socks are knit in GGH/Muench *Wollywasch* (Color #98, 100% wool, 137 yd./50g ball, 6 sts per inch). They have a picot hemmed cuff and a stockinette stitch heel flap. The lace pattern is carried onto the instep up to the beginning of the wedge toe shaping.

The pale green socks are knit in www.fancyimageyarn.com *Machine Washable Merino* (hand-dyed, 100% merino wool, 240 yd./4 oz. hank, 6 sts per inch). They are knit in an allover 2x2 rib and have a heel stitch flap and wedge toe shaping.

The reverse stockinette stitch stripe gray marl socks are knit in Brown Sheep *Wildfoote* (Color #SY39, 75% wool/25% nylon, 215 yd./50 g skein, 7 sts per inch). They have a 2x2 ribbed cuff, a heel stitch flap, and star toe shaping.

How to Make the Socks

When making socks, you have a number of options: cuff stitch, leg stitch, heel stitch, and toe shaping. Because these socks are worked from the top down, stitch patterns will be upside-down. If you want to apply your own color pattern or motif, remember to work it upside-down. You make two socks exactly the same.

ALL STYLES: CAST ON

1 CO the number of sts specified for your size and gauge in Table 3.

Note: It is important to cast on loosely so that the socks pull on easily. If necessary, use a needle two or three sizes larger for casting on.

2 Divide sts evenly onto 3 dpns (use the fourth as the working needle), place marker (pm), and join rnd, taking care not to twist sts.

3 Go to the directions for the desired cuff style under "Make Cuff," below.

Table 3. Cast On for Socks	
Gauge	**No. of Sts to CO**
4 sts/in.	24 (24, 28, 32, 36) sts
5 sts/in.	28 (32, 36, 40, 44) sts
6 sts/in.	32 (36, 44, 48, 56) sts
7 sts/in.	36 (44, 48, 56, 64) sts

Note: Be sure your stitch count is compatible with the stitch pattern you choose. Most of the leg patterns are worked on a multiple of 4 sts and will work with all the stitch counts in Table 3. However, there are a few that can be worked only on a multiple of 8 sts.

MAKE CUFF

1x1 Ribbed Cuff (Even No. of Sts)

This easy rib is one of the most common cuff styles, and it works well with just about any leg pattern.

1 *K1, p1; rep from * to end of rnd.

2 Rep step 1, sl marker beg every rnd, until cuff measures 1 (1, 1¼, 1¼, 1½) inches or desired length.

3 Go to the directions for the desired leg style under "Make Leg," page 80.

CONTINUED ON NEXT PAGE

Easy Ribbed Socks

A sock with a 1x1 or 2x2 ribbed cuff *and* leg has a handsome look and a nice, snug fit. For this type of sock, you continue the rib as established until the sock measures 2½ (3, 4, 5, 6) inches from the CO row for ankle socks or 4 (5, 6, 7, 8) inches for midcalf-length socks. Then you go to the heel directions.

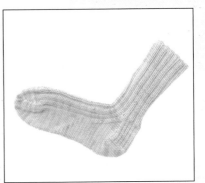

2x2 Ribbed Cuff (Mult of 4 Sts)

This rib produces a very elastic cuff. It works well with leg stitch patterns that are worked over a multiple of 4 stitches.

1 *K2, p2; rep from * to end of rnd.

2 Rep step 1, sl marker beg every rnd, until cuff measures 1 (1, 1¼, 1¼, 1½) inches or desired length.

3 Go to the directions for the desired leg style under "Make Leg," below.

Hemmed Cuff (Any No. of Sts)

This type of cuff looks pretty, but it doesn't hug the leg like the ribbed cuff. It's great for fancy and delicate ankle socks.

1 Using needles one size smaller than the needles needed to obtain gauge, knit all rnds, sl marker beg every rnd, until piece measures 1 (1¼, 1¼, 1½, 1½) inches from CO edge.

2 Switch to needles needed to obtain gauge. Purl next rnd to form folding ridge.

   Note: *For a picot hem, as shown in the photo here, work the folding ridge as an eyelet row by repeating [k2tog, yo] around.*

3 Knit all rnds until piece measures 1 (1¼, 1¼, 1½, 1½) inches from CO edge.

4 Go to the directions for the desired leg style under "Make Leg," below.

MAKE LEG

Stockinette Stitch Leg (Any No. of Sts)

This pattern, which is worked over any number of stitches, is a good basic pattern that can be used with any yarn and works especially well with variegated yarns.

1 Knit every rnd until sock measures 2½ (3, 4, 5, 6) inches from CO row for ankle sock or 4 (5, 6, 7, 8) inches for midcalf-length sock.

2 Go to "Divide for Heel: All Socks," page 83.

Reverse Stockinette Striped Leg (Any No. of Sts)

This pattern, which can be worked over any number of stitches, produces fun ridges.

1 Knit 4 rnds.

2 Purl 2 rnds.

3 Rep steps 1 and 2 until sock measures 2½ (3, 4, 5, 6) inches from CO row for ankle sock or 4 (5, 6, 7, 8) inches for midcalf-length sock.

4 Go to "Divide for Heel: All Socks," page 83.

Lace Leg (Mult of 8 Sts)

This pretty pattern works best in yarns no thicker than 5 sts per inch.

1 Rnd 1: *P2, yo, k2tog, p2, [k 2nd st then 1st st on left needle and sl both sts off needle tog]; rep from * to end of rnd.

2 Rnds 2 and 4: *P2, k2; rep from * to end of rnd.

3 Rnd 3: *P2, k2tog, yo, p2, [k 2nd st then 1st st on left needle and slip both sts off needle tog]; rep from * to end of rnd.

4 Rep rnds 1–4 until sock measures 2½ (3, 4, 5, 6) inches from CO row for ankle sock or 4 (5, 6, 7, 8) inches for midcalf-length sock.

Note: Make a note of which row of the pattern you worked last if you want to continue the pattern on the instep stitches after the heel and gusset shaping.

5 Go to "Divide for Heel: All Socks," page 83.

CONTINUED ON NEXT PAGE

Diagonal Rib Leg (Mult of 4 Sts)

This pattern works well with the 2x2 ribbed cuff.

1 Rnds 1 and 2: *K2, p2; rep from * to end of rnd.

2 Rnds 3 and 4: P1, *k2, p2; rep from * to last 3 sts, k2, p1.

3 Rnds 5 and 6: *P2, k2; rep from * to end of rnd.

4 Rnds 7 and 8: K1, *p2, k2; rep from * to last 3 sts, p2, k1.

5 Rep rnds 1–8 until sock measures 2½ (3, 4, 5, 6) inches from CO row for ankle sock or 4 (5, 6, 7, 8) inches for midcalf-length sock.

> **Note:** *Make a note of which row of the pattern you worked last if you want to continue the pattern on the instep stitches after the heel and gusset shaping.*

6 Go to "Divide for Heel: All Socks," on the next page.

Round Cabled Leg (Mult of 8 Sts)

This pattern looks great on socks for a man, woman, or child. The reverse stockinette stitch background offsets the cable nicely.

1 Rnd 1: *P2, [slip next st onto cable needle (cn) and hold at back of work, knit next st on needle, then knit st from cn], [slip next st onto cn and hold at front of work, knit next st on needle, then knit st from cn], p2; rep from * to end of rnd.

2 Rnds 2 and 4: *P2, k4, p2; rep from * to end of rnd.

3 Rnd 3: *P2, [slip next st onto cn and hold at front of work, knit next st on needle, then knit st from cn], [slip next st onto cn and hold at back of work, knit next st on needle, then knit st from cn], p2; rep from * to end of rnd.

4 Rep rnds 1–4 until sock measures 2½ (3, 4, 5, 6) inches from CO row for ankle sock or 4 (5, 6, 7, 8) inches for midcalf-length sock.

> **Note:** *Make a note of which row of the pattern you worked last if you want to continue the pattern on the instep stitches after the heel and gusset shaping.*

5 Go to "Divide for Heel: All Socks," on the next page.

DIVIDE FOR HEEL: ALL SOCKS

You must divide the stitches to work the heel. You put aside half the stitches for the instep and work the other half back and forth in rows to shape the heel. Here's how you do it.

1. Starting at the beg of the rnd, knit the number of sts specified for your size and gauge in Table 4.

2. Turn and purl across the sts you knit in step 1. Set aside needle from which sts were purled.

3. Do not turn. Using same needle, continue across beg/end of rnd (marker) to purl across the same number of sts on the third needle as you did in step 1. Half your total sock sts will be on one needle. These are the heel sts. Check Table 5 to ensure that you have the correct number of heel sts for your size and gauge.

4. Put rem sts (these will be the instep) onto holders, if desired; if your needles aren't slippery, leave them on the dpn(s).

5. Go to the directions for the desired heel flap, under "Make Heel Flap," page 84.

Table 4. Divide for Heel	
Gauge	**No. of Sts to Knit**
4 sts/in.	6 (6, 7, 8, 9) sts
5 sts/in.	7 (8, 9, 10, 11) sts
6 sts/in.	8 (9, 11, 12, 14) sts
7 sts/in.	9 (11, 12, 14, 16) sts

Table 5. Total Number of Heel Stitches	
Gauge	**No. of Sts for Heel**
4 sts/in.	12 (12, 14, 16, 18) sts
5 sts/in.	14 (16, 18, 20, 22) sts
6 sts/in.	16 (18, 22, 24, 28) sts
7 sts/in.	18 (22, 24, 28, 32) sts

CONTINUED ON NEXT PAGE

MAKE HEEL FLAP

Stockinette Stitch Heel Flap

This heel flap is worked in stockinette stitch. It is flat but not as strong as a heel flap worked in heel stitch. You can reinforce it with thread later.

1 Beg with a knit row (RS), work in St st for the number of rows specified for your size and gauge in Table 6.

2 Go to "Turn Heel: All Socks," on the next page.

Table 6. Number of Rows to Work for Heel Flap	
Gauge	**No. of Rows to Work for Heel Flap**
4 sts/in.	12 (12, 14, 16, 18) rows
5 sts/in.	14 (16, 18, 20, 22) rows
6 sts/in.	16 (18, 22, 24, 28) rows
7 sts/in.	18 (22, 24, 28, 32) rows

Note: The heel flap should be approximately square.

Heel Stitch Flap

This flap is worked in a slip 1, knit 1 pattern that produces a sturdy heel.

1 Row 1 (RS): *Sl1 purlwise wyib, k1; rep from * to end of row.

2 Row 2: Sl1 purlwise wyif, purl to end of row.

3 Rep rows 1 and 2 until you have worked the number of rows specified for your size and gauge in Table 6.

Note: Use a row counter to keep track of rows. The heel flap should be approximately square.

4 Go to "Turn Heel: All Socks," on the next page.

FAQ

I am worried that my knit socks will wear at the heels and ruin all my hard work. What can I do to reinforce the heel?

You should reinforce the heel if your yarn is not already strengthened with nylon. Here's what you do:

1 When you start the heel flap, carry a strand of matching polyester sewing thread or very fine yarn along with your knitting yarn.

2 Work the heel flap to the end, carrying along the thread. Break it off after step 1 of the gusset instructions, after you have worked halfway across the heel sts.

TURN HEEL: ALL SOCKS

In order to make the angle that joins the leg to the foot, you must turn the heel. The instructions for turning a heel look more complicated than they really are. If you read carefully as you work, you'll have a beautifully turned heel in no time.

① Row 1 (RS): Knit half the stitches in the row, k2, sl1 purlwise wyib, k1, psso, k1, turn work without finishing row.

② Row 2 (WS): Sl1 purlwise wyif, p5, p2tog, p1, turn work again without finishing row.

③ Row 3: Sl1 purlwise wyib, knit across to 1 st before the gap caused by turning, sl1 purlwise wyib, k1, psso, k1, turn.

④ Row 4: Sl1 purlwise wyif, purl to 1 st before turning gap, p2tog, p1, turn.

⑤ Rep rows 3 and 4, sl first st beg every row, and working tog the 2 sts, as established, on each side of the turning gap, until all sts have been worked into the center and there are no more gaps, ending with a WS row.

   Note: On the last dec row(s), you may not have enough sts to end the row with a k1 or p1. End these rows with the decrease.

⑥ After turning the heel, you should have rem the number of heel sts specified for your size and gauge in Table 7.

⑦ Go to "Make Gusset: All Socks," below.

Table 7. Number of Heel Stitches Remaining After Turning	
Gauge	**No. of Heel Sts Rem After Turning**
4 sts/in.	8 (8, 10, 10, 12) sts
5 sts/in.	10 (10, 12, 12, 14) sts
6 sts/in.	10 (12, 14, 14, 16) sts
7 sts/in.	12 (14, 14, 16, 18) sts

MAKE GUSSET: ALL SOCKS

① With RS facing you, use an empty needle to knit halfway across heel sts, placing split-ring marker on last st worked, if necessary.

   Note: This is the same point where the rnd ended and began when you were working the leg.

② Using another empty needle (this will be called needle #1), knit across rem heel sts; then, using same needle, pick up and knit the number of sts specified for your size and gauge in Table 8 along right edge of heel flap. You will have on needle #1 the number of sts specified for your size and gauge in the third column of Table 8.

   Note: The number of sts picked up along the edge corresponds to the number of slipped edge stitches along the side of the heel flap.

③ Using another empty needle, work across the instep sts from their needle or holder. (This set of sts will be needle #2.)

Table 8. Number of Stitches to Pick Up Along Right Edge of Heel Flap		
Gauge	**No. of Sts to Pick Up Along Right Edge of Heel Flap**	**Total No. of Sts on Needle #1 at This Point**
4 sts/in.	6 (6, 7, 8, 9) sts	10 (10, 12, 13, 15) sts
5 sts/in.	7 (8, 9, 10, 11) sts	12 (13, 15, 16, 18) sts
6 sts/in.	8 (9, 11, 12, 14) sts	13 (15, 18, 19, 22) sts
7 sts/in.	9 (11, 12, 14, 16) sts	15 (18, 19, 22, 25) sts

CONTINUED ON NEXT PAGE

4 Using a fourth needle, pick up and knit the number of sts specified for your size and gauge in Table 9 along the left side of the heel flap. Then, using the same needle, knit across the first half of the heel sts to marker. (These picked-up sts and heel sts will be on needle #3.) You should now have all sts on three needles, ready to begin first rnd of foot; the third column of Table 9 shows how many stitches you should have in all at this point.

Note: You should have the same number of sts (one-quarter the total number of sts) on needles #1 and #3 and half the stitches on needle #2.

5 Go to "Shape Gusset: All Socks," below.

Table 9. Number of Stitches to Pick Up Along Left Edge of Heel Flap		
Gauge	**No. of Sts to Pick Up Along Left Edge of Heel Flap**	**Total No. of Sts at This Point**
4 sts/in.	6 (6, 7, 8, 9) sts	32 (32, 38, 42, 48) sts
5 sts/in.	7 (8, 9, 10, 11) sts	38 (42, 48, 52, 58) sts
6 sts/in.	8 (9, 11, 12, 14) sts	42 (48, 58, 62, 72) sts
7 sts/in.	9 (11, 12, 14, 16) sts	48 (58, 62, 72, 82) sts

SHAPE GUSSET: ALL SOCKS

1 Rnd 1: K to last 3 sts of needle #1, k2tog, k1; k across instep sts on needle #2; on needle #3, k1, ssk, k to end of rnd. You have decreased 2 sts for gusset.

2 Rnd 2: Knit.

3 Rep rnds 1 and 2 until you have the number of sts specified for your size and gauge in Table 10.

4 Go to "Work Foot: All Socks," below.

Table 10. Total Number of Stitches After Gusset Shaping	
Gauge	**No. of Sts Rem After Gusset Shaping**
4 sts/in.	24 (24, 28, 32, 36) sts
5 sts/in.	28 (32, 36, 40, 44) sts
6 sts/in.	32 (36, 44, 48, 56) sts
7 sts/in.	36 (44, 48, 56, 64) sts

WORK FOOT: ALL SOCKS

You can work the foot in stockinette stitch as described here, or, if you worked the leg in one of the pattern stitches, you can continue in that pattern, on the instep stitches only, down to the beginning of the toe shaping.

1 Knit all rnds without decreasing, until foot (from heel back) measures approx 2¾–5¼ (5–6, 5¼–6¾, 6½–8, 7¾–9¼) inches, depending on the size of the foot you're knitting for.

Note: If none of the foot lengths is suitable for the size foot for which you're knitting, work until foot measures approx 1¼ (1½, 1¾, 2, 2¼) inches shorter than desired total foot length.

2 Go to the directions for the desired toe shaping under "Shape Toe," on the next page.

SHAPE TOE

Star Toe Shaping

This toe shaping is achieved by knitting 2 stitches together 4 times evenly around. It results in a nice round toe that requires no extra finishing.

Note: You can reinforce the toe by carrying along with your yarn a strand of polyester sewing thread.

1. Place a split-ring marker halfway across the stitches on needle #2, dividing them in half.

2. Rnd 1: K to last 2 sts on needle #1, k2tog; k to last 2 sts before marker on needle #2, k2tog; k to last 2 sts on needle #2, k2tog; k to last 2 sts on needle #3, k2tog. You have now decreased 4 sts.

3. Rnd 2: Knit.

4. Rep rnds 1 and 2 until you have rem the number of sts specified for your size and gauge in Table 11.

5. Rep rnd 1 every rnd until 8 sts rem.

6. Cut yarn, leaving an 8-inch tail. Thread tail through rem sts and tighten.

    Note: For a longer toe, work more non-decrease rnds between dec rnds. For a shorter toe, beg working dec rnd every rnd earlier than specified above.

7. Go to "Finish the Sock: All Socks," page 88.

Table 11. Number of Stitches Remaining After Decreasing 4 Stitches Every Other Round	
Gauge	**No. of Stitches After Gusset Shaping**
4 sts/in.	12 (12, 16, 16, 16) sts
5 sts/in.	16 (16, 16, 20, 20) sts
6 sts/in.	16 (16, 20, 24, 28) sts
7 sts/in.	16 (20, 24, 28, 32) sts

Wedge Toe Shaping

This toe shaping results in a rounded, fitted toe. You can finish it by drawing the tail through the remaining stitches and tightening, or you can graft the remaining stitches together by using Kitchener stitch.

Note: You can reinforce the toe by carrying along with your yarn a strand of polyester sewing thread.

1. Rnd 1: K to last 3 sts on needle #1, k2tog, k1; k1, ssk the first 3 sts on needle #2; k to last 3 sts of needle #2, k2tog, k1; k1, ssk over the first 3 sts of needle #3, k to end of needle #3 (end of rnd). You have just decreased 4 sts.

2. Rnd 2: Knit.

3. Rep rnds 1 and 2 until you have rem the number of sts specified for your size and gauge in Table 11.

4. Rep rnd 1 every rnd until 8 sts rem.

5. Graft rem sts using Kitchener st (see pages 258–259) or cut yarn, leaving an 8-inch tail, thread tail through rem sts, and tighten.

6. Go to "Finish the Sock: All Socks," page 88.

CONTINUED ON NEXT PAGE

FINISH THE SOCK: ALL SOCKS

1 Weave in loose ends.

2 Block socks using sock blockers to match the size of your socks, or, if your yarn's care instructions allow, lightly steam to block, taking care not to mash stitch patterns.

TIP

Monogrammed Socks

Handknit socks make such wonderful gifts that you'll probably want to knit many pairs. You can take those gifts a step further and personalize the socks—as long as the leg is worked in stockinette stitch—by embroidering initials onto them in duplicate stitch. It's easy to do, and the added color will liven up a blank sock. Here's how to do it:

1 Chart the initial(s) onto graph paper, as shown.

2 Frame the area on the sock leg where you want the initials to be—usually on the outside of the leg—with safety pins.

3 Choose a contrast color yarn that is visible against the sock background and thread a long strand of it into a tapestry needle.

4 Work the initial(s) in duplicate stitch within the frame, starting at the lower-right corner. (For instructions on working duplicate stitch, see page 274.)

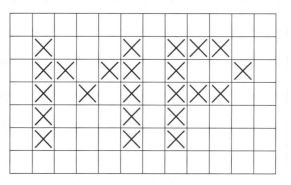

Although it's not as common as the top-down method, you can also make socks from the toe up. Setting up the toe stitches takes a little ingenuity, but once you master it with the first sock, the second will come easily. The benefit of working socks this way is that you can try them on as you go and customize the fit more easily and accurately than with the cuff-to-toe method.

This sock pattern is written for one size and gauge, just to show you how it works. The sample shown here is knit in self-patterning yarn, or yarn that has been dyed at intervals along the strand so that a stripe pattern forms as you knit. It's fun to watch the design appear.

Specifications

SIZES

Approximate foot circumference: 8 inches

MATERIALS

2 balls elann.com *Sock It to Me Collection: Puzzle* (Color #717, 75% wool/25% nylon, 230 yd./50g ball)

1 set of double-pointed needles in size 2 or 3 (2.5–3.25mm) or size needed to obtain gauge

Split-ring markers to fit your needle size

Tapestry needle

Row counter

GAUGE

7 sts per inch

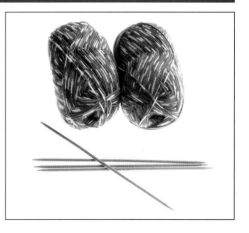

CONTINUED ON NEXT PAGE

How to Make the Socks

Make two of these fun toe-up socks exactly the same.

MAKE THE TOE

1. Using 1 dpn, CO 36 sts. Do not divide sts onto 3 or 4 dpn or work in the round yet.

2. Row 1: *Sl1, k1; rep from * to end of row.

3. Row 2: Rep row 1.

4. Divide the sts between 2 dpns: Holding the dpn with the sts on it in your left hand and 2 more dpns in your right hand, alternate slipping the knit stitches onto one needle and the sl sts onto the other needle until you have 18 sts parallel to each other on each of the 2 dpns. Slip a marker, if needed, onto the needle opposite the working yarn, for beg of rnd. Now you are ready to shape the toe.

   Note: The toe is worked in the round with stitches held on 2 dpns, using a third dpn as the working needle.

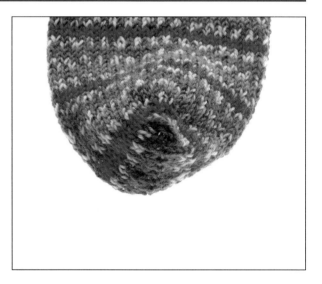

5. Rnd 1: *K1 (to join rnd), m1, k to last st on first needle, m1, k1; on second needle, k1, m1, k to last st on second needle, m1, k1—40 sts.

6. Rnd 2: Knit.

7. Rep last 2 rnds until you have 56 sts.

8. Go to "Make the Foot," below.

MAKE THE FOOT

1. If you're working with a set of 5 dpns, divide the sts over 4 dpns so that there are 14 sts on each needle. If you are using a set of 4 dpns, divide the sts so that 28 sts are on the first needle and 14 sts each are on the second and third needles.

2. Knit every rnd, without further shaping, until sock is approx 2 inches shorter than the desired foot length.

3. Arrange the sts to prepare for heel shaping: Put the first 28 stitches, for the instep, onto a loose strand of scrap yarn. Then place the rem 28 sts for the heel onto a second needle.

4. Go to "Make the Heel," on the next page.

MAKE THE HEEL

The short-row heel is worked back and forth in rows.

1. Row 1: K27, bring yarn to front of work, sl1 purlwise to right needle, turn.

2. Row 2: Sl1 (the unworked st from the last row) purlwise wyif to right needle, p to last st, bring yarn to back of work, and sl1 to the right needle, turn.

   Note: You have now wrapped 1 st on each end.

3. Row 3: Sl1 wyib, k to the st before the wrapped st, bring yarn to front of work, sl1 purlwise to right needle, turn.

4. Row 4: Sl1 wyif, p to the st before the wrapped st, bring yarn to back of work, sl1 to the right needle, turn.

5. Rep rows 3 and 4 until you have 8 wrapped sts on each end and 12 unwrapped sts in the middle, ready to work a RS row.

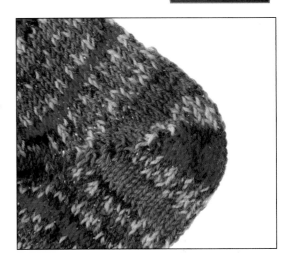

6. Beg back of heel: Sl1 to complete wrap, k to the first wrapped st, [insert the right needle knitwise into both the wrap and the wrapped st, knit the wrap and the wrapped st as 1 st], bring yarn to front of work, sl1 (the next wrapped st), turn. (This last slipped st will now have 2 wraps.)

7. Sl1 (the st with 2 wraps), p to the first wrapped st, [insert the right needle from back to front through the back loop of the wrap, lift the wrap, and place it onto the left needle with the wrapped st, p the wrap and the st as 1 st], bring yarn to back, sl1.

8. Rep steps 6 and 7, but pick up both wraps and knit or purl them together with their accompanying st, until you have worked all sts and have 28 unwrapped sts and are ready to beg a knit row.

9. Knit across the heel sts once more so that you're ready to rejoin the rnd.

10. Go to "Make the Leg and Cuff," below.

MAKE THE LEG AND CUFF

1. Slip 14 heel sts (half the heel sts) onto a second dpn. Place the instep sts back onto a dpn. Join rnd and begin working all 56 sts in the rnd again.

   Note: You might want to pick up a st between the heel and instep sts if a gap occurs at the two points where they meet. If you do, be sure to decrease back down to 56 sts next rnd.

2. Work until sock leg is approximately 4 inches for an ankle sock and approximately 6 inches for a midcalf-length sock, or length desired, minus the cuff.

3. Work the cuff in 1x1 ribbing for approximately 2 inches, or desired length.

4. BO loosely in rib.

5. Go to "Finish the Sock," below.

FINISH THE SOCK

1. Weave in loose ends.

2. Block socks using sock blockers to match the size of your socks, or, if your yarn's care instructions allow, lightly steam to block, taking care not to mash stitch patterns.

chapter 6

Mittens, Gloves, and Hand Warmers

Mittens are easier to make than they appear—they're basically a tube for the hand with a smaller tube coming off for the thumb. Fit is not as crucial with mittens as with gloves, so they make excellent gifts for people of all ages.

As for gloves, don't be scared off by the fingers: Knitting them does add a little more time to your project, but the result is so elegant that it's worth it.

The hand warmers you'll find in this chapter are basically fingerless and thumbless gloves—great for those days when you just need a little warmth and still want the use of your uncovered fingers.

Mittens and gloves come in all shapes and sizes and can be knit in all kinds of yarn. You can add a personal touch by choosing from one of the many cuff styles presented at the beginning of this chapter. Hand coverings ideally should be warm and soft, but aside from that, they can be colorful, playful, or completely practical.

CUFF TREATMENTS

Here are a few basic cuff options that work well for either mittens or gloves. The ribbed cuff is the most common, probably because the elasticity of the stitch pattern helps keep the mitten on the hand. For this master pattern, you can work the ribbed cuff in single (1x1) rib, or, if your stitch count is divisible by four, in double (2x2) rib. You can double the cuff length if you prefer to fold it over for added warmth or a different look.

Reverse stockinette stitch stripe cuff

Seed stitch cuff

Ribbed cuff

Here are some playful cuff treatments. The loop stitch cuff requires a little extra yarn, but the result is worth it. You can also work your cuff in a novelty yarn like the one shown here for added texture and color. Just be sure to choose a novelty yarn that is warm and not itchy to the sensitive skin on the underside of the wrist.

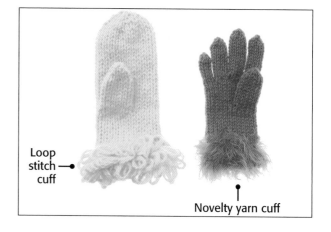

Loop stitch cuff

Novelty yarn cuff

THE THUMB

There are a few different ways to work a thumb. Some mitten patterns involve increasing along one side to form a gusset. The master pattern in this chapter uses a thumb that requires no added shaping to the body and lies flat when the mitten or glove is off the hand. To work this thumb, you slip a thumb's width worth of stitches onto a holder and cast on the same number of stitches in their place—much as you work a buttonhole—and continue knitting until the rest of the mitten or glove is finished. Then you slip the stitches from the holder back to the needle, pick up the same number of stitches plus a couple more around the edge of the thumbhole, and knit the thumb in the round to the desired length. Working the body of a mitten or glove in a repeating stitch or color pattern is easier when this type of thumb is used. You can also have a little fun and knit this type of thumb in an accent color.

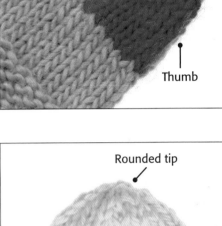

Thumb

MITTEN TIP TREATMENTS

After you have worked the cuff and knit the body of the mitten to the desired length, you can shape the tip as either a rounded tip or a pointed tip. The rounded tip is achieved by working a short series of decrease rounds and then pulling the cut tail through the last remaining stitches, cinching it tight, and fastening it off.

Rounded tip

The pointed tip is created by working decreases on opposite sides of every round until you have only one or two stitches left. You then cut the yarn, pull the tail through the last remaining stitch or stitches, and pull it tight.

Pointed tip

You can use this master pattern to knit mittens and gloves for the whole family, from toddler to adult men's. Choose from several different cuff treatments or create your own. Instructions for rounded-tip mittens, pointed-tip mittens, and basic gloves are presented together: Simply follow the instructions for the style of your choice.

Specifications

SIZES

XS (S, M, L, XL)

Hand circumference: 5 (6, 7, 8, 9) inches

Note: Instructions for gloves in the two smallest sizes are not included for 3 sts per inch, and instructions for the smallest size are not included for 4 sts per inch.

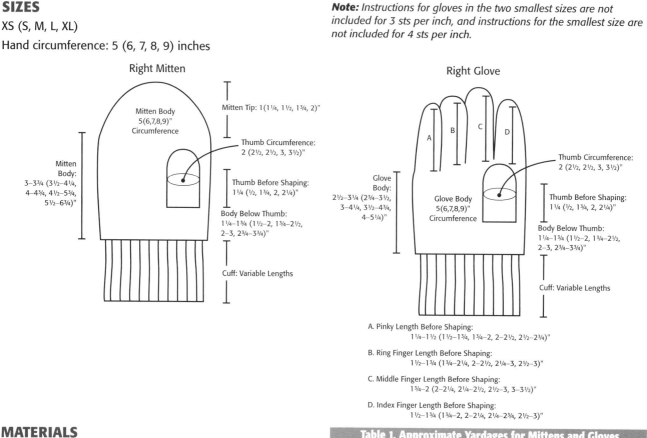

Right Mitten

Mitten Body 5(6,7,8,9)" Circumference

Mitten Tip: 1(1¼, 1½, 1¾, 2)"

Thumb Circumference: 2 (2½, 2½, 3, 3½)"

Mitten Body: 3–3¾ (3½–4¼, 4–4¾, 4½–5¾, 5½–6¾)"

Thumb Before Shaping: 1¼ (½, 1¾, 2, 2¼)"

Body Below Thumb: 1¼–1¾ (1½–2, 1¾–2½, 2–3, 2¾–3¾)"

Cuff: Variable Lengths

Right Glove

Thumb Circumference: 2 (2½, 2½, 3, 3½)"

Glove Body: 2½–3¼ (2¾–3½, 3–4¼, 3½–4¾, 4–5¼)"

Glove Body 5(6,7,8,9)" Circumference

Thumb Before Shaping: 1¼ (½, 1¾, 2, 2¼)"

Body Below Thumb: 1¼–1¾ (1½–2, 1¾–2½, 2–3, 2¾–3¾)"

Cuff: Variable Lengths

A. Pinky Length Before Shaping: 1¼–1½ (1½–1¾, 1¾–2, 2–2½, 2½–2¾)"

B. Ring Finger Length Before Shaping: 1½–1¾ (1¾–2¼, 2–2½, 2¼–3, 2½–3)"

C. Middle Finger Length Before Shaping: 1¾–2 (2–2¼, 2¼–2½, 2½–3, 3–3½)"

D. Index Finger Length Before Shaping: 1½–1¾ (1¾–2, 2–2¼, 2¼–2¾, 2½–3)"

MATERIALS

Desired yarn, in the amount specified in Table 1

10–20 yards of second color yarn (B) for two-color cuff styles

1 set of double-pointed needles in size needed to obtain gauge

1 set of double-pointed needles one size smaller than size needed to obtain gauge (for some cuff edgings)

Stitch marker to fit your needle size

Tapestry needle

Table 1. Approximate Yardages for Mittens and Gloves		
Gauge (in Stockinette Stitch)	Mittens: Approximate Yardage	Gloves: Approximate Yardage
3 sts/in.	50–175 yd.	75–200 yd.
4 sts/in.	75–225 yd.	85–225 yd.
5 sts/in.	75–250 yd.	95–250 yd.
6 sts/in.	100–300 yd.	100–300 yd.
7 sts/in.	100–375 yd.	100–400 yd.

NOTES ON THE SAMPLES

The brown gloves are knit in Brown Sheep *Lamb's Pride Bulky* (Color #M02, 85% wool/15% mohair, 125 yd./4 oz. skein, 3 sts per inch). They have a corrugated rib cuff.

The light yellow mittens are knit in Cascade *Cloud 9* (Color #106, 50% merino wool/50% angora, 109 yd./50g ball, 4 sts per inch), with two strands held together. They have a rounded top and loop stitch cuff.

The orange gloves are knit in elann.com *Peruvian Collection Uros* (Color #3052, 50% wool/50% llama, 90 yd./50g ball, 4 sts per inch). The novelty yarn cuff is worked in GGH/Muench *Apart* (Color #11, 100% nylon, 121 yd./50g ball, 4 sts per inch).

The small lime mittens are knit in Cascade *Pastaza* (Colors #042 and #061, 50% wool/50% llama, 132 yd./100g hank, 4 sts per inch). They are worked with a reverse stockinette stitch stripe cuff and have a rounded tip; the thumb is worked in the second color. The mitten chain is a twisted cord made from the two colors.

The light brown mittens with the striped ribbed cuff are knit in elann.com *Peruvian Collection Highland Chunky* (Color #0208, 100% wool, 76 yd./50g ball, 4 sts per inch). They are worked with a 2x2 striped ribbed cuff and have a pointed tip.

The olive green gloves are knit in Plymouth *Checkheaton Country 8-ply* (Color #2250, 100% wool, 104 yd./50g skein, 6 sts per inch). They have a diagonal stripe cuff.

How to Make the Mittens and Gloves

CAST ON (MITTENS AND GLOVES)

You can choose to make regular-length cuffs or the longer gauntlet-style cuffs.

All Cuff Styles Except Gauntlet: Casting On

1 Using smaller needles, loosely CO sts for your size and gauge, according to Table 2, dividing sts as evenly as possible onto 3 dpns.

Note: *Instructions are not included for the first and second sizes of gloves at 3 sts per inch or for the first size at 4 sts per inch. These sizes are too small for such thick yarns.*

2 Place marker (pm) and join rnd, taking care not to twist sts.

3 Go to the directions for the desired cuff style under "Make the Cuff," page 99.

Table 2. Cast On for Mittens and Gloves	
Gauge	**No. of Sts to CO**
3 sts/in.	16 (18, 22, 24, 28) sts
4 sts/in.	20 (24, 28, 32, 36) sts
5 sts/in.	26 (30, 36, 40, 44) sts
6 sts/in.	30 (36, 42, 48, 54) sts
7 sts/in.	36 (42, 48, 56, 64) sts

CONTINUED ON NEXT PAGE

Gauntlet Cuff: Casting On and Working

This is an old-fashioned cuff that creates a unique mitten or glove. Consider applying a color or stitch pattern.

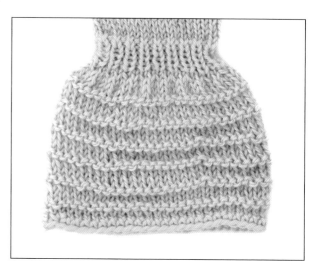

1. Using smaller needles, loosely CO sts for your size and gauge, according to Table 3.

2. Place marker (pm) and join rnd, taking care not to twist sts.

3. Rnds 1, 3, and 4: Knit.

4. Rnd 2: Purl.

5. Rep rnds 1–4, sl marker beg every rnd; until cuff measures approx 2½ (3, 3½, 4, 4½) inches from CO edge, ending with rnd 2, 3, or 4.

6. Next rnd: *K1, k2tog; rep from * to end of rnd. You will have the number of sts rem indicated for your size and gauge in Table 4.

7. Next 5–10 rnds: *K1, p1; rep from * to end of rnd.

   Note: *You can work this ribbed section as long as you want, but at least 1 inch is recommended. For an even tighter fit, you can work this section on needles two sizes smaller than the needles used for the rest of the project.*

8. Go to "Make Body Below Thumb Opening: All Mittens and Gloves," page 103.

Table 3. Cast On for Gauntlet-Style Mittens and Gloves	
Gauge	**No. of Sts to CO**
3 sts/in.	24 (27, 33, 36, 42) sts
4 sts/in.	30 (36, 42, 48, 54) sts
5 sts/in.	39 (45, 54, 60, 66) sts
6 sts/in.	45 (54, 63, 72, 81) sts
7 sts/in.	54 (63, 72, 84, 96) sts

Table 4. Number of Stitches Remaining After Decrease Round for Gauntlet Cuff	
Gauge	**No. of Sts Rem After Dec Rnd**
3 sts/in.	16 (18, 22, 24, 28) sts
4 sts/in.	20 (24, 28, 32, 36) sts
5 sts/in.	26 (30, 36, 40, 44) sts
6 sts/in.	30 (36, 42, 48, 54) sts
7 sts/in.	36 (42, 48, 56, 64) sts

MAKE THE CUFF

The cuff you choose for your mittens or gloves gives it character, and because there is no shaping to interrupt your knitting, you can have fun with it. The following are some of the possibilities.

1x1 Ribbed Cuff (Even No. of Sts)

This basic rib can be worked over any even number of stitches. It provides a nice elastic cuff.

1 Rnd 1: *K1, p1; rep from * to end of rnd.

2 Rep rnd 1, sl marker beg every rnd, until cuff measures 1½–2 (2–2½, 2¼–2½, 2½–3, 3–3¼) inches or desired length.

3 Go to "Make Body Below Thumb Opening: All Mittens and Gloves," page 103.

2x2 Ribbed Cuff (Mult of 4 Sts)

This rib, which makes a wrist-hugging, stretchy cuff, is worked over a multiple of 4 sts.

1 Rnd 1: *K2, p2; rep from * to end of rnd.

2 Rep rnd 1, sl marker beg every rnd, until cuff measures 1½–2 (2–2½, 2¼–2½, 2½–3, 3–3¼) inches or desired length.

3 Go to "Make Body Below Thumb Opening: All Mittens and Gloves," page 103.

Seed Stitch Cuff (Even No. of Sts)

Seed stitch is worked over an even number of stitches. This cuff will not hug the wrist like a ribbed cuff, so you may want to work it on needles two sizes smaller than the needles you use for the body.

1 Rnd 1: *K1, p1; rep from * to end of rnd.

2 Rnd 2: *P1, k1; rep from * to end of rnd.

3 Rep rnds 1 and 2, sl marker beg every rnd, until cuff measures 1½–2 (2–2½, 2¼–2½, 2½–3, 3–3¼) inches or desired length.

4 Go to "Make Body Below Thumb Opening: All Mittens and Gloves," page 103.

CONTINUED ON NEXT PAGE

Reverse Stockinette Stitch Stripe Cuff (Any No. of Sts)

This stitch, which can be worked over any number of stitches, produces a springy, playful cuff.

1 Purl 3 rnds, sl marker beg every rnd.

2 Knit 3 rnds.

3 Rep step 1.

Note: For a longer cuff, rep steps 2–3 to desired length.

4 Go to "Make Body Below Thumb Opening: All Mittens and Gloves," page 103.

Striped Ribbed Cuff (Even No. of Sts)

You can work this as 2x2 rib if your stitch count is divisible by 4. Either way, choose a contrast color (B) that looks nice with the main color (A).

1 Rnd 1: Using A, *K1, p1; rep from * to end of rnd.

2 Rep rnd 1, sl marker beg every rnd, for 3 more rnds.

3 Change to B and knit 1 rnd.

4 Still using B, work rib as set in step 1, for 2 more rnds.

5 Change back to A and knit 1 rnd.

6 Work rib for 3 rnds.

7 Rep steps 3–6.

8 Go to "Make Body Below Thumb Opening: All Mittens and Gloves," page 103.

Corrugated Rib Cuff (Even No. of Sts)

You can work this as 2x2 rib if your stitch count is divisible by 4. This cuff uses two colors, A and B. You cast on in A.

1 Rnd 1: *K1 in A, k1 in B; rep from * to end of rnd.

2 Rnd 2: *K1 in A, p1 in B; rep from * to end of rnd.

3 Rep rnd 2, sl marker beg every rnd, until cuff measures 1½–2 (2–2½, 2¼–2½, 2½–3, 3–3¼) inches or desired length.

4 Go to "Make Body Below Thumb Opening: All Mittens and Gloves," page 103.

Checkered Pattern Cuff (Even No. of Sts)

This fun cuff uses two colors, A and B. You cast on in A.

1 Knit 1 rnd, sl marker beg every rnd.

2 Purl 1 rnd.

3 Beg check patt—Rnd 1: *K1 in A, k1 in B; rep from * to end of rnd.

4 Rnd 2: *K1 in B, k1 in A; rep from * to end of rnd.

5 Rep rnds 1 and 2 until cuff measures approx 1½–2 (2–2½, 2¼–2½, 2½–3, 3–3¼) inches from CO edge, ending with rnd 1.

6 Go to "Make Body Below Thumb Opening: All Mittens and Gloves," page 103.

Leaf Pattern Cuff (Mult of 4 Sts)

This cuff, which must be worked over a multiple of 4 stitches, uses two colors, A and B. You cast on in A.

1 Purl 2 rnds in A, sl marker beg every rnd.

2 Knit 2 rnds in B.

3 Knit 1 rnd in A.

4 Knit 1 rnd in B.

5 Beg leaf patt—Rnds 1 and 7: *K1 in B, k3 in A; rep from * to end of rnd.

6 Rnds 2 and 6: *K3 in A, k1 in B; rep from * to end of rnd.

7 Rnds 3 and 5: *K2 in A, k1 in B, k1 in A; rep from * to end of rnd.

8 Rnd 4: *K2 in B, k1 in A, k1 in B; rep from * to end of rnd.

9 After completing all 7 rnds of patt, knit 1 rnd in B.

10 Knit 1 rnd in A.

11 Knit 2 rnds in B.

12 Knit 1 rnd in A.

13 Purl 2 rnds in A.

14 Go to "Make Body Below Thumb Opening: All Mittens and Gloves," page 103.

CONTINUED ON NEXT PAGE

Diagonal Stripe Cuff (Mult of 4 Sts)

This cuff must be worked over a multiple of 4 stitches. You use two colors, A and B, casting on in A.

1 Purl 2 rnds in A, sl marker beg every rnd.

2 Beg stripe patt—Rnds 1 and 5: *K2 in A, k2 in B; rep from * to end of rnd.

3 Rnd 2: K1 in A, k2 in B, *k2 in A, k2 in B; rep from * to last st, k1 in A.

4 Rnd 3: *K2 in B, k2 in A; rep from * to end of rnd.

5 Rnd 4: K1 in B, k2 in A, *k2 in B, k2 in A; rep from * to last st, k1 in B.

6 Knit 1 rnd in A.

7 Purl 2 rnds in A.

8 Go to "Make Body Below Thumb Opening: All Mittens and Gloves," on the next page.

Zigzag Stripe Cuff (Mult of 4 Sts)

This cuff, which must be worked over a multiple of 4 stitches, uses two colors, A and B. You cast on in A.

1 Purl 2 rnds in A, sl marker beg every rnd.

2 Beg zigzag patt—Rnds 1, 5, 11, and 15: *K2 in B, k2 in A; rep from * to end of rnd.

3 Rnds 2, 6, 10, and 14: K1 in A, k2 in B, *k2 in A, k2 in B; rep from * to last st, k1 in A.

4 Rnds 3, 7, 9, and 13: *K2 in A, k2 in B; rep from * to end of rnd.

5 Rnds 4, 8, and 12: K1 in B, k2 in A, *k2 in B, k2 in A; rep from * to last st, k1 in B.

6 After completing all 15 rnds of patt; k1 rnd in A.

7 Purl 2 rnds in A.

8 Go to "Make Body Below Thumb Opening: All Mittens and Gloves," on the next page.

Novelty Yarn Cuff (Any No. of Sts)

This simple garter stitch cuff works well with hairy or fuzzy yarns.

1 Rnd 1: Knit.

2 Rnd 2: Purl.

3 Rep rnds 1 and 2, sl marker beg every rnd, until cuff measures 1½–2 (2–2½, 2¼–2½, 2½–3, 3–3¼) inches or desired length.

4 Go to "Make Body Below Thumb Opening: All Mittens and Gloves," on the next page.

Loop Stitch Cuff (Any No. of Sts)

This cuff is fun to work and produces a fun and fashionable accent to girls' and women's mittens and gloves. It uses the following stitch:

loop 1: Knit into next st but don't drop it off the needle. Bring the yarn to the front, between the needles, and loop it over your thumb, then bring it between the needles to the back. Knit into the st again, this time bringing it up and off the left needle. You will have 2 sts on the right needle. Pass the 1st st over the 2nd and off. This secures the loop.

1 Rnd 1: Purl, sl marker beg every rnd.

2 Rnd 2: *Loop 1; rep from * to end of rnd.

3 Rep rnd 2 until cuff measures 1½–2 (2–2½, 2¼–2½, 2½–3, 3–3¼) inches from CO edge or desired length.

4 Go to "Make Body Below Thumb Opening: All Mittens and Gloves," below.

MAKE BODY BELOW THUMB OPENING: ALL MITTENS AND GLOVES

1 Change to larger needles and knit every rnd (or work in desired stitch patt) for 1¼–2 (1½–2¼, 1¾–2¾, 2–3¼, 2¾–4) inches.

Note: These measurements are approximate. For the most accurate fit, try mitten or glove on a hand that is close in size to that of the intended wearer. The thumb opening should be placed at the crook of the thumb.

2 Go to "Make Thumb Opening: All Mittens and Gloves," page 104.

CONTINUED ON NEXT PAGE

MAKE THUMB OPENING: ALL MITTENS AND GLOVES

1 K1 at beg of rnd, then slip the number of sts indicated for your size and gauge in Table 5 onto a holder or safety pin.

2 CO the same number of sts as specified in Table 5 to the right (working) needle, using simple cast-on (see page 244), and k to end of rnd.

3 Go to the directions for mittens or gloves under "Make Body Above Thumb Opening," below.

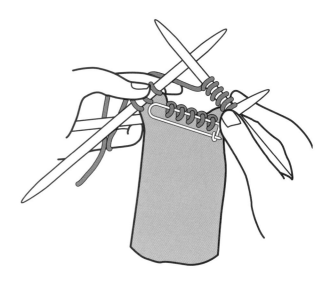

Table 5. Number of Stitches to Put on Holder for Thumb Opening	
Gauge	*No. of Sts to Put on Holder for Thumb Opening*
3 sts/in.	3 (4, 4, 5, 5) sts
4 sts/in.	4 (5, 5, 6, 7) sts
5 sts/in.	5 (7, 7, 8, 9) sts
6 sts/in.	6 (7, 7, 9, 11) sts
7 sts/in.	7 (9, 9, 11, 12) sts

MAKE BODY ABOVE THUMB OPENING

This is where the directions for mittens and gloves diverge.

Mitten Body

1 Knit every rnd until body of mitten measures approx 3–3¾ (3½–4¼, 4–4¾, 4½–5¾, 5½–6¾) inches from top of cuff/beg of body.

Note: These measurements are approximate. For accurate fit, begin tip shaping above tip of pinky.

2 Go to desired mitten tip shaping under "Shape Mitten," on the next page.

Glove Body

1 Knit every rnd until body of glove measures approx 2½–3¼ (2¾–3½, 3–4¼, 3½–4¾, 4–5¼) inches from top of cuff/beg of body.

Note: These measurements are approximate. For accurate fit, measure the hand the gloves are being knit for from wrist to base of fingers. Stop knitting the glove body at the base of the fingers.

2 Go to the directions for working the fingers under "Work Fingers: Right Glove," page 107, or "Work Fingers: Left Glove," page 112.

SHAPE MITTEN

There are two basic styles of mitten tips: rounded and pointed. If you use the rounded style, you work both mittens the same. If you use the pointed style, you end up with a left and a right mitten, and you shape their tips slightly differently.

Rounded Mitten Tip Shaping

1 Work dec rnd as specified for your size and gauge in Table 6. You should have rem the number of sts indicated for your size and gauge in the third column of Table 6.

2 Next rnd: Knit.

Table 6. First Decrease Round for Rounded-Tip Mitten		
Gauge	*Work Dec Rnd*	*No. of Sts Rem After First Dec Rnd*
3 sts/in.	*K2, k2tog; rep from * to last 0 (2, 2, 0, 0) sts, k0 (2, 2, 0, 0).	12 (14, 17, 18, 21) sts
4 sts/in.	*K2, k2tog; rep from * to end.	15 (18, 21, 24, 27) sts
5 sts/in.	*K2, k2tog; rep from * to last 2 (2, 0, 0, 0) sts, k2 (2, 0, 0, 0).	20 (23, 27, 30, 33) sts
6 sts/in.	*K2, k2tog; rep from * to last 2 (0, 2, 0, 2) sts, k2 (0, 2, 0, 2).	23 (27, 32, 36, 41) sts
7 sts/in.	*K2, k2tog; rep from * to last 0 (2, 0, 0, 0) sts, k0 (2, 0, 0, 0).	27 (32, 36, 42, 48) sts

CONTINUED ON NEXT PAGE

3 Work dec rnd as specified for your size and gauge in Table 7. You should have rem the number of sts indicated for your size and gauge in the third column of Table 7.

4 Next rnd: Knit.

5 Next rnd: *K2tog; rep from * to end of rnd.

6 If you have 7 or fewer sts rem, skip to step 8. Otherwise, knit 1 rnd.

7 Rep steps 5–6 until you have 7 or fewer sts.

> **Note:** *If you have an odd number of sts, [k2tog] around to last st, end k1.*

8 Cut yarn, leaving a 6-inch tail. Pull through rem sts and secure.

9 Go to "Work Thumb: All Mittens and Gloves," page 112.

Table 7. Second Decrease Round for Rounded Tip Mitten		
Gauge	**Work Dec Rnd**	**No. of Sts Rem After Second Dec Rnd**
3 sts/in.	*K1, k2tog; rep from * to last 0 (2, 2, 0, 0) sts, k0 (2, 2, 0, 0).	8 (10, 12, 12, 14) sts
4 sts/in.	*K1, k2tog; rep from * to end.	10 (12, 14, 16, 18) sts
5 sts/in.	*K1, k2tog; rep from * to last 2 (2, 0, 0, 0) sts, k2 (2, 0, 0, 0).	14 (16, 18, 20, 22) sts
6 sts/in.	*K1, k2tog; rep from * to last 2 (0, 2, 0, 2) sts, k2 (0, 2, 0, 2).	16 (18, 22, 24, 28) sts
7 sts/in.	*K1, k2tog; rep from * to last 0 (2, 0, 0, 0) sts, k0 (2, 0, 0, 0).	18 (22, 24, 28, 32) sts

Pointed Mitten Tip: Right Mitten Shaping

1 Arrange the sts on the 3 needles as shown in Table 8 to prepare for shaping. Needle #1 is the one that begins the rnd. The stitches on needles #1 and #2 form the palm.

2 Rnd 1: Ssk the first 2 sts on needle #1; k to last 2 sts on needle #2, k2tog; ssk the first 2 sts on needle #3, k to last 2 sts on needle #3, k2tog—4 sts dec.

3 Rnd 2: Knit.

4 Rep rnds 1 and 2—4 more sts dec.

5 Rep rnd 1 until 4 or 6 sts rem.

6 Cut yarn, leaving a 6-inch tail. Pull through rem sts and secure.

7 Go to "Work Thumb: All Mittens and Gloves," page 112.

Table 8. Arrangement of Stitches on 3 dpns for Right Mitten		
Gauge	**No. of Sts on Needle #1**	**No. of Sts on Needle #2**	**No. of Sts on Needle #3**
3 sts/in.	4 (4, 5, 6, 7) sts	4 (5, 6, 6, 7) sts	8 (9, 11, 12, 14) sts
4 sts/in.	5 (6, 7, 8, 9) sts	5 (6, 7, 8, 9) sts	10 (12, 14, 16, 18) sts
5 sts/in.	6 (7, 9, 10, 11) sts	7 (8, 9, 10, 11) sts	13 (15, 18, 20, 22) sts
6 sts/in.	7 (9, 10, 12, 13) sts	8 (9, 11, 12, 14) sts	15 (18, 21, 24, 27) sts
7 sts/in.	9 (10, 12, 14, 16) sts	9 (11, 12, 14, 16) sts	18 (21, 24, 28, 32) sts

Pointed Tip: Left Mitten Shaping

① Arrange the sts on the 3 needles as indicated in Table 9 to prepare for shaping. Needle #1 is the one that begins the rnd. The sts on needles #1 and #3 form the palm.

② Rnd 1: K to last 2 sts on needle #1, k2tog; ssk first 2 sts on needle #2, k to last 2 sts on needle #2, k2tog; ssk the first 2 sts on needle #3, k to end—4 sts dec.

③ Rnd 2: Knit.

④ Rep rnds 1 and 2—4 more sts dec.

⑤ Rep rnd 1 until 4 or 6 sts rem.

⑥ Cut yarn, leaving a 6-inch tail. Pull through rem sts and secure.

⑦ Go to "Work Thumb: All Mittens and Gloves," page 112.

Table 9. Arrangement of Stitches on 3 dpns for Left Mitten			
Gauge	*No. of Sts on Needle #1*	*No. of Sts on Needle #2*	*No. of Sts on Needle #3*
3 sts/in.	4 (4, 5, 6, 7) sts	8 (9, 11, 12, 14) sts	4 (5, 6, 6, 7) sts
4 sts/in.	5 (6, 7, 8, 9) sts	10 (12, 14, 16, 18) sts	5 (6, 7, 8, 9) sts
5 sts/in.	6 (7, 9, 10, 11) sts	13 (15, 18, 20, 22) sts	7 (8, 9, 10, 11) sts
6 sts/in.	7 (9, 10, 12, 13) sts	15 (18, 21, 24, 27) sts	8 (9, 11, 12, 14) sts
7 sts/in.	9 (10, 12, 14, 16) sts	18 (21, 24, 28, 32) sts	9 (11, 12, 14, 16) sts

WORK FINGERS: RIGHT GLOVE

The fingers of the glove are worked one at a time, beginning with the pinky. Each finger is made up of a few stitches from the back of the hand and a few stitches from the palm, plus a few cast-on stitches. Many knitters are put off by the idea of knitting all those fingers, but it's really not that much extra work, and the elegance of the end result is certainly worth the effort.

CONTINUED ON NEXT PAGE

Right Pinky

① K across the number of sts indicated for your size and gauge in the second column of Table 10 and then put those same sts aside onto a strand of loose yarn.

② K across the number of sts indicated for your size and gauge in the third column of Table 10. Leave these sts on the needle and put all rem sts aside on a second strand of loose yarn.

③ Going back to the sts on the needle, with working yarn still attached, use simple cast-on (see page 244) to CO the number of sts indicated for your size and gauge in the fourth column of Table 10.

④ You should have on your needle for the pinky the number of sts indicated for your size and gauge in the fifth column of Table 10. Divide these sts as evenly as possible over 3 dpns. Join these sts into a rnd for the pinky.

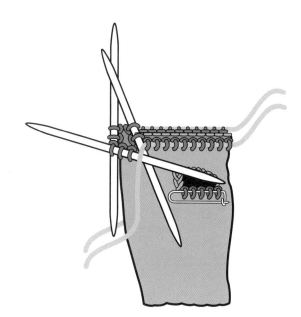

⑤ Knit until the pinky measures approx 1¼–1½ (1½–1¾, 1¾–2, 2–2½, 2½–2¾) inches from beg.

⑥ Next rnd: *K2tog; rep from * to end of rnd.

Note: *If you have an odd number of sts, work as specified to last 3 sts, k3tog.*

⑦ Cut yarn, leaving a 6-inch tail. Pull through rem sts and secure.

⑧ Go to "Top of Hand," on the next page.

Table 10. Right Pinky Setup					
Gauge	**Step 1: Knit Across**	**Step 2: Knit Across**	**Step 3: CO to Close Gap**	**No. of Pinky Sts**	**No. of Sts on Holders**
3 sts/in.	– (–, 9, 9, 11) sts	– (–, 5, 6, 7) sts	– (–, 1, 1, 1) st	– (–, 6, 7, 8) sts	– (–, 17, 18, 21) sts
4 sts/in.	– (10, 11, 12, 14) sts	– (5, 7, 8, 9) sts	– (1, 1, 1, 1) st	– (6, 8, 9, 10) sts	– (19, 21, 24, 27) sts
5 sts/in.	10 (12, 14, 15, 17) sts	6 (7, 9, 10, 11) sts	1 (1, 1, 2, 2) sts	7 (8, 10, 12, 13) sts	20 (23, 27, 30, 33) sts
6 sts/in.	12 (12, 14, 17, 19) sts	7 (8, 10, 12, 14) sts	2 (2, 2, 2, 2) sts	9 (10, 12, 14, 16) sts	23 (28, 32, 36, 40) sts
7 sts/in.	14 (17, 19, 22, 24) sts	8 (9, 11, 13, 16) sts	2 (2, 2, 2, 2) sts	10 (11, 13, 15, 18) sts	28 (33, 37, 43, 48) sts

Top of Hand

Before beginning the ring finger, you must put all the remaining hand stitches back onto the needles and work for about ¼ inch to account for the crook between the ring finger and the middle finger being higher than the crook between the pinky and the ring finger.

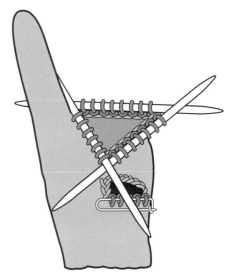

1 Put first set of sts held on loose yarn back onto a dpn. Put second set of sts held on loose yarn onto second dpn.

2 Rejoin working yarn and pick up and knit–from base of pinky at CO sts–the number of sts indicated for your size and gauge in the second column of Table 11. This is the new end of rnd.

3 You should have on the needles the number of sts indicated for your size and gauge in the third column of Table 11. Divide these sts as evenly as possible over 3 dpns, maintaining beg of rnd after picked-up sts.

4 Rejoin rnd and work the number of rnds indicated for your size and gauge in the fourth column of Table 11.

5 Go to "Right Ring Finger," below.

Table 11. Top of Hand Setup			
Gauge	**Step 2: Pick Up and Knit**	**No. of Sts for Top of Hand**	**Step 4: No. of Rnds to Work**
3 sts/in.	– (–, 1, 1, 1) st	– (–, 18, 19, 22) sts	1 (1, 1, 1, 2) rnds
4 sts/in.	– (1, 1, 1, 2) sts	–(20, 22, 25, 29) sts	1 (1, 1, 2, 2) rnds
5 sts/in.	2 (2, 2, 2, 2) sts	22 (25, 29, 32, 35) sts	2 (2, 2, 3, 3) rnds
6 sts/in.	2 (2, 2, 2, 2) sts	25 (30, 34, 38, 42) sts	2 (3, 3, 3, 4) rnds
7 sts/in.	2 (2, 2, 2, 2) sts	30 (35, 39, 45, 50) sts	3 (4, 4, 5, 5) rnds

Right Ring Finger

1 Place onto a dpn the number of sts from the beg of rnd indicated for your size and gauge in the second column of Table 12.

Table 12. Ring Finger Setup					
Gauge	**Place on Needle #1**	**Place on Needle #2**	**Place on Holder**	**CO to Close Gap**	**No. of Ring Finger Sts**
3 sts/in.	– (–, 3, 3, 4) sts	– (–, 3, 4, 4) sts	– (–, 12, 12, 14) sts	– (–, 1, 1, 1) st	– (–, 7, 8, 9) sts
4 sts/in.	– (3, 4, 4, 5) sts	– (4, 4, 5, 5) sts	– (13, 14, 16, 19) sts	– (1, 1, 1, 1) st	– (8, 9, 10, 11) sts
5 sts/in.	3 (4, 5, 5, 5) sts	4 (5, 6, 6, 7) sts	15 (16, 18, 21, 23) sts	2 (2, 2, 2, 2) sts	9 (11, 13, 13, 14) sts
6 sts/in.	3 (5, 6, 6, 6) sts	5 (7, 7, 7, 8) sts	17 (18, 21, 25, 28) sts	2 (2, 2, 2, 3) sts	10 (14, 15, 15, 17) sts
7 sts/in.	4 (6, 7, 7, 8) sts	6 (7, 8, 9, 9) sts	20 (22, 24, 29, 33) sts	2 (2, 2, 2, 3) sts	12 (15, 17, 18, 20) sts

CONTINUED ON NEXT PAGE

2 Place onto a 2nd dpn the number of sts from the end of rnd (this includes the picked-up sts at base of pinky) indicated for your size and gauge in the third column of Table 12.

3 Put rem sts indicated in fourth column of Table 12 onto a holder or strand of loose yarn.

4 Going back to the sts on the needles, with working yarn still attached, k across the number of sts from the beg of rnd indicated in the second column of Table 12.

5 Use simple cast-on (page 244) to CO the number of sts indicated for your size and gauge in the fifth column of Table 12. This covers the gap between the palm and the back of the hand.

6 You should have on the needles for the ring finger the number of sts indicated for your size and gauge in the sixth column of Table 12. Join these sts into a rnd after the CO sts, then k to end of sts from the third column of Table 12. Pm for beg/end of rnd here. Divide sts as evenly as possible over 3 dpns.

7 Knit until the finger measures approx 1½–1¾ (1¾–2¼, 2–2½, 2¼–3, 2½–3) inches from beg.

8 Next rnd: *K2tog; rep from * to end of rnd.

Note: If you have an odd number of sts, work as specified to last 3 sts, k3tog.

9 Cut yarn, leaving a 6-inch tail. Pull through rem sts and secure.

10 Go to "Right Middle Finger," below.

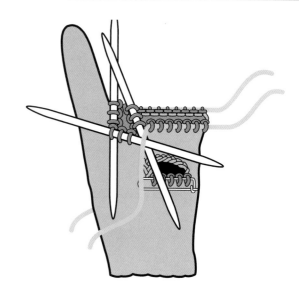

Right Middle Finger

1 Taking from the sts held on the loose yarn for the back of the hand, place onto a dpn the number of sts indicated for your size and gauge in the second column of Table 13.

2 Place onto a 2nd dpn the number of sts held on the loose yarn for the palm indicated for your size and gauge in the third column of Table 13.

3 Keep rem sts indicated in fourth column of Table 13 on holder or strand of loose yarn.

4 Beg with the palm side sts, rejoin working yarn and k across.

5 Pick up and k from the base of the ring finger the number of sts indicated for your size and gauge in the fifth column of Table 13.

6 Use a third needle to k across the back-of-hand sts, then use simple cast-on (page 244) to CO the number of sts indicated for your size and gauge in the sixth column of Table 13 to close gap between palm and back of hand.

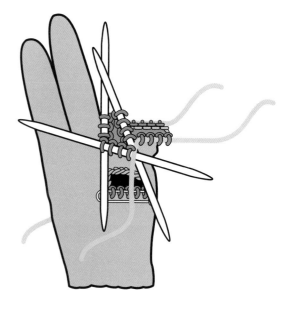

7 You should have on the needles for the middle finger the number of sts indicated for your size and gauge in the seventh column of Table 13. Divide these sts as evenly as possible onto 3 dpns. Join these sts into a rnd for the middle finger.

8 Knit until the finger measures approx 1¾–2 (2–2¼, 2¼–2½, 2½–3, 3–3½) inches from beg.

9 Next rnd: *K2tog; rep from * to end of rnd.

   Note: *If you have an odd number of sts, work as specified to last 3 sts, k3tog.*

10 If you are knitting the largest size at 6 sts per inch or any of the four largest sizes at 7 sts per inch, rep last rnd.

11 Cut yarn, leaving a 6-inch tail. Pull through rem sts and secure.

12 Go to "Right Index Finger," below.

	Table 13. Middle Finger Setup					
Gauge	**Place on Needle #1**	**Place on Needle #2**	**Place on Holder**	**Pick Up and Knit**	**CO to Close Gap**	**No. of Middle Finger Sts**
3 sts/in.	– (–, 3, 3, 3) sts	– (–, 3, 3, 4) sts	– (–, 6, 6, 7) sts	– (–, 1, 2, 2) sts	– (–, 1, 1, 1) st	– (–, 8, 9, 10) sts
4 sts/in.	– (3, 3, 4, 4) sts	– (3, 4, 4, 5) sts	– (7, 7, 8, 10) sts	– (2, 2, 2, 2) sts	– (1, 1, 1, 2) sts	– (9, 10, 11, 13) sts
5 sts/in.	3 (3, 4, 5, 5) sts	4 (4, 4, 5, 6) sts	8 (9, 10, 11, 12) sts	2 (2, 2, 2, 3) sts	2 (2, 2, 2, 2) sts	11 (11, 12, 14, 16) sts
6 sts/in.	4 (4, 5, 6, 7) sts	4 (5, 6, 6, 7) sts	9 (9, 10, 13, 14) sts	2 (2, 2, 2, 2) sts	2 (3, 3, 3, 3) sts	12 (14, 16, 17, 19) sts
7 sts/in.	5 (5, 6, 7, 8) sts	5 (6, 6, 7, 8) sts	10 (11, 12, 15, 17) sts	2 (2, 2, 2, 2) sts	3 (3, 3, 3, 3) sts	15 (16, 17, 19, 21) sts

Right Index Finger

1 Put rem sts held on loose yarn onto 2 dpns, dividing evenly.

2 Rejoin working yarn and pick up and k from the base of the middle finger at the CO sts the number of sts indicated for your size and gauge in the second column of Table 14. You should have on the needles for the index finger the number of sts indicated for your size and gauge in the third column of Table 14. Join these sts into a rnd for the index finger.

3 Knit until the finger measures approx 1½–1¾ (1¾–2, 2–2¼, 2¼–2¾, 2½–3) inches from beg.

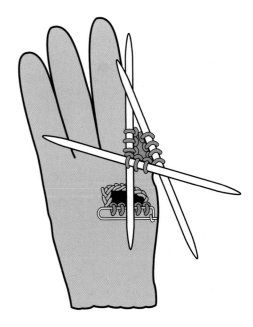

	Table 14. Index Finger Setup	
Gauge	**Pick Up and K**	**No. of Index Finger Sts**
3 sts/in.	– (–, 1, 2, 2) sts	– (–, 7, 8, 9) sts
4 sts/in.	– (1, 2, 2, 2) sts	– (8, 9, 10, 12) sts
5 sts/in.	2 (2, 2, 2, 3) sts	10 (11, 12, 13, 15) sts
6 sts/in.	2 (3, 3, 3, 3) sts	11 (12, 13, 16, 17) sts
7 sts/in.	3 (3, 3, 3, 3) sts	13 (14, 15, 18, 20) sts

CONTINUED ON NEXT PAGE

4 Next rnd: *K2tog; rep from * to end of rnd.

Note: *If you have an odd number of sts, work as specified to last 3 sts, k3tog.*

5 If you are knitting the largest size at 6 sts per inch or either of the two largest sizes at 7 sts per inch, rep last rnd.

6 Cut yarn, leaving a 6-inch tail. Pull through rem sts and secure.

7 Go to "Work Thumb: All Mittens and Gloves," below.

WORK FINGERS: LEFT GLOVE

The left glove is worked essentially the same as the right, except that you rearrange the stitches on the needles so that the thumb opening is moved to the left edge of the palm.

1 Knit across the number of sts indicated in Table 15.

2 Rearrange the sts on the needles and pm so that the rnd begins after the sts knit across in Table 15.

3 Work as for right-hand fingers from here, beginning with step 1 of right pinky, only remember that for the left hand, "back of hand" now refers to "palm of hand" and vice versa.

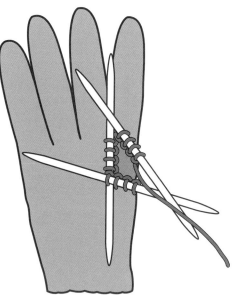

New beginning of round

Table 15. Set Up to Work Left Fingers	
Gauge	No. of Sts to K Across to New Beg of Rnd
3 sts/in.	– (–, 6, 7, 7) sts
4 sts/in.	– (7, 7, 8, 9) sts
5 sts/in.	7 (9, 9, 10, 11) sts
6 sts/in.	8 (9, 9, 11, 13) sts
7 sts/in.	9 (11, 11, 13, 14) sts

WORK THUMB: ALL MITTENS AND GLOVES

1 Join yarn and use a dpn to knit across the thumb sts from the holder.

2 Using a 2nd dpn, pick up and k1 st at left side of thumb opening, then pick up and k from the top of the thumb opening half the number of sts that were on holder for the thumb earlier (refer to Table 5, page 104).

Note: *If the number of sts on the holder for the thumb was an odd number, pick up 1 st fewer than half.*

3 Using a 3rd dpn, pick up and k the remaining sts around the top of the thumb opening–half the number of sts that were on the holder, plus 1 at the side of the thumb opening. You should have on your 3 dpns the number of sts indicated for your size and gauge in Table 16.

4 Pm and join rnd.

5 Knit every rnd until thumb measures approx 1¼ (1½, 1¾, 2, 2¼) inches, or to midpoint of the thumbnail.

6 Work dec rnd as specified for your size and gauge in Table 17.

7 Knit 1 rnd.

8 Next rnd: *K2tog; rep from * to end of rnd.

   Note: If you have an odd number of sts, k2tog around to last st, end k1.

9 Rep last 2 rnds until you have 4 or 3 sts rem.

10 Cut yarn, leaving a 6-inch tail. Pull through rem sts and secure.

11 Go to the appropriate instructions under "Finish the Mittens and Gloves," page 114.

Table 16. Number of Thumb Stitches	
Gauge	**No. of Thumb Sts**
3 sts/in.	8 (10, 10, 12, 12) sts
4 sts/in.	10 (12, 12, 14, 16) sts
5 sts/in.	12 (16, 16, 16, 20) sts
6 sts/in.	14 (16, 16, 20, 24) sts
7 sts/in.	16 (20, 20, 24, 26) sts

Table 17. First Decrease Round for Tip of Thumb		
Gauge	**Work Dec Rnd**	**No. of Sts Rem After Dec Rnd**
3 sts/in.	*K2, k2tog; rep from * to last 0 (2, 2, 0, 0) sts, k0 (2, 2, 0, 0).	6 (8, 8, 9, 9) sts
4 sts/in.	*K2, k2tog; rep from * to last 2 (0, 0, 2, 0) sts, k2 (0, 0, 2, 0).	8 (9, 9, 11, 12) sts
5 sts/in.	*K2, k2tog; rep from * to end.	9 (12, 12, 12, 15) sts
6 sts/in.	*K2, k2tog; rep from * to last 2 (0, 0, 0, 0) sts, k2 (0, 0, 0, 0).	11 (12, 12, 15, 18) sts
7 sts/in.	*K2, k2tog; rep from * to last 0 (0, 0, 0, 2) sts, k0 (2, 0, 0, 2).	12 (15, 15, 18, 20) sts

CONTINUED ON NEXT PAGE

FINISH THE MITTENS AND GLOVES

Finishing Mittens

① Weave in yarn ends, stitching up holes at beg of thumb, if necessary.

② Lightly steam to block, if yarn's care instructions allow.

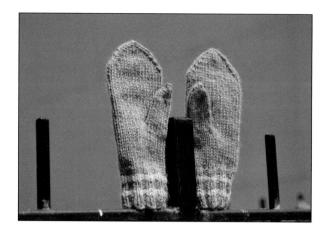

Finishing Gloves

① Weave in yarn ends, stitching up holes at beg of thumb and between fingers, if necessary.

② Lightly steam or wet to block, if yarn's care instructions allow.

TIP

No More Lost Mittens

It would be a shame if one of the mittens or gloves you lovingly knit were to fall out of a pocket into the snow and get lost. You can join a pair of mittens or gloves with a mitten chain to ensure that this doesn't happen. Mitten chains can be worked as crocheted cords, twisted cords, or even knitted cords—and they're not necessarily just for children. If you make a chain in matching and contrast colors, you can add a lively twist to your plain old mittens or gloves, without going to a lot of trouble.

Simply sew the chain ends to the inside wrist corners of the cuffs and then thread the mittens or gloves through the sleeves of a winter coat. For instructions on how to make mitten chains, see "Making Knitted and Twisted Cords," page 271.

Hand warmers, or fingerless gloves, make excellent gifts. They're less demanding to make than mittens or gloves, and their simplicity makes it easy to add interesting stitch patterns or cables. Hand warmers can also be worn on top of knitted or leather gloves for extra warmth. Many of the stitch patterns for the hand warmers can be used for mitten or glove cuffs as well.

Specifications

SIZES

XS (S, M, L, XL)

Hand circumference: 5 (6, 7, 8, 9) inches

5 (6, 7, 8, 9)"

1"

4 (5, 6, 7, 8)"

5 (6, 7, 8, 9)" Circumference

MATERIALS

Desired yarn, in the amount specified in Table 18

1 set of double-pointed needles in size needed to obtain gauge

Stitch marker to fit your needle size

Cable needle (for cabled rib hand warmers)

Tapestry needle

CONTINUED ON NEXT PAGE

Table 18. Approximate Yardage for Hand Warmers	
Gauge (in Stockinette Stitch)	**Approximate Yardage**
2 sts/in.	40–100 yd.
3 sts/in.	50–125 yd.
4 sts/in.	65–150 yd.
5 sts/in.	75–175 yd.
6 sts/in.	75–200 yd.

NOTES ON THE SAMPLES

The 2x2 rib hand warmers are worked using Plymouth Yarn *Baby Alpaca Grande* (Color #3317, 100% baby alpaca, 110 yd./100g hank, 4 sts per inch).

The orange broken rib hand warmers are worked using one strand each Brown Sheep *Lamb's Pride Worsted* (Color #M-22, 85% wool/15% mohair, 190 yd./100g skein, 4.5 sts per inch) and Plymouth Yarn *Baby Alpaca Brush* (Color #1004, 80% baby alpaca/20% acrylic, 110 yd./50g ball, 3.5 sts per inch) held together, resulting in a gauge of 3 sts per inch.

The lace rib hand warmers are worked using elann.com *Peruvian Collection Highland Wool* (Color #0741, 100% wool, 109 yd./50g ball, 5 sts per inch).

The bobble border hand warmers are worked using elann.com *Peruvian Collection Highland Chunky* (Color #87M2, 100% wool, 76 yd./50g ball, 4 sts per inch).

The simple seed stitch hand warmers are worked using elann.com *Peruvian Collection Uros* (Color #4148, 50% wool/50% llama, 90 yd/50g ball, 4 sts per inch).

The loop stitch hand warmers are worked using Cascade *Lana Grande* (Color #6033, 100% wool, 87 yd./100g ball, 2 sts per inch).

The cabled rib hand warmers are worked using Plymouth Yarn *Baby Alpaca Grande* (Color #3317, 100% baby alpaca, 110 yd./100g hank, 4 sts per inch).

The corrugated rib hand warmers are worked using elann.com *Peruvian Collection Highland Chunky* (Color #0208, 100% wool, 76 yd./50g ball, 4 sts per inch) and elann.com *Peruvian Collection Uros* (color #4148, 50% wool/50% llama, 90 yd./50g ball, 4 sts per inch).

How to Make the Hand Warmers

CAST ON

1. CO sts for your size and gauge, according to Table 19, dividing sts as evenly as possible onto 3 dpns.

2. Place marker (pm) and join rnd, taking care not to twist sts.

3. Go to the directions for the desired hand warmer pattern under "Make Body," below.

MAKE BODY

Because there is no shaping involved in hand warmers, you can use almost any stitch pattern you like. Here are a few to get you started.

Table 19. Cast On for Hand Warmers	
Gauge	*No. of Sts to CO*
2 sts/in	– (–, 14, 16, 18) sts
3 sts/in.	16 (18, 20, 24, 28) sts
4 sts/in.	20 (24, 28, 32, 36) sts
5 sts/in.	24 (30, 36, 40, 44) sts
6 sts/in.	30 (36, 42, 48, 54) sts

2x2 Ribbed Hand Warmer (Mult of 4 Sts)

This stretchy rib is worked over a multiple of 4 sts.

1 Rnd 1: *K2, p2; rep from * to end of rnd.

2 Rep rnd 1, sl marker beg every rnd, until hand warmer measures 4 (5, 6, 7, 8) inches from beg.

3 Go to "Make Thumbhole: All Styles," page 121, and work thumbhole as specified.

4 Cont in patt for approx 1 inch more.

5 BO in patt.

6 Go to "Finish: All Styles," page 121.

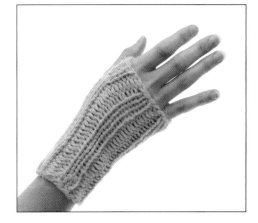

Broken Rib Hand Warmer (Even No. of Sts)

This easy pattern looks very different on the front and on the back but is attractive on both sides, so you could wear these hand warmers on either side.

1 Rnd 1: *K1, p1; rep from * to end of rnd.

2 Rnd 2: Knit.

3 Rep rnds 1 and 2, sl marker beg every rnd, until hand warmer measures 4 (5, 6, 7, 8) inches from beg.

4 Go to "Make Thumbhole: All Styles," page 121, and work thumbhole as specified.

5 Cont in patt from where you left off for approx 1 inch more, ending with rnd 2.

6 BO in patt.

7 Go to "Finish: All Styles," page 121.

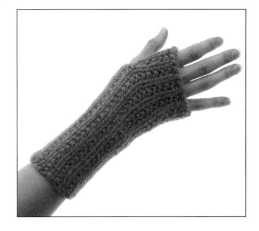

Lace Rib Hand Warmer (Even No. of Sts)

This hand warmer works well worn over knit or leather gloves.

1 Rnds 1 and 2: *K1, p1; rep from * to end of rnd.

2 Rnd 3: *Yo, k2tog; rep from * to end of rnd.

3 Rep rnds 1–3 until hand warmer measures 4 (5, 6, 7, 8) inches from beg, ending with a rnd 1 or 2.

4 Go to "Make Thumbhole: All Styles," page 121, and work thumbhole as specified.

5 Cont in patt from where you left off for approx 1 inch more, ending with a rnd 1 or 3.

6 BO in patt.

7 Go to "Finish: All Styles," page 121.

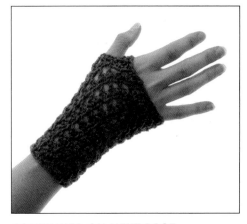

CONTINUED ON NEXT PAGE

Bobble Border Hand Warmer (Even No. of Sts)

This hand warmer has a small bobbled border on each end. It uses the following stitch:

> make bobble (mb): Knit into the front, back, front, back, and front (that's five times) of the next stitch. Without turning work, use the left needle to pick up the 4th stitch and pass it over the 5th and off the needle; pass the 3rd stitch over the 5th and off the needle; pass the 2nd stitch over the 5th and off the needle; and finally, pass the 1st stitch over the 5th and off the needle.

1. Purl 2 rnds.
2. Knit 1 rnd.
3. *Mb, k1; rep from * to end of rnd.
4. Knit 1 rnd.
5. Purl 2 rnds.
6. Knit every rnd until hand warmer measures 4 (5, 6, 7, 8) inches from beg.
7. Go to "Make Thumbhole: All Styles," page 121, and work thumbhole as specified.
8. Knit 1 rnd.
9. Rep steps 1–5.
10. BO knitwise.
11. Go to "Finish: All Styles," page 121.

Simple Seed Stitch Hand Warmer (Mult of 4 Sts)

This easy hand warmer begins and ends with a seed stitch border, with the body made up of simple seed stitch.

1. Rnds 1, 3, and 5: *K1, p1; rep from * to end of rnd.
2. Rnds 2, 4, and 6: *P1, k1; rep from * to end of rnd.
3. Rnd 7: K2, p1, *k3, p1; rep from * to last st, k1.
4. Rnds 8 and 10: Knit.
5. Rnd 9: *P1, k3; rep from * to end of rnd.
6. Rep rnds 7–10 until hand warmer measures 4 (5, 6, 7, 8) inches from beg, ending with a rnd 7 or 9.
7. Go to "Make Thumbhole: All Styles," page 121, and work thumbhole as specified.
8. Rep Rnds 1–6.
9. BO in patt.
10. Go to "Finish: All Styles," page 121.

Loop Stitch Hand Warmer (Even No. of Sts)

This hand warmer has a cuff made up of a fun fabric of thick loops. Loop stitch may take a little practice to master, but once you get going, it feels natural. It uses the following stitch:

> loop 1: Knit into next st but don't drop it off the needle. Bring the yarn to the front, between the needles, and loop it over your thumb, then bring it between the needles to the back. Knit into the st again, this time bringing it up and off the left needle. You will have 2 sts on the right needle. Pass the 1st st over the 2nd and off. This secures the loop.

1. Rnd 1: Knit.
2. Rnds 2 and 4: Purl.
3. Rnd 3: *K1, loop 1; rep from * to end of rnd.
4. Rnd 5: *Loop 1, k1; rep from * to end of rnd.
5. Rep rnds 2–4 once more.
6. Knit every rnd until hand warmer measures 4 (5, 6, 7, 8) inches from beg.
7. Go to "Make Thumbhole: All Styles," page 121, and work thumbhole as specified.
8. Knit every rnd for approx 1 inch more.
9. BO purlwise.
10. Go to "Finish: All Styles," page 121.

Cabled Rib Hand Warmer (Mult of 6 Sts)

The cable pattern for this hand warmer is worked on a multiple of 6 sts. It produces a 2x4 rib, where the k4 is actually at 4-stitch cable.

1. Rnds 1–3: *P2, k4; rep from * to end of rnd.
2. Rnd 4: *P2, sl2 to cn and hold at front, k2, k2 from cn; rep from * to end of rnd.
3. Rep rnds 1–4 for cable patt, slipping marker beg every rnd, until hand warmer measures 4 (5, 6, 7, 8) inches from beg, ending with a rnd 1 or 2.
4. Go to "Make Thumbhole: All Styles," page 121, and work thumbhole as specified.
5. Cont in patt from where you left off for approx 1 inch more, ending with a rnd 1 or 2.
6. BO in patt.
7. Go to "Finish: All Styles," page 121.

CONTINUED ON NEXT PAGE

Corrugated Rib Hand Warmer (Even No. of Sts)

This is a fun rib to work and is a good way to practice 2-color knitting. You can work it as a 2x2 rib if your stitch count is divisible by 4. You need two colors, A and B, and you cast on in A.

1 Rnd 1: *K1 in A, k1 in B; rep from * to end of rnd.

2 Rnd 2: *K1 in A, p1 in B; rep from * to end of rnd.

3 Rep rnd 2 until hand warmer measures 4 (5, 6, 7, 8) inches from beg.

4 Go to "Make Thumbhole: All Styles," on the next page, and work thumbhole as specified.

5 Cont in patt for approx 1 inch more.

6 BO purlwise in A.

7 Go to "Finish: All Styles," on the next page.

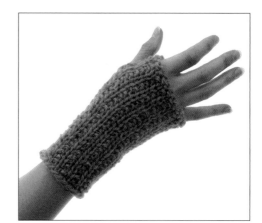

FAQ

I would like to make hand warmers using the master pattern, but I want to substitute a stitch pattern that is written for working back and forth in rows. Is there a way to convert it so I can knit it in the round?

Yes, you can substitute a new stitch pattern as long as the pattern repeat is compatible with the stitch count. Some stitch patterns can be a little tricky to convert, but with some experimentation, you should be able to adapt a lot of patterns.

Remember that when you are working in the round, all rows—rounds, actually—are RS rows. So when you rewrite your pattern, all RS rows can be worked in the round as they are written. For a WS row, you need to keep in mind the following:

1 Remember that purl sts on the WS are knit sts on the RS.

2 Read written instructions backward and write them out so that you don't get confused.

3 Read all rows of charted patterns from right to left.

4 For WS instructions that say *wyib* substitute *wyif* and vice versa.

See the boxes at right for a sample conversion.

Before
Row 1 (RS): *K1, p3; rep from * to end.
Row 2 (WS): *K1, sl 1 wyib, k1, p1; rep from * to end.

After
Rnd 1: *K1, p3; rep from * to end.
Rnd 2: *K1, p1, sl 1 wyif, p1; rep from * to end.

MAKE THUMBHOLE: ALL STYLES

The thumbhole is worked the same as a one-row buttonhole.

1. Work first 2 sts of rnd in patt.

2. Bring the yarn to the front, slip the next st from the left needle as if to purl, and bring the yarn to the back.

3. Slip the next st from the left needle to the right and pass the first slipped st over it and off the needle.

4. Rep step 3, keeping the yarn at the back, until you have bound off a length that is approx ¾–1 (1, 1¼, 1½, 1¾) inches. Make a note of how many sts you bound off.

5. Slip the last bound-off st back to the left needle.

6. Turn your work so that the WS is facing and bring the yarn to the back.

7. Insert the right needle between the 1st and 2nd sts on the left needle and wrap the yarn around the right needle as if to knit. Bring the loop through to the front as if to knit, but instead of slipping the old stitch off the left needle, use the right needle to place the new loop onto the left needle.

8. Rep step 7 the same number of times you bound off sts in step 4.

   You have cast on 1 more than the number of sts you bound off in step 4.

9. Turn your work so that the RS is facing again. Bring the yarn to the back and slip the first stitch from the left needle to the right needle; pass the additional CO st over the slipped st to close the thumbhole.

10. Work in patt to the end of the rnd as usual.

11. Return to patt for your style.

FINISH: ALL STYLES

1. Weave in ends.

2. Steam to block, if necessary, and if yarn's care instructions allow.

3. Reinforce thumbhole with buttonhole stitch, as described on page 261.

chapter **7**

Vests

Vests have all the potential versatility of sweaters, without the added labor of sleeves. They make excellent layering options, providing warmth, style, and color—minus the bulk of an entire sweater. These vests can be made as pullovers or cardigans, and they can have either round or v-neck shaping.

Vests are essentially sleeveless sweaters, and the style possibilities are limitless. This chapter covers just a few of the options. Once you grasp the concepts, you can easily create your own unique vest styles.

THE VERSATILITY OF VESTS

Knitted vests can take numerous forms: a plain v-neck pullover, a buttoned-up cardigan, a cropped accent over a long shirt, a sleeveless tunic, perhaps even a sleeveless dress. Vests are also the perfect layer for children and babies because they keep little ones warm while allowing them to move freely. Consider knitting a vest to match a knit sweater for added warmth.

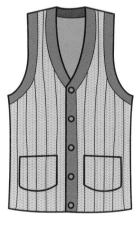

PULLOVERS AND CARDIGANS

A pullover vest can be very easy to make. Except for the neck shaping that takes place on the front, the front and back pieces are essentially the same. A cardigan vest is knit in three pieces—the back, the left front, and the right front. You will probably want to work a ribbing or some other sort of edging along the armholes and neck of a pullover vest. A button band, neckband, and buttonhole band are usually worked along the front edges of a cardigan vest after the main pieces are knit and assembled.

ARMHOLE SHAPING

Some sweaters require no armhole shaping, but you will most likely want to shape the armholes of a vest for a more tailored look. The vests in this chapter use a rounded armhole, which requires binding off a few stitches where the armhole begins and then decreasing a few more stitches gradually over a series of rows.

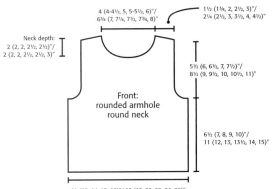

4 (4-4½, 5, 5-5½, 6)"/
6¾ (7, 7¼, 7½, 7¾, 8)"

1½ (1¾, 2, 2½, 3)"/
2¼ (2½, 3, 3½, 4, 4½)"

Neck depth:
2 (2, 2, 2½, 2½)"/
2 (2, 2, 2½, 2½, 3)"

5½ (6, 6½, 7, 7½)"/
8½ (9, 9½, 10, 10½, 11)"

Front:
rounded armhole
round neck

6½ (7, 8, 9, 10)"/
11 (12, 13, 13½, 14, 15)"

11 (12, 14, 15, 16)"/ 18 (19, 20, 22, 24, 26)"

NECK TREATMENTS

Most vests use one of two neck shaping options: the crew-neck or the v-neck. The crewneck, rounded and high, involves binding off or leaving on a holder several stitches at the center of the front and then decreasing a few stitches gradually on either side of the neck. The v-neck is usually worked by decreasing—beginning at a point just above where the arm-hole shaping begins—one stitch on each side of the V every other row. Most cardigan vests have v-neck shaping.

EDGINGS

When you finish knitting your vest and sewing the pieces together, you will probably want to work some kind of edging along the armholes, neck, and, if it is a cardigan, front edges. To do this, you use a flexible circular needle to pick up stitches evenly around the edge you're working. Then you can do a number of things: You can work these edges in ribbing, seed stitch, or garter stitch—these are traditional—or you can try a bobbled edge, a crocheted edge, a lace edge, or even a ruffle.

Vest: Master Pattern

You will be surprised by how quickly you can knit a vest. The added knitting and finishing time for sweater sleeves is considerable—and so is the added yarn yardage. This master pattern includes instructions for both a pullover and a cardigan, with a number of variations, and a broad range of sizes. Take careful measurements when choosing a size to knit. Babies and children grow quickly, so for practical reasons, the baby/child sizing allows generous ease. That way, your lovingly knit vest will fit comfortably for at least a year or two.

Specifications

SIZES

Baby/Child Vest

6–18 mos. (2–4 yrs., 4–6 yrs., 6–8 yrs., 8–10 yrs.)

Finished chest: 22 (24, 28, 30, 32) inches

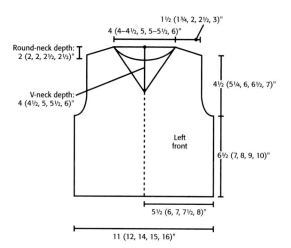

Round-neck depth: 2 (2, 2, 2½, 2½)"

V-neck depth: 4 (4½, 5, 5½, 6)"

1½ (1¾, 2, 2½, 3)"

4 (4–4½, 5, 5–5½, 6)"

4½ (5¼, 6, 6½, 7)"

Left front

6½ (7, 8, 9, 10)"

5½ (6, 7, 7½, 8)"

11 (12, 14, 15, 16)"

Adult Vest

XS (S, M, L, XL, XXL)

Finished chest: 36 (38, 40, 44, 48, 52) inches

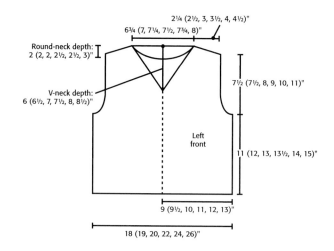

Round-neck depth: 2 (2, 2, 2½, 2½, 3)"

V-neck depth: 6 (6½, 7, 7½, 8, 8½)"

2¼ (2½, 3, 3½, 4, 4½)"

6¾ (7, 7¼, 7½, 7¾, 8)"

7½ (7½, 8, 9, 10, 11)"

Left front

11 (12, 13, 13½, 14, 15)"

9 (9½, 10, 11, 12, 13)"

18 (19, 20, 22, 24, 26)"

MATERIALS

Desired yarn, in the amount specified in Table 1

1 pair straight needles in size needed to obtain gauge

Circular needle one size smaller than needles used for vest body (to work some edgings)

2 stitch holders

Row counter

Tapestry needle

Buttons for cardigan (5 for baby/child sizes, 7 for adult sizes)

Table 1. Approximate Yardage for Vest		
Gauge (in Stockinette Stitch)	**Approximate Yardage**	
	Baby/Child Vest	**Adult Vest**
2 sts/in.	200–400 yd.	350–750 yd.
3 sts/in.	300–450 yd.	450–900 yd.
4 sts/in.	400–600 yd.	600–1,100 yd.
5 sts/in.	450–700 yd.	750–1,200 yd.
6 sts/in.	500–800 yd.	950–1,750 yd.

NOTES ON THE SAMPLES

The men's v-neck vest is knit in Brown Sheep *Lamb's Pride Bulky* (Color #M02, 85% wool/15% mohair, 190 yd./4 oz. skein, 3 sts per inch). It has a braided cable running up the center front and is trimmed in 1x1 rib.

The striped baby vest is knit in GGH/Muench *Bali* (Colors #86, #22, and #21, 50% cotton/50% acrylic, 154 yd./50g ball, 5 sts per inch). It is worked in a stripe pattern of 8 rows of the main color and 3 rows of the contrast color. The hem, armholes, and crewneck are worked in 2x2 rib in a third color.

Edging Stitch Patterns

You usually want to include an edging to ensure a neat fit for your vest. Ribbings and hems also keep the edges from stretching and flaring. You might want to knit your edging in needles one or two sizes smaller than those used for the vest body to guarantee a firm edge.

1X1 RIBBED EDGING (EVEN NO. OF STS)

This edging is the most common choice for vests and sweaters, and it is easy to do.

1 Row 1: *K1, p1; rep from * to end of row.

2 Rep row 1 to desired length.

CONTINUED ON NEXT PAGE

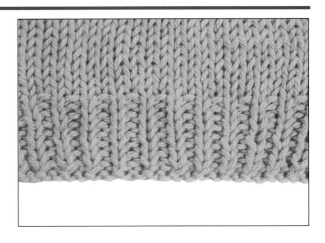

2X2 RIBBED EDGING (EVEN NO. OF STS)

This edging creates a nice elastic trim. For a multiple of 4 sts, work as follows:

1 Row 1 (RS): *K2, p2; rep from * to end of row.

2 Rep row 1 to desired length.

For a multiple of 4 sts plus 2, work as follows:

1 Row 1 (RS): K2, *p2, k2; rep from * to end of row.

2 Row 2 (WS): *P2, *k2, p2; rep from * to end of row.

3 Rep rows 1 and 2 to desired length.

> *Note: You can make a ribbed edging using virtually any number of stitches. For example, the adult sweater shown in Chapter 8 uses a 3x2 ribbed edging. Creating a unique edging is a powerful design technique.*

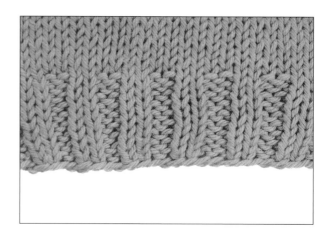

ROLLED EDGING (ANY NO. OF STS)

To make this easy edging tidy, use needles one size smaller than those used for the vest body.

1 Row 1 (RS): Knit.

2 Row 2 (WS): Purl.

3 Rep rows 1 and 2 for about 1 inch or to desired length.

> *Note: If you are using this edging for the bands around the neck, armholes, or cardigan fronts and you have picked up stitches from the RS, begin edging with row 2.*

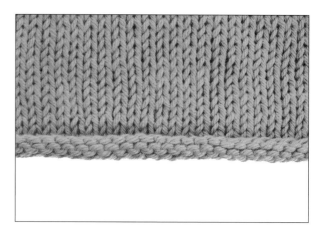

GARTER STITCH EDGING (ANY NO. OF STS)

To make this flat edging firm, use needles one size smaller than those used for the vest body.

1 Row 1 (RS): Knit.

2 Rep row 1 to desired length.

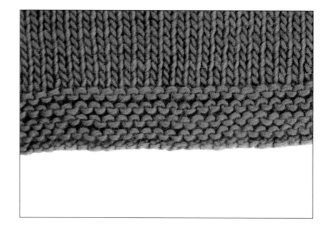

SEED STITCH EDGING (ANY NO. OF STS)

Seed stitch has a tendency to work up in a looser gauge than stockinette stitch, so use needles one or two sizes smaller to make it firm. For an even number of sts, work as follows:

1 Row 1 (RS): *K1, p1; rep from * to end of row.

2 Row 2 (WS): *P1, k1; rep from * to end of row.

3 Rep rows 1 and 2 to desired length.

For an odd number of sts, work as follows:

1 Row 1 (RS): K1, *p1, k1; rep from * to end of row.

2 Rep row 1 to desired length.

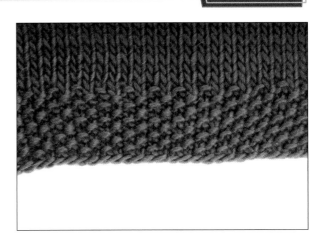

TURNED HEM (ANY NO. OF STS)

This edging produces a smooth and elegant line. Use needles one size smaller than those used for the vest body for steps 1–4 for a firm hem.

1 Row 1 (RS): Knit.

2 Row 2 (WS): Purl.

3 Rep rows 1 and 2 for approximately 1 inch.

4 Next row (RS): Purl across row to form folding ridge.

Note: For a picot hem, work the folding ridge as an eyelet row by repeating k2tog, yo across, ending k1 if necessary.

5 Change to larger needles to beg working body of vest.

Note: Measure from the folding ridge when pattern specifies to measure from the beginning.

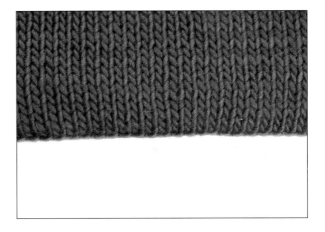

On the Edge

An easy way to liven up a vest is to work the ribbing or garter stitch border in an accent color or stripes. Alternatively, you can dress up a vest with edgings other than the ones presented here. Ruffles, scalloped edges, and lacey borders are just a few options. See "Fancy Knitted Borders" on page 287 for more ideas.

CONTINUED ON NEXT PAGE

How to Make the Baby/Child Vests

The back is worked the same way for both the pullover and the cardigan vest. The instructions for the baby/child version and the adult version of the vests are separate.

MAKE BACK: ALL BABY/CHILD VESTS

1. CO sts for your size and gauge according to Table 2.

2. Choose one of the edgings from pages 127–129 and work for 1 (1¼, 1½, 1¾, 2) inches, desired length, or length specified for your edging choice, ending with a WS row.

   Note: *If you want to work an edging that requires a different number of sts than that specified for your size and gauge in Table 2, you can cast on 1 or 2 fewer sts and work the edging to one row before the end. Increase back to the stitch count specified in Table 2 on the last edging row.*

3. Beg with a knit row, work in St st until back measures 6½ (7, 8, 9, 10) inches from CO edge, ending with a WS row.

4. Next row (RS)—Beg armhole shaping: Beg next 2 rows, BO the number of sts specified for your gauge in Table 3.

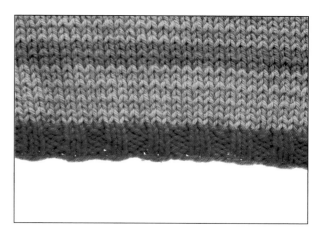

Table 2. Cast On for Baby/Child Vest Back	
Gauge	**No. of Sts to CO**
2 sts/in.	22 (24, 28, 30, 32) sts
3 sts/in.	33 (36, 42, 45, 48) sts
4 sts/in.	44 (48, 56, 60, 64) sts
5 sts/in.	55 (60, 70, 75, 80) sts
6 sts/in.	66 (72, 84, 90, 96) sts

Table 3. Baby/Child Vest Back: Begin Armhole Shaping	
Gauge	**No. of Sts to BO Beg Next 2 Rows**
2 sts/in.	2 sts
3 sts/in.	3 sts
4 sts/in.	4 sts
5 sts/in.	5 sts
6 sts/in.	6 sts

5. Beg next row (RS), dec 1 st each end every RS row the number of times specified for your size and gauge in the second column of Table 4. You should have rem the number of sts specified for your size and gauge in the third column of Table 4.

6. Cont without further shaping until armhole measures 4½ (5¼, 6, 6½, 7) inches, ending with a WS row.

7. Beg shoulder shaping: Beg next 2 rows, BO the number of sts specified for your size and gauge in Table 5.

8. Beg next 2 rows, BO the number of sts specified for your size and gauge in the second column in Table 6. You should have rem the number of neck sts specified for your gauge and size in the third column of Table 6.

9. Cut yarn and put rem neck sts onto holder or spare needle for later; this should be the number of sts specified in the third column of Table 6.

10. Go to instructions for desired front style under "Make Front: Baby/Child Vests," page 132.

Table 4. Baby/Child Vest Back: Armhole Shaping

Gauge	No. of Times to Dec 1 St Each End Every RS Row	No. of Sts After Armhole Shaping
2 sts/in.	2 (2, 3, 3, 2) times	14 (16, 18, 20, 24) sts
3 sts/in.	3 (4, 5, 4, 3) times	21 (22, 26, 31, 36) sts
4 sts/in.	4 (5, 6, 5, 4) times	28 (30, 36, 42, 48) sts
5 sts/in.	5 (6, 7, 6, 5) times	35 (38, 46, 53, 60) sts
6 sts/in.	6 (7, 9, 7, 6) times	42 (46, 54, 64, 72) sts

Table 5. Baby/Child Vest Back: Begin Shoulder Shaping

Gauge	No. of Sts to BO Beg Next 2 Rows
2 sts/in.	2 (2, 2, 3, 3) sts
3 sts/in.	2 (3, 3, 4, 5) sts
4 sts/in.	3 (3, 4, 5, 6) sts
5 sts/in.	4 (4, 5, 6, 8) sts
6 sts/in.	5 (5, 6, 8, 9) sts

Table 6. Baby/Child Vest Back: Finish Shoulder Shaping

Gauge	No. of Sts to BO Beg Next 2 Rows	No. of Neck Sts After Shoulder Shaping
2 sts/in.	1 (2, 2, 2, 3) sts	8 (8, 10, 10, 12) sts
3 sts/in.	2 (2, 2, 3, 4) sts	13 (12, 16, 17, 18) sts
4 sts/in.	3 (3, 4, 5, 6) sts	16 (18, 20, 22, 24) sts
5 sts/in.	3 (4, 5, 6, 7) sts	21 (22, 26, 29, 30) sts
6 sts/in.	4 (4, 6, 7, 9) sts	24 (28, 30, 34, 36) sts

CONTINUED ON NEXT PAGE

MAKE FRONT: BABY/CHILD VESTS

You can choose from several styles for the vest front. If you're making a pullover, you can shape the neck with either the round neck, which is high, or the v-neck, which is probably the most common neck shaping style for vests. You can also make a v-neck cardigan vest, which allows more opportunity to embellish with ribbings and buttons.

Baby/Child Pullover Vest: Round-Neck Front

1 Work as for vest back, including armhole, until front measures 9 (10¼, 12, 13, 14½) inches from CO edge, ending with a RS row.

2 Shape right neck and shoulder: Work across the number of sts specified for your size and gauge in Table 7.

3 Turn and put rem sts, as specified for your size and gauge in Table 8, onto holder or spare needle.

4 Working right shoulder sts only, dec 1 st at neck edge every row for the number of rows specified for your size and gauge in Table 9.

Table 7. Baby/Child Round-Neck Pullover Vest Front: Begin Neck Shaping	
Gauge	**No. of Sts to Work Across**
2 sts/in.	6 (7, 7, 8, 9) sts
3 sts/in.	9 (9, 10, 12, 13) sts
4 sts/in.	12 (12, 14, 16, 18) sts
5 sts/in.	14 (15, 18, 20, 22) sts
6 sts/in.	17 (18, 21, 24, 27) sts

Table 8. Baby/Child Round-Neck Pullover Vest Front: Left Shoulder Stitches on Holder	
Gauge	**No. of Unworked Sts on Holder for Left Shoulder**
2 sts/in.	8 (9, 11, 12, 15) sts
3 sts/in.	12 (13, 16, 19, 23) sts
4 sts/in.	16 (18, 22, 26, 30) sts
5 sts/in.	21 (23, 28, 33, 38) sts
6 sts/in.	25 (28, 33, 40, 45) sts

Table 9. Baby/Child Round-Neck Pullover Vest Front: Begin Right Neck Shaping	
Gauge	**No. of Rows to Dec 1 St at Neck Edge**
2 sts/in.	2 (2, 2, 2, 2) rows
3 sts/in.	3 (2, 3, 3, 2) rows
4 sts/in.	3 (3, 3, 3, 3) rows
5 sts/in.	4 (4, 4, 4, 4) rows
6 sts/in.	4 (5, 5, 5, 5) rows

5. Beg next row, dec 1 st at neck edge every other row the number of times specified for your size and gauge in the second column of Table 10. You should have rem the number of sts specified for your size and gauge in the third column of Table 10.

6. AT THE SAME TIME, when armhole measures 4½ (5¼, 6, 6½, 7) inches, ending with a RS row, begin shaping shoulders. Beg next row (WS), BO the number of sts specified for your size and gauge in Table 11.

7. Next row (RS): Knit.

8. Next row (WS)—Finish shoulder shaping: BO rem shoulder sts, as indicated for your size and gauge in Table 12.

Table 10. Baby/Child Round-Neck Pullover Vest Front: Finish Right Neck Shaping

Gauge	No. of Times to Dec 1 St at Neck Edge Every Other Row	No. of Sts After Shaping Right Neck
2 sts/in.	All sizes: 1 time	3 (4, 4, 5, 6) sts
3 sts/in.	All sizes: 2 times	4 (5, 5, 7, 9) sts
4 sts/in.	All sizes: 3 times	6 (6, 8, 10, 12) sts
5 sts/in.	3 (3, 4, 4, 3) times	7 (8, 10, 12, 15) sts
6 sts/in.	4 (4, 4, 4, 4) times	9 (9, 12, 15, 18) sts

Table 11. Baby/Child Round-Neck Pullover Vest Front: Begin Shoulder Shaping

Gauge	No. of Sts to BO Beg This Row, Begin Shaping Shoulders
2 sts/in.	2 (2, 2, 3, 3) sts
3 sts/in.	2 (3, 3, 4, 5) sts
4 sts/in.	3 (3, 4, 5, 6) sts
5 sts/in.	4 (4, 5, 6, 8) sts
6 sts/in.	5 (5, 6, 8, 9) sts

Table 12. Baby/Child Round-Neck Pullover Vest Front: Finish Shoulder Shaping

Gauge	No. of Sts to BO Beg This Row, Finish Shaping Shoulders
2 sts/in.	1 (2, 2, 2, 3) sts
3 sts/in.	2 (2, 2, 3, 4) sts
4 sts/in.	3 (3, 4, 5, 6) sts
5 sts/in.	3 (4, 5, 6, 7) sts
6 sts/in.	4 (4, 6, 7, 9) sts

CONTINUED ON NEXT PAGE

9 Beg left neck and shoulder shaping: Slip the number of sts indicated for your size and gauge in Table 13 onto another holder for the center neck.

10 Slip rem sts, as indicated for your size and gauge in Table 14, onto your needle.

11 Beg with a RS row, rejoin yarn and knit.

12 Shape left neck and shoulder as right neck and shoulder, reversing sides.

13 Go to "Block: All Vests," page 146.

Table 13. Baby/Child Round-Neck Pullover Vest Front: Center Neck Stitches on Holder	
Gauge	**No. of Sts on Holder for Center**
2 sts/in.	2 (2, 4, 4, 6) sts
3 sts/in.	3 (4, 6, 7, 10) sts
4 sts/in.	4 (6, 8, 10, 12) sts
5 sts/in.	7 (8, 10, 13, 16) sts
6 sts/in.	8 (10, 12, 16, 18) sts

Table 14. Baby/Child Round-Neck Pullover Vest Front: Begin Left Neck Shaping	
Gauge	**No. of Sts on Needle for Left Neck Shaping**
2 sts/in.	6 (7, 7, 8, 9) sts
3 sts/in.	9 (9, 10, 12, 13) sts
4 sts/in.	12 (12, 14, 16, 18) sts
5 sts/in.	14 (15, 18, 20, 22) sts
6 sts/in.	17 (18, 21, 24, 27) sts

Baby/Child Pullover Vest: V-Neck Front

1 Work as for back until armhole measures ½ (¾, 1, 1, 1) inches, ending with a WS row.

2 If you are working on an odd number of sts, work to the center st and put the center st onto a safety pin or holder. If you are working on an even number of sts, work halfway across row, m1. Put this new st onto a safety pin or holder.

3 Put rem unworked right shoulder sts onto another holder or spare needle.

4 Turn and beg working left shoulder sts only.

5 Next row (WS): Purl.

6. Cont to shape armhole as established, and AT THE SAME TIME, beg v-neck shaping: Dec 1 st at neck edge by k2tog at end of every RS row until you have rem the number of sts indicated for your size and gauge in Table 15.

7. Cont without further shaping until front measures same as back at beg shoulder shaping, ending with a WS row.

8. Next row (RS)–Beg shoulder shaping: BO beg this row the number of sts specified for your size and gauge in Table 16.

9. Next row (WS): Purl.

10. Next row (RS): Finish shoulder shaping: BO rem shoulder sts; this should be the number of sts specified for your size and gauge in Table 17.

11. Put right shoulder sts back onto needle, leaving center st on holder for later. Finish armhole, right neck, and shoulder as for left, reversing shaping and shaping right v-neck by beg every RS row with ssk.

12. Go to "Block: All Vests," page 146.

Table 15. Baby/Child V-Neck Pullover Vest Front: Shoulder Stitches Remaining After Left Neck Shaping

Gauge	No. of Sts After Shaping Armhole and Left V-Neck
2 sts/in.	3 (4, 4, 5, 6) sts
3 sts/in.	4 (5, 5, 7, 9) sts
4 sts/in.	6 (6, 8, 10, 12) sts
5 sts/in.	7 (8, 10, 12, 15) sts
6 sts/in.	9 (9, 12, 15, 18) sts

Table 16. Baby/Child V-Neck Pullover Vest Front: Begin Shoulder Shaping

Gauge	No. of Sts to BO Beg This Row, Begin Shaping Shoulders
2 sts/in.	2 (2, 2, 3, 3) sts
3 sts/in.	2 (3, 3, 4, 5) sts
4 sts/in.	3 (3, 4, 5, 6) sts
5 sts/in.	4 (4, 5, 6, 8) sts
6 sts/in.	5 (5, 6, 8, 9) sts

Table 17. Baby/Child V-Neck Pullover Vest Front: Finish Shoulder Shaping

Gauge	No. of Sts to BO Beg This Row, Finish Shaping Shoulders
2 sts/in.	1 (2, 2, 2, 3) sts
3 sts/in.	2 (2, 2, 3, 4) sts
4 sts/in.	3 (3, 4, 5, 6) sts
5 sts/in.	3 (4, 5, 6, 7) sts
6 sts/in.	4 (4, 6, 7, 9) sts

CONTINUED ON NEXT PAGE

Baby/Child Cardigan Vest: Left Front

1 CO sts for your size and gauge according to Table 18.

> **Note:** *If you want to work an edging that requires a different number of sts than that specified for your size and gauge in Table 18, you can cast on 1 or 2 fewer sts and work the edging to one row before the end. Increase back to the stitch count specified in Table 18 on the last edging row.*

2 Work edging to same length as back edging, then cont in St st until left front measures 6½ (7, 8, 9, 10) inches from CO edge, ending with a WS row.

3 Next row (RS)—Beg armhole shaping: BO beg this row the number of sts indicated for your size and gauge in Table 19.

4 Next row (WS): Purl.

5 Beg next row, dec 1 st beg every RS row the number of times indicated for your size and gauge in Table 20.

Table 18. Cast On for Baby/Child Cardigan Vest Front

Gauge	No. of Sts to CO
2 sts/in.	11 (12, 14, 15, 16) sts
3 sts/in.	16 (18, 21, 22, 24) sts
4 sts/in.	22 (24, 26, 30, 32) sts
5 sts/in.	27 (30, 35, 37, 40) sts
6 sts/in.	33 (36, 42, 45, 48) sts

Table 19. Baby/Child Cardigan Vest Front: Begin Armhole Shaping

Gauge	No. of Sts to BO Beg This Row
2 sts/in.	2 sts
3 sts/in.	3 sts
4 sts/in.	4 sts
5 sts/in.	5 sts
6 sts/in.	6 sts

Table 20. Baby/Child Cardigan Vest Front: Finish Armhole Shaping

Gauge	No. of Times to Dec 1 St Beg Every RS Row
2 sts/in.	2 (2, 3, 3, 2) times
3 sts/in.	3 (4, 5, 4, 3) times
4 sts/in.	4 (5, 6, 5, 4) times
5 sts/in.	5 (6, 7, 6, 5) times
6 sts/in.	6 (7, 9, 7, 6) times

6 AT THE SAME TIME, when armhole measures ½ (¾, 1, 1, 1) inches, begin neck shaping: Dec 1 st by k2tog at end of every RS row until you have rem the number of sts indicated for your size and gauge in Table 21.

7 Work without further shaping until front measures same as back to beg shoulder shaping, ending with a WS row.

8 Next row (RS)—Beg shoulder shaping: BO beg this row the number of sts indicated for your size and gauge in the second column of Table 22. You should have rem the number of sts indicated for your size and gauge in the third column of Table 22.

9 Next row (WS): Purl.

10 Next row (RS): BO rem sts.

11 Go to "Baby/Child Cardigan Vest: Right Front," below.

Table 21. Baby/Child Cardigan Vest Front: Shoulder Stitches Remaining After Left Neck and Armhole Shaping	
Gauge	No. of Sts After Shaping Left Neck
2 sts/in.	3 (4, 4, 5, 6) sts
3 sts/in.	4 (5, 5, 7, 9) sts
4 sts/in.	6 (6, 8, 10, 12) sts
5 sts/in.	7 (8, 10, 12, 15) sts
6 sts/in.	9 (9, 12, 15, 18) sts

Table 22. Baby/Child Cardigan Vest Front: Begin Shoulder Shaping		
Gauge	No. of Sts to BO Beg Next RS Row	No. of Shoulder Sts After First BO
2 sts/in.	2 (2, 2, 3, 3) sts	1 (2, 2, 2, 3) sts
3 sts/in.	2 (3, 3, 4, 5) sts	2 (2, 2, 3, 4) sts
4 sts/in.	3 (3, 4, 5, 6) sts	3 (3, 4, 5, 6) sts
5 sts/in.	4 (4, 5, 6, 8) sts	3 (4, 5, 6, 7) sts
6 sts/in.	5 (5, 6, 8, 9) sts	4 (4, 6, 7, 9) sts

Baby/Child Cardigan Vest: Right Front

1 Work as for left front, reversing armhole and shoulder shaping and working neck shaping by beg every RS row with ssk.

2 Go to "Block: All Vests," page 146.

CONTINUED ON NEXT PAGE

How to Make the Adult Vests

MAKE BACK: ALL ADULT VESTS

1 CO sts for your size and gauge according to Table 23.

> **Note:** *If you want to work an edging that requires a different number of sts than that specified for your size and gauge in Table 23, you can cast on 1 or 2 fewer sts and work the edging to one row before the end. Increase back to the stitch count specified in Table 23 on the last edging row.*

2 Choose from one of the edgings on pages 127–129 and work for desired length, ending with a WS row.

3 Beg with a knit row, work in St st until back measures 11 (12, 13, 13½, 14, 15) inches from CO edge, ending with a WS row.

4 Beg armhole shaping: Beg next 2 rows, BO the number of sts specified for your size and gauge in Table 24.

Table 23. Cast On for Adult Vest Back	
Gauge	**No. of Sts to CO**
2 sts/in.	36 (38, 40, 44, 48, 52) sts
3 sts/in.	54 (57, 60, 66, 72, 78) sts
4 sts/in.	72 (76, 80, 88, 96, 104) sts
5 sts/in.	90 (95, 100, 110, 120, 130) sts
6 sts/in.	108 (114, 120, 132, 144, 156) sts

Table 24. Adult Vest Back: Begin Armhole Shaping	
Gauge	**No. of Sts to BO Beg Next 2 Rows**
2 sts/in.	3 (3, 3, 3, 3, 4) sts
3 sts/in.	4 (4, 4, 5, 5, 6) sts
4 sts/in.	6 (6, 6, 7, 7, 8) sts
5 sts/in.	7 (7, 7, 8, 8, 9) sts
6 sts/in.	9 (9, 9, 10, 10, 10) sts

5. Armhole shaping: Beg next row, dec 1 st each end every RS row the number of times specified for your size and gauge in the second column of Table 25. You should have rem the number of sts specified for your size and gauge in the third column of Table 25.

6. Cont without further shaping until armhole measures 7½ (7½, 8, 9, 10, 11) inches.

7. Beg shoulder shaping: Beg next 2 rows, BO the number of sts specified for your size and gauge in Table 26.

8. Finish shoulder shaping: Beg next 2 rows, BO the number of sts specified for your size and gauge in the second column of Table 27.

9. Cut yarn and put rem neck sts onto a holder or spare needle for later; this should be the number specified in the third column of Table 27.

10. Go to the directions for the desired front style under "Make Front: Adult Vests," page 140.

Table 25. Adult Vest Back: Armhole Shaping

Gauge	No. of Times to Dec 1 St Each End Every RS Row	No. of Sts After Armhole Shaping
2 sts/in.	3 (4, 4, 4, 5, 5) times	24 (24, 26, 30, 32, 34) sts
3 sts/in.	6 (6, 6, 7, 7, 8) times	34 (37, 40, 42, 48, 50) sts
4 sts/in.	7 (8, 7, 8, 10, 10) times	46 (48, 54, 58, 62, 68) sts
5 sts/in.	9 (10, 10, 11, 13, 13) times	58 (61, 66, 72, 78, 86) sts
6 sts/in.	11 (12, 11, 12, 15, 17) times	68 (72, 80, 88, 94, 102) sts

Table 26. Adult Vest Back: Begin Shoulder Shaping

Gauge	No. of Sts to BO Beg Next 2 Rows
2 sts/in.	3 (3, 3, 4, 4, 5) sts
3 sts/in.	4 (4, 5, 5, 6, 7) sts
4 sts/in.	5 (5, 6, 7, 8, 9) sts
5 sts/in.	6 (7, 8, 9, 10, 12) sts
6 sts/in.	7 (8, 9, 11, 12, 14) sts

Table 27. Adult Vest Back: Finish Shoulder Shaping

Gauge	No. of Sts to BO Beg Next 2 Rows	No. of Neck Sts After Shaping Shoulders
2 sts/in.	2 (2, 3, 3, 4, 4) sts	14 (14, 14, 16, 16, 16) sts
3 sts/in.	3 (4, 4, 5, 6, 6) sts	20 (21, 22, 22, 24, 24) sts
4 sts/in.	4 (5, 6, 7, 8, 9) sts	28 (28, 30, 30, 30, 32) sts
5 sts/in.	6 (6, 7, 8, 10, 11) sts	34 (35, 36, 38, 38, 40) sts
6 sts/in.	7 (7, 9, 10, 12, 13) sts	40 (42, 44, 46, 46, 48) sts

CONTINUED ON NEXT PAGE

MAKE FRONT: ADULT VESTS

You have a few choices for the vest front: a pullover with a round neck, a pullover with a v-neck, or a cardigan with a v-neck. Within this range of choices are numerous opportunities to make your vest unique with edgings, ribbings, buttons, clasps, ruffles, embroidery, or other embellishments at the finishing stage.

Adult Pullover Vest: Round-Neck Front

1 Work as for vest back, including armhole, until front measures 16½ (17½, 19, 20, 21½, 23) inches from CO edge, ending with a RS row.

2 Shape right neck and shoulder: Work across the number of sts specified for your size and gauge in the second column of Table 28.

3 Turn and put rem sts onto a holder or spare needle for later; this should be the number specified in the third column of Table 28.

4 Working right shoulder sts only, dec 1 st at neck edge every row for the number of rows specified for your size and gauge in Table 29.

Table 28. Adult Round-Neck Pullover Vest Front: Divide for Neck Shaping		
Gauge	No. of Sts to Work Across	No. of Sts on Holder for Later
2 sts/in.	9 (9, 9, 11, 12, 12) sts	15 (15, 17, 19, 20, 22) sts
3 sts/in.	12 (13, 14, 15, 17, 18) sts	22 (24, 26, 27, 31, 32) sts
4 sts/in.	16 (17, 19, 21, 23, 25) sts	30 (31, 35, 37, 39, 43) sts
5 sts/in.	21 (22, 24, 26, 29, 32) sts	37 (39, 42, 46, 49, 54) sts
6 sts/in.	24 (25, 28, 32, 34, 37) sts	44 (47, 52, 56, 60, 65) sts

Table 29. Adult Round-Neck Pullover Vest Front: Begin Right Neck Shaping	
Gauge	No. of Rows to Dec 1 St at Neck Edge
2 sts/in.	2 rows
3 sts/in.	3 rows
4 sts/in.	4 rows
5 sts/in.	5 rows
6 sts/in.	6 rows

⑤ Dec 1 st at neck edge every other row the number of times specified for your size and gauge in the second column of Table 30. You should have rem the number of sts specified for your size and gauge in the third column of Table 30.

⑥ AT THE SAME TIME, when armhole measures 7½ (7½, 8, 9, 10, 11) inches, ending with a RS row, begin shaping shoulders. Beg next row (WS), BO the number of sts specified for your size and gauge in Table 31.

⑦ Next row (RS): Knit.

⑧ Next row (WS): Finish shoulder shaping: BO rem shoulder sts; this should be the number of sts specified for your size and gauge in Table 32.

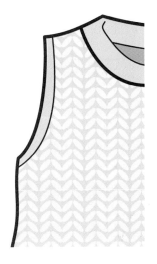

Table 30. Adult Round-Neck Pullover Vest Front: Finish Right Neck Shaping

Gauge	No. of Times to Dec 1 St at Neck Edge Every Other Row	No. of Sts After Shaping Right Neck
2 sts/in.	2 (2, 1, 2, 2, 1) times	5 (5, 6, 7, 8, 9) sts
3 sts/in.	All sizes: 2 times	7 (8, 9, 10, 12, 13) sts
4 sts/in.	All sizes: 3 times	9 (10, 12, 14, 16, 18) sts
5 sts/in.	All sizes: 4 times	12 (13, 15, 17, 20, 23) sts
6 sts/in.	4 (4, 4, 5, 4, 4) times	14 (15, 18, 21, 24, 27) sts

Table 31. Adult Round-Neck Pullover Vest Front: Begin Shoulder Shaping

Gauge	No. of Sts to BO Beg This Row, Begin Shaping Shoulders
2 sts/in.	3 (3, 3, 4, 4, 5) sts
3 sts/in.	4 (4, 5, 5, 6, 7) sts
4 sts/in.	5 (5, 6, 7, 8, 9) sts
5 sts/in.	6 (7, 8, 9, 10, 12) sts
6 sts/in.	7 (8, 9, 11, 12, 14) sts

Table 32. Adult Round-Neck Pullover Vest Front: Finish Shoulder Shaping

Gauge	No. of Sts to BO Beg This Row, Finish Shaping Shoulders
2 sts/in.	2 (2, 3, 3, 4, 4) sts
3 sts/in.	3 (4, 4, 5, 6, 6) sts
4 sts/in.	4 (5, 6, 7, 8, 9) sts
5 sts/in.	6 (6, 7, 8, 10, 11) sts
6 sts/in.	7 (7, 9, 10, 12, 13) sts

CONTINUED ON NEXT PAGE

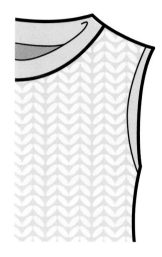

9. Shape left neck and shoulder: Slip the number of center neck sts indicated for your size and gauge in Table 33 onto a holder for later.

10. Slip rem sts, as indicated for your size and gauge in Table 34, onto your needle.

11. Rejoin yarn to RS and knit 1 row.

12. Shape left neck and shoulder as right neck and shoulder, reversing sides.

13. Go to "Block: All Vests," page 146.

Table 33. Adult Round-Neck Pullover Vest Front: Center Neck Stitches on Holder	
Gauge	**No. of Sts on Holder for Center**
2 sts/in.	6 (6, 8, 8, 8, 10) sts
3 sts/in.	10 (11, 12, 12, 14, 14) sts
4 sts/in.	14 (14, 16, 16, 16, 18) sts
5 sts/in.	16 (17, 18, 20, 20, 22) sts
6 sts/in.	20 (22, 24, 24, 26, 28) sts

Table 34. Adult Round-Neck Pullover Vest Front: Begin Left Neck Shaping	
Gauge	**No. of Sts on Needle for Left Neck and Shoulder**
2 sts/in.	9 (9, 9, 11, 12, 12) sts
3 sts/in.	12 (13, 14, 15, 17, 18) sts
4 sts/in.	16 (17, 19, 21, 23, 25) sts
5 sts/in.	21 (22, 24, 26, 29, 32) sts
6 sts/in.	24 (25, 28, 32, 34, 37) sts

Adult Pullover Vest: V-Neck Front

1. Work as for pullover back until armhole measures 1½ (1, 1, 1½, 2, 2½) inches, ending with a WS row.

2. If you are working on an odd number of sts, work to the center st and put the center st onto a safety pin or holder. If you are working on an even number of sts, work halfway across row, m1. Put this new st onto a safety pin or holder.

3. Put rem unworked right shoulder sts onto another holder or spare needle.

4. Turn and beg working left shoulder sts only.

5. Next row (WS): Purl.

⑥ Cont to shape armhole as established for back, and AT THE SAME TIME, beg v-neck shaping: Dec 1 st at neck edge by k2tog at end of every RS row until you have rem the number of sts indicated for your size and gauge in Table 35.

⑦ Cont without further shaping until front measures same as back to beg shoulder shaping, ending with a WS row.

⑧ Next row (RS)—Beg shoulder shaping: BO beg this row the number of sts specified for your size and gauge in Table 36.

⑨ Next row (WS): Purl.

⑩ Finish shoulder shaping (RS): BO rem shoulder sts; this should be the number of sts specified for your size and gauge in Table 37.

⑪ Put right shoulder sts back onto needle, leaving center st on holder for later. Finish right armhole, neck, and shoulder as for left, reversing shaping and shaping right v-neck by beg every RS row with ssk.

⑫ Go to "Block: All Vests," page 146.

Table 35. Adult V-Neck Pullover Vest Front: Shoulder Stitches Remaining After Left Neck Shaping

Gauge	No. of Sts After Shaping Left V-Neck
2 sts/in.	5 (5, 6, 7, 8, 9) sts
3 sts/in.	7 (8, 9, 10, 12, 13) sts
4 sts/in.	9 (10, 12, 14, 16, 18) sts
5 sts/in.	12 (13, 15, 17, 20, 23) sts
6 sts/in.	14 (15, 18, 21, 24, 27) sts

Table 36. Adult V-Neck Pullover Vest Front: Begin Shoulder Shaping

Gauge	No. of Sts to BO Beg This Row, Beg Shaping Shoulders
2 sts/in.	3 (3, 3, 4, 4, 5) sts
3 sts/in.	4 (4, 5, 5, 6, 7) sts
4 sts/in.	5 (5, 6, 7, 8, 9) sts
5 sts/in.	6 (7, 8, 9, 10, 12) sts
6 sts/in.	7 (8, 9, 11, 12, 14) sts

Table 37. Adult V-Neck Pullover Vest Front: Finish Shoulder Shaping

Gauge	No. of Sts to BO Beg This Row, Finish Shaping Shoulders
2 sts/in.	2 (2, 3, 3, 4, 4) sts
3 sts/in.	3 (4, 4, 5, 6, 6) sts
4 sts/in.	4 (5, 6, 7, 8, 9) sts
5 sts/in.	6 (6, 7, 8, 10, 11) sts
6 sts/in.	7 (7, 9, 10, 12, 13) sts

CONTINUED ON NEXT PAGE

Adult Cardigan Vest: Left Front

1 CO sts for your size and gauge according to Table 38.

Note: If you want to work an edging that requires a different number of sts than that specified for your size and gauge in Table 38, you can cast on 1 or 2 fewer sts and work the edging to one row before the end. Increase back to the stitch count specified in Table 38 on the last edging row.

2 Work edging to same length as back edging and then cont in St st until left front measures 11 (12, 13, 13½, 14, 15) inches from CO edge, ending with a WS row.

3 Next row (RS)—Beg armhole shaping: BO beg this row the number of sts indicated for your size and gauge in Table 39.

4 Next row (WS): Purl.

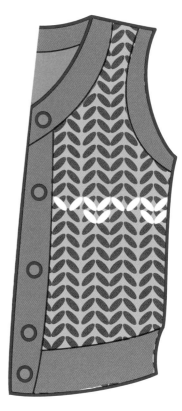

Table 38. Cast On for Adult Cardigan Vest Front	
Gauge	**No. of Sts to CO**
2 sts/in.	18 (19, 20, 22, 24, 26) sts
3 sts/in.	27 (28, 30, 33, 36, 39) sts
4 sts/in.	36 (38, 40, 44, 48, 52) sts
5 sts/in.	45 (47, 50, 55, 60, 65) sts
6 sts/in.	54 (57, 60, 66, 72, 78) sts

Table 39. Adult Cardigan Vest Front: Begin Armhole Shaping	
Gauge	**No. of Sts to BO Beg This Row**
2 sts/in.	3 (3, 3, 3, 3, 4) sts
3 sts/in.	4 (4, 4, 5, 5, 6) sts
4 sts/in.	6 (6, 6, 7, 7, 8) sts
5 sts/in.	7 (7, 7, 8, 8, 9) sts
6 sts/in.	9 (9, 9, 10, 10, 10) sts

5 Beg next row, dec 1 st beg every RS row the number of times indicated for your size and gauge in Table 40.

6 AT THE SAME TIME, when armhole measures 1½ (1, 1, 1½, 2, 2½) inches, beg neck shaping: Dec 1 st by k2tog at end of every RS row until you have rem the number of sts indicated for your size and gauge in Table 41.

7 Work without further shaping until front measures same as back to beg shoulder shaping, ending with a WS row.

8 Next row (RS)—Beg shoulder shaping: BO beg this row the number of sts indicated for your size and gauge in the second column of Table 42. You should have rem the number of sts indicated for your size and gauge in the third column of Table 42.

9 Next row (WS): Purl.

10 Next row (RS): BO rem sts.

11 Go to "Adult Cardigan Vest: Right Front," below.

Table 40. Adult Cardigan Vest Front: Armhole Shaping	
Gauge	**No. of Times to Dec 1 St Beg Every RS Row**
2 sts/in.	3 (4, 4, 4, 5, 5) times
3 sts/in.	6 (6, 6, 7, 7, 8) times
4 sts/in.	7 (8, 7, 8, 10, 10) times
5 sts/in.	9 (10, 10, 11, 13, 13) times
6 sts/in.	11 (12, 11, 12, 15, 17) times

Table 41. Adult Cardigan Vest Front: Shoulder Stitches Remaining After Left Neck and Armhole Shaping	
Gauge	**No. of Sts After Shaping Left V-Neck**
2 sts/in.	5 (5, 6, 7, 8, 9) sts
3 sts/in.	7 (8, 9, 10, 12, 13) sts
4 sts/in.	9 (10, 12, 14, 16, 18) sts
5 sts/in.	12 (13, 15, 17, 20, 23) sts
6 sts/in.	14 (15, 18, 21, 24, 27) sts

Table 42. Adult Cardigan Vest Front: Begin Shoulder Shaping		
Gauge	**No. of Sts to BO Beg Next RS Row**	**No. of Shoulder Sts After BO**
2 sts/in.	3 (3, 3, 4, 4, 5) sts	2 (2, 3, 3, 4, 4) sts
3 sts/in.	4 (4, 5, 5, 6, 7) sts	3 (4, 4, 5, 6, 6) sts
4 sts/in.	5 (5, 6, 7, 8, 9) sts	4 (5, 6, 7, 8, 9) sts
5 sts/in.	6 (7, 8, 9, 10, 12) sts	6 (6, 7, 8, 10, 11) sts
6 sts/in.	7 (8, 9, 11, 12, 14) sts	7 (7, 9, 10, 12, 13) sts

Adult Cardigan Vest: Right Front

1 Work as for left front, reversing armhole and shoulder shaping and working neck shaping by beg every RS row with ssk.

2 Go to "Block: All Vests," page 146.

CONTINUED ON NEXT PAGE

How to Complete All Vests

For many knitters, finishing is the most difficult part of completing a project. You can look at this stage as the opportunity to present your work in the best possible frame. You should use care when sewing seams and definitely take time to block. Now is also the time to make your blank slate of a vest unique through the use of edgings and embellishments.

BLOCK: ALL VESTS

1 Weave in loose ends.

2 Block vest pieces to measurements, if yarn's care instructions allow.

3 Go to the instructions for the neckband for your vest style, under "Make Neckband," below.

MAKE NECKBAND

When making a neckband, button bands, or armbands, be sure to pick up sts evenly. When picking up stitches along a vertical or shaped edge, remember that row height is less than stitch width: Pick up approximately 3 stitches every 4 rows or 4 stitches every 5 rows. Also, if you are working an edging that requires a certain multiple of sts, be sure to work that in when picking up sts. For more information on picking up stitches, see pages 262–263.

Round-Neck Pullover Vest Neckband

You work this edging using a short circular needle or double-pointed needles so you can comfortably pick up stitches all the way around the neck opening. Even though it's on a circular needle, you work it back and forth in rows.

1 Sew right shoulder seam and steam, if yarn's care instructions allow. (For information on seams, see pages 163 and 253–256.)

2 With RS facing, use a short circ needle or dpns one size smaller than the needles used for the vest body to pick up and k sts evenly down left front neck to holder, k across the center neck sts from holder, pick up and k same number of sts up right front neck to shoulder seam as picked up for left front neck, and k across the back neck sts from holder.

3 Work in edging of your choice to desired length.

4 BO in patt.

5 Sew left shoulder seam, including neckband.

6 Go to "Make Armbands: All Vests," page 148.

V-Neck Pullover Vest Neckband

You work this edging in rounds, using a short circular needle or double-pointed needles one size smaller than the needles used for the vest body.

1. Sew both shoulder seams and steam, if yarn's care instructions allow. (For information on seams, see pages 163 and 253–256.)

2. With RS facing, pick up and k sts evenly down left front neck to v-neck center, k the center st from holder, and mark it with a split-ring marker or scrap yarn, pick up and k same number of sts up right front neck to shoulder seam as picked up for left front neck, and k across the back neck sts from holder.

3. Place marker for beg of rnd, join rnd, and work in chosen edging, shaping center v-neck as foll.

4. Rnd 1: Work patt to within 2 sts of center st, k2tog, k center st, ssk, work in patt to end of rnd.

5. Rnd 2: Work edging patt without shaping.

6. Rep rnds 1 and 2 to desired length, ending with rnd 2.

7. BO in patt, working the dec at center v-neck as in previous rnds.

8. Go to "Make Armbands: All Vests," page 148.

Cardigan Vest Neckband and Button Bands

You work this edging on a long circular needle so you can comfortably pick up stitches all the way around the fronts and neck. Even though it's on a circular needle, you work back and forth in rows.

1. Sew both shoulder seams and steam, if yarn's care instructions allow. (For information on seams, see pages 163 and 253–256.)

2. Place markers (pm) for buttons (on left front for females and right front for males): Pm ½ inch up from hem, pm ½ inch down from beg neck shaping, and place 3 or 5 more markers, evenly spaced, between these two.

3. With RS facing and beg at right front hem, use long circ needle one size smaller than needles used for the vest body to pick up and k sts evenly up right front to shoulder seam, k across the back neck sts from holder, and pick up and k the same number of sts down left front to hem as picked up for right front.

4. Work in edging of your choice for one row.

5. Next row: Work in edging patt and work buttonholes opposite markers this row. (See pages 260–261 for buttonhole techniques.)

6. Cont in patt to desired length.

7. BO in patt.

8. Go to "Make Armbands: All Vests," page 148.

CONTINUED ON NEXT PAGE

MAKE ARMBANDS: ALL VESTS

You work the armband edging using a circular needle so as to be able to comfortably pick up stitches all the way around the armhole. You work it back and forth in rows.

1 With RS facing, use a circular needle one size smaller than the needles used for the vest body to pick up and knit sts evenly up the left front armhole to shoulder seam and then the same number of sts down left back armhole to end.

2 Work in chosen edging patt to desired length.

3 BO in patt.

4 Rep for right armband, except start picking up sts on the back.

5 Go to "Finish: All Vests," below.

FINISH: ALL VESTS

1 Weave in rem loose ends.

2 Before sewing side seams, lightly steam shoulder seams to neaten, if yarn's care instructions allow.

3 Sew side seams, including armband edges. (For information on seams, see pages 163 and 253–256.)

4 Lightly steam side seams to neaten, taking care not to mash or stretch out ribbings.

5 For cardigan, sew buttons opposite buttonholes. Reinforce buttonholes, if necessary. (See page 261 for instructions.)

FAQ

I don't want a thick ribbing around the edges of my vest. If I leave it raw, it looks sloppy. Is there something I can do to neaten it?

Yes, you can work a quick knit row around these edges:

1 Pick up stitches around the edge that you want to work as instructed on the previous pages.

2 Knit 1 row (or round).

Note: For buttonholes, follow instructions on page 147 to place markers. Work buttonholes opposite markers this first row and then knit 1 more row before proceeding to step 3.

3 Bind off knitwise.

The vest is such an adaptable garment that you can alter the master pattern in a few simple ways to make it into something entirely different than the classic version. You can do any number of things: add a stripe or two across the chest or across the bottom ribbing, or add cables, remembering to increase the number of stitches to account for the pulling. But a really beautiful tweed yarn may be all you need. Here are a just a few more suggestions.

NO-EDGING VEST

If you work your vest neatly in a stitch pattern that lies flat, you can get away with omitting the edgings. This vest is knit in a garter stitch stripe pattern that consists of six rows of stockinette stitch alternated with eight rows of garter stitch. If you're knitting a cardigan like the one shown, one change you will have to make to the master pattern is to cast on about an extra ½ inch worth of stitches to each front piece. This allows the front pieces to overlap for buttoning, as the buttonholes are worked directly into the front piece rather than on a knit-in band. Before you work the front piece that will have the buttonholes, simply place markers for buttons on the opposite front piece and work the buttonholes 2 or 3 stitches in from the front vertical edge, opposite the markers.

COLORFUL VEST

In addition to working the master pattern in a compatible stitch pattern, you can work it in a color pattern that works with your stitch count. This easy vest is knit in several colors but uses only two colors per piece. To work this vertical stripe pattern, simply knit 2 stitches in the first color, then 2 stitches in the second color. Repeat this across the row, turn, and work the same pattern in purl stitches. You need to have a stitch count that is a multiple of 4 stitches to work it this way. Knitting in two colors in an easy repeat like this is also a great way to practice holding one color in the left hand and one color in the right hand.

CONTINUED ON NEXT PAGE

TURTLENECK TOP

You can easily make a round-neck vest into an elegant sleeveless turtle-neck top. The only variation to the master pattern is to work the neckband for about 8 to 10 inches for a folded turtleneck or 4 to 5 inches for a mock turtleneck. It's that simple.

CROPPED VEST

If you work the body of the vest—the part that comes before the armhole shaping—a few or several inches shorter than the master pattern indicates, you will have a cropped vest. This would make an excellent layer over a dress, t-shirt, or billowy blouse. The cardigan and the pullover work equally well cropped. This style requires less yarn than the master pattern calls for, so it's a good way to make a sweater without a big investment in yarn.

LONG VEST

If you work the body below the armhole shaping several inches longer than the master pattern specifies, you will end up with a tunic. Remember that you need quite a bit more yarn for this than specified in the master pattern, depending on how many inches are added. Measure from the underarm down to determine the length desired. You may also want to work a longer edging at the hem and sew the side seams, beginning above the edging, to form side slits for a more easy fit.

Here is a project that uses the master pattern as a starting point to produce something new. Adding a few inches to the body length, tapering the sides, and changing the neck shaping transform the classic vest into a flattering women's tunic. The instructions here describe how to make it with either a straight or tapered body.

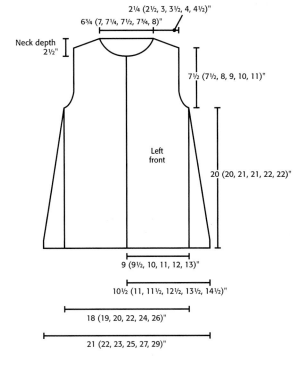

Specifications

SIZES

XS (S, M, L, XL, XXL)

Finished chest measurements: 36 (38, 40, 44, 48, 52) inches

MATERIALS

Desired yarn, in the amount specified in Table 43

1 pair straight needles in size needed to obtain gauge

Circular needle 1 size smaller than needles used for vest body to work edgings

1 large stitch holder

Row counter

Tapestry needle

5 buttons

Table 43. Approximate Yardage for Adult Tunic	
Gauge (in Stockinette Stitch)	**Adult Vest: Approximate Yardage**
2 sts/in.	400–700 yd.
3 sts/in.	600–950 yd.
4 sts/in.	750–1,250 yd.
5 sts/in.	850–1,350 yd.
6 sts/in.	950–1,600 yd.

CONTINUED ON NEXT PAGE

2¼ (2½, 3, 3½, 4, 4½)"

6¾ (7, 7¼, 7½, 7¾, 8)"

Neck depth 2½"

7½ (7½, 8, 9, 10, 11)"

Left front

20 (20, 21, 21, 22, 22)"

9 (9½, 10, 11, 12, 13)"

10½ (11, 11½, 12½, 13½, 14½)"

18 (19, 20, 22, 24, 26)"

21 (22, 23, 25, 27, 29)"

NOTES ON THE SAMPLE

The tunic is knit in elann.com *Peruvian Collection Highland Wool* (Colors #1068 and #0306, 100% wool, 109 yd./50g ball, 5 sts per inch). It uses the tapered shaping and seed stitch edging. The neckband was worked in seed stitch for 1 inch. The buttons were placed with one button ½ inch down from neck, another button 12 inches up from hem, and three more evenly spaced between those two. The armbands were knit in seed stitch for ¾ inch.

How to Make the Tunic

MAKE TUNIC BACK

You have two options for the tunic back: the straight style or the tapered style. The straight style is easiest—it's really just like the master pattern, but longer below the armhole. The tapered style produces an a-line shape and is more feminine.

Straight Tunic Back

1 CO and work desired edging as for vest back on pages 138–139.

> **Note:** *Remember that ribbing will pull the hem in. This may not be a desirable look for the edging. Try an edging that lays flat.*

2 Work body in St st without shaping until back measures 20 (20, 21, 21, 22, 22) inches from CO edge.

3 Shape armholes and shoulders and finish back as for vest back on pages 138–139.

4 Go to the appropriate directions under "Make Tunic Front," page 154.

Tapered Tunic Back

1 CO sts for your size and gauge according to Table 44.

> **Note:** *If you want to work an edging that requires a different number of sts than that specified for your size and gauge in Table 44, you can cast on 1 or 2 fewer sts and work the edging to one row before the end. Increase back to the stitch count specified in Table 44 on the last edging row.*

Table 44. Cast On for Tapered Tunic Back	
Gauge	**No. of Sts to CO**
2 sts/in.	42 (44, 46, 50, 54, 58) sts
3 sts/in.	64 (67, 70, 76, 82, 88) sts
4 sts/in.	84 (88, 92, 100, 108, 116) sts
5 sts/in.	106 (111, 116, 126, 136, 146) sts
6 sts/in.	126 (132, 138, 150, 162, 174) sts

2. Choose one of the edgings from pages 127–129 and work for the desired length, ending with a WS row.

Note: Remember that ribbing will pull the hem in. This may not be a desirable look for the tunic. Try an edging that lays flat. The sample shown uses seed st for the edging, and the edging is worked for 1¼ inches.

3. If your edging is shorter than 4 inches, beg with a knit row, work in St st until back measures 4 inches from CO edge, ending with a WS row.

4. Shape sides by dec 1 st each end on specified rows the number of times indicated for your size and gauge in Table 45.

Note: Refer to your gauge swatch to determine your row gauge. If the row gauge you are achieving is not listed for your stitch gauge, choose the closest one for your stitch gauge. Don't use the instructions for any other stitch gauge, even if the row gauge matches yours, or the math will be off.

Table 45. Tapered Tunic Back: Side Shaping		
Stitch Gauge	**Row Gauge**	**Dec 1 St Each End Every**
2 sts/in.	2½ rows/in.	13th (13th, 14th, 14th, 15th, 15th) row, 3 times
2 sts/in.	3 rows/in.	16th (16th, 17th, 17th, 18th, 18th) row, 3 times
3 sts/in.	4 rows/in.	12th (12th, 13th, 13th, 14th, 14th) row, 5 times
3 sts/in.	4½ rows/in.	14th (14th, 15th, 15th, 16th, 16th) row, 5 times
4 sts/in.	5 rows/in.	13th (13th, 14th, 14th, 15th, 15th) row, 6 times
4 sts/in.	5½ rows/in.	14th (14th, 15th, 15th, 16th, 16th) row, 6 times
5 sts/in.	6 rows/in.	12th (12th, 13th, 13th, 13th, 13th) row, 8 times
5 sts/in.	7 rows/in.	14th (14th, 15th, 15th, 16th, 16th) row, 8 times
6 sts/in.	7½ rows/in.	13th (13th, 14th, 14th, 15th, 15th) row, 9 times
6 sts/in.	8 rows/in.	14th (14th, 15th, 15th, 16th, 16th) row, 9 times

CONTINUED ON NEXT PAGE

You should have rem the number of sts indicated for your size and gauge in Table 46.

⑤ Cont without further shaping until back measures 20 (20, 21, 21, 22, 22) inches from CO edge.

⑥ Shape armholes and shoulders and finish back as for vest back on pages 138–139.

⑦ Go to the appropriate directions under "Make Tunic Front," below.

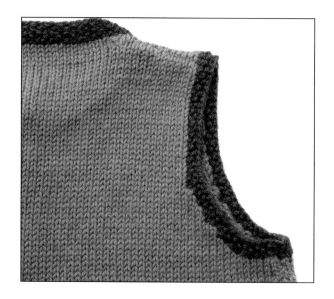

Table 46. Tapered Tunic Back: Stitches Remaining After Side Shaping	
Gauge	**No. of Sts After Shaping Sides**
2 sts/in.	36 (38, 40, 44, 48, 52) sts
3 sts/in.	54 (57, 60, 66, 72, 78) sts
4 sts/in.	72 (76, 80, 88, 96, 104) sts
5 sts/in.	90 (95, 100, 110, 120, 130) sts
6 sts/in.	108 (114, 120, 132, 144, 156) sts

MAKE TUNIC FRONT

The directions here are for a cardigan tunic with a round neck, in both the straight and tapered styles.

Straight Tunic: Left Front

① CO as for adult cardigan left front on page 144 and work desired edging as for tunic back.

② Work body in St st without shaping until left front measures 20 (20, 21, 21, 22, 22) inches from CO edge, ending with a WS row.

③ Shape armholes as for adult cardigan left front on pages 144–145.

④ AT THE SAME TIME, when armhole measures 5 (5, 5½, 6½, 7½, 8½) inches, beg neck shaping on next WS row: Beg this row (neck edge), BO the number of sts indicated for your gauge in Table 47.

Table 47. Tunic Left Front: Begin Neck Shaping	
Gauge	**No. of Sts to BO Beg Next WS Row**
2 sts/in.	4 sts
3 sts/in.	6 sts
4 sts/in.	8 sts
5 sts/in.	10 sts
6 sts/in.	12 sts

5 Dec 1 st at neck edge *every* row the number of times indicated for your size and gauge in Table 48.

6 Dec 1 st at neck edge every other row the number of times indicated for your size and gauge in Table 49.

Note: *If the number of times indicated for your size and gauge is 0, skip ahead to step 7.*

7 Work without further neck shaping until front measures same as back to beg shoulder shaping, ending with a WS row. After neck and armhole shaping, you should have rem the number of sts indicated for your size and gauge in Table 50.

8 Shape and finish shoulder as for adult cardigan left front on page 145.

9 Go to "All Tunics: Right Front," page 157.

Table 48. Tunic Left Front: Neck Shaping	
Gauge	No. of Times to Dec 1 St at Neck Edge Every Row
2 sts/in.	2 (2, 2, 3, 3, 3) times
3 sts/in.	2 (2, 4, 4, 5, 5) times
4 sts/in.	4 (4, 5, 5, 5, 6) times
5 sts/in.	4 (4, 5, 7, 7, 8) times
6 sts/in.	4 (5, 7, 8, 8, 10) times

Table 49. Tunic Left Front: Finish Neck Shaping	
Gauge	No. of Times to Dec 1 St at Neck Edge Every Other Row
2 sts/in.	1 (1, 1, 1, 1, 3) times
3 sts/in.	2 (2, 1, 1, 1, 1) times
4 sts/in.	All sizes: 2 times
5 sts/in.	3 (3, 3, 2, 2, 2) times
6 sts/in.	4 (4, 3, 3, 3, 2) times

Table 50. Tunic Left Front: Shoulder Stitches Remaining After Neck and Armhole Shaping	
Gauge	No. of Sts After Shaping Armhole and Neck
2 sts/in.	5 (5, 6, 7, 8, 9) sts
3 sts/in.	7 (8, 9, 10, 12, 13) sts
4 sts/in.	9 (10, 12, 14, 16, 18) sts
5 sts/in.	12 (13, 15, 17, 20, 23) sts
6 sts/in.	14 (15, 18, 21, 24, 27) sts

CONTINUED ON NEXT PAGE

Tapered Tunic: Left Front

1. CO sts for your size and gauge according to Table 51.

2. Work edging as for tapered tunic back (see page 153).

3. Shape side by dec 1 st at beg of specified RS rows or end of specified WS rows the number of times indicated for your size and gauge in Table 52.

Table 51. Cast On for Tapered Tunic Left Front	
Gauge	**No. of Sts to CO**
2 sts/in.	21 (22, 23, 25, 27, 29) sts
3 sts/in.	32 (33, 35, 38, 41, 44) sts
4 sts/in.	42 (44, 46, 50, 54, 58) sts
5 sts/in.	53 (55, 58, 63, 68, 73) sts
6 sts/in.	63 (66, 69, 75, 81, 87) sts

Table 52. Tapered Tunic Left Front: Side Shaping		
Stitch Gauge	**Row Gauge**	**Dec 1 St Each End Every**
2 sts/in.	2½ rows/in.	13th (13th, 14th, 14th, 15th, 15th) row, 3 times
2 sts/in.	3 rows/in.	16th (16th, 17th, 17th, 18th, 18th) row, 3 times
3 sts/in.	4 rows/in.	12th (12th, 13th, 13th, 14th, 14th) row, 5 times
3 sts/in.	4½ rows/in.	14th (14th, 15th, 15th, 16th, 16th) row, 5 times
4 sts/in.	5 rows/in.	13th (13th, 14th, 14th, 15th, 15th) row, 6 times
4 sts/in.	5½ rows/in.	14th (14th, 15th, 15th, 16th, 16th) row, 6 times
5 sts/in.	6 rows/in.	12th (12th, 13th, 13th, 13th, 13th) row, 8 times
5 sts/in.	7 rows/in.	14th (14th, 15th, 15th, 16th, 16th) row, 8 times
6 sts/in.	7½ rows/in.	13th (13th, 14th, 14th, 15th, 15th) row, 9 times
6 sts/in.	8 rows/in.	14th (14th, 15th, 15th, 16th, 16th) row, 9 times

You should have rem the number of sts indicated for your size and gauge in Table 53.

④ Cont without further shaping until front measures 20 (20, 21, 21, 22, 22) inches from CO edge, ending with a WS row.

⑤ Shape armholes, neck, and shoulder as for straight tunic left front (see pages 154–155).

⑥ Go to "All Tunics: Right Front," below.

| Table 53. Tapered Tunic Left Front: Stitches Remaining After Side Shaping ||
Gauge	No. of Sts After Shaping Side
2 sts/in.	18 (19, 20, 22, 24, 26) sts
3 sts/in.	27 (28, 30, 33, 36, 39) sts
4 sts/in.	36 (38, 40, 44, 48, 52) sts
5 sts/in.	45 (47, 50, 55, 60, 65) sts
6 sts/in.	54 (57, 60, 66, 72, 78) sts

All Tunics: Right Front

① Work as for your left front, reversing armhole, neck, and shoulder shaping.

② Go to "Make Neckband, Button Bands, and Armbands: All Tunics," page 158.

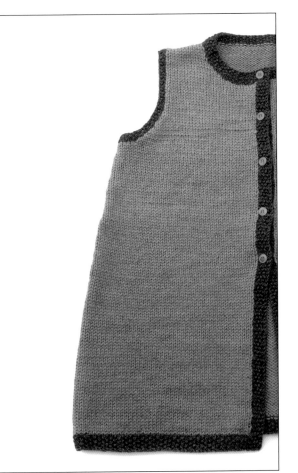

CONTINUED ON NEXT PAGE

MAKE NECKBAND, BUTTON BANDS, AND ARMBANDS: ALL TUNICS

When making a neckband, button bands, or armbands, be sure to pick up sts evenly. When picking up stitches along a vertical or shaped edge, remember that row height is less than stitch width: pick up approximately 3 stitches every 4 rows or 4 stitches every 5 rows. If you are working an edging that requires a certain multiple of sts, work that in when picking up sts. For more information on picking up stitches, see pages 262–263.

Neckband

You work this edging back and forth in rows on a long circular needle one size smaller than the needles used for the tunic body.

1 Sew both shoulder seams and steam, if yarn's care instructions allow. (For information on seams, see pages 163 and 253–256.)

2 With RS facing and starting at beg right neck shaping, use circ needle to pick up and k sts up the right neck to shoulder seam, k across the back neck sts from holder, and pick up and k the same number of sts down left front neck as picked up for right neck.

3 Work in edging of your choice to desired length.

4 BO in patt.

5 Go to "Button Bands," below.

Button Bands

You work this edging on a long circular needle so you can comfortably pick up stitches all the way up the front. Even though it's on a circular needle, you work it back and forth in rows.

1 With RS facing, use circ needle one size smaller than that used for tunic body to pick up and k sts evenly down center left front edge from top to hem.

2 Work in edging of your choice to desired length.

3 BO in patt.

4 Place markers for buttons on left front as desired, starting ½ inch down from beg neck shaping.

5 With RS facing and beg at right front hem, use circ needle to evenly pick up and k same number of sts as for left button band up center right front edge to top.

6 Work in edging patt for 1 row.

7 Next row: Cont in edging patt, but work buttonholes opposite markers this row. (See pages 260–261 for buttonhole techniques.)

8 Cont in patt to same length as left button band.

9 BO in patt.

10 Go to "Armbands," on the next page.

Armbands

The armbands are worked on a circular needle but worked back and forth in rows.

1. With RS facing, use a short circular needle one size smaller than that used for vest body to pick up and k sts evenly up left front armhole to shoulder seam and then the same number of sts down left back armhole to end.

2. Work in chosen edging patt to desired length.

3. BO in patt.

4. Rep for right armband, except start picking up sts on the back.

5. Go to "Finish Tunic: All Tunics," below.

FINISH TUNIC: ALL TUNICS

1. Sew side seams, leaving a slit 3–4 inches up from hem, if desired. (For information on seams, see pages 163 and 253–256.)

2. Work in any rem ends.

3. Lightly steam seams, if yarn's care instructions allow.

4. Sew buttons opposite buttonholes.

8

Sweaters

Pullover, cardigan, coat, and tunic—these are just a few types of sweaters. You can try your hand at all these styles by following the master pattern included in this chapter. Or simply consult the pattern for math purposes, or use it as a stepping-stone to designing a distinctive fashion all your own.

Sweater Styles

It is impossible to cover in one book even a fraction of the possible sweater options; however, numerous armhole and neck shapes—over a broad size range—do appear in these pages. Follow the master pattern closely to create a classic pullover; or simply use it as a starting point to create your own look.

THE PULLOVER

The pullover is the most basic of sweaters. First you knit the back, and then you knit the front—which is almost identical to the back, except for the neck shaping. The neck must be large enough to pull over the head, unless a placket is used on the back neck, front neck, or shoulder. You make two sleeves just alike.

THE CARDIGAN

The cardigan is made up of five pieces: a back, two fronts, and two sleeves. The fronts are mirror images of each other; so once you have worked the first front, the second front is easy—all you have to do is reverse the sides where the armhole and neck shaping takes place.

ARMHOLE SHAPING

Some sweaters require no armhole shaping; for example, a straight armhole results in a drop-shouldered look. For a little less drop to the shoulder, you can use the square armhole, or the angled armhole, with a matching sleeve cap. For an even more tailored look, you can use the rounded or raglan armhole. Remember that the type of armhole shaping determines the sleeve cap shaping.

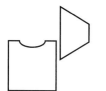

Straight armhole with straight sleeve cap

Square armhole with set-in sleeve

Angled armhole with angular sleeve cap

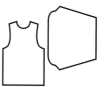

Rounded armhole with rounded sleeve cap

Raglan armhole with raglan sleeve

Before you start sewing your sweater pieces together, take a few minutes to read about the order of assembly and what seaming technique is best for each part.

ORDER OF ASSEMBLY

Generally, sweaters that are knit flat in pieces are joined first at the shoulders. Then the sleeves are attached. Finally, the side and underarm seams are sewn. You use long straight pins to pin pieces together before seaming. You should neaten up seams by lightly steaming them with an iron after sewing them together.

WHICH SEAM FOR WHICH PART?

Sometimes knitting instructions specify the best seaming technique for a given join. If no specific technique is indicated, you can always safely use the backstitch seam for the shoulders, whether they are shaped or not. If the shoulders are not shaped, you can try using the invisible horizontal seam or the three-needle bind-off. The invisible vertical seam is an excellent choice for side and underarm seams; but again, a backstitch seam is perfectly acceptable for those joins. The following table shows when to use various seams, and pages 253–256 describe how to accomplish the different seams.

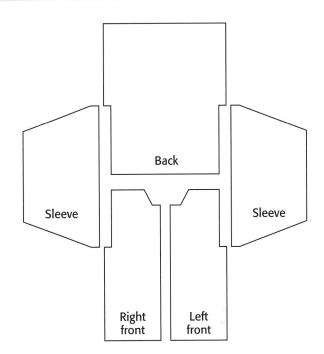

Type of Seam	Use It to Join	Examples
Invisible horizontal seam	Two horizontal edges	Bound-off shoulder seams
Backstitch seam	All edges	Shaped shoulders, side seams, add-on collars
Invisible vertical seam	Two vertical edges	Sweater sides and underarm seams
Invisible vertical-to-horizontal seam	A bound-off edge to a side edge	Joining a sleeve cap to an armhole
Grafted seam	Two horizontal edges	Unshaped shoulders, toes of socks, and mitten tips

Sweater: Master Pattern

This master pattern covers pullovers and cardigans with round or v-necks, four different armhole styles, and numerous edgings. Try adding a stitch or color pattern—always checking your gauge beforehand—to liven things up. You can also adjust the size by shortening or lengthening the body below the armholes, as needed.

Take careful measurements when choosing a size to knit. Babies and children grow quickly, so for practical reasons, the baby/child sizing allows generous ease. That way, your lovingly knit sweater will fit comfortably for at least a year or two.

Specifications

SIZES

Baby/Child Sweater

6–18 mos. (2–4 yrs., 4–6 yrs., 6–8 yrs., 8–10 yrs.)
Finished chest measurements: 22 (24, 28, 30, 32) inches

Adult Sweater

XS (S, M, L, XL, XXL)
Finished chest measurements: 36 (38, 40, 44, 48, 52) inches

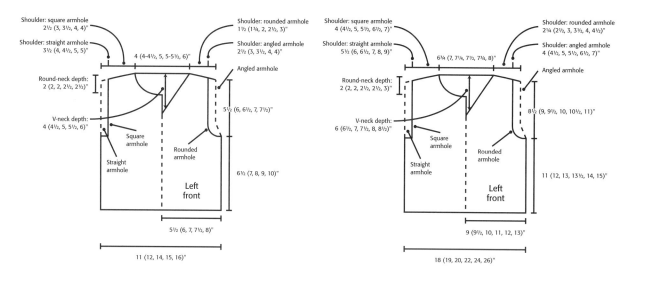

MATERIALS

Desired yarn, in the amount specified in Table 1

1 pair straight needles in size needed to obtain gauge

Circular needle one size smaller than needles used for sweater body (to work some edgings)

Tapestry needle

2 stitch holders

Row counter

Buttons for cardigan (5 for baby/child sizes, 7 for adult sizes)

Table 1. Approximate Yardage for Sweater		
Gauge (in Stockinette Stitch)	Baby/Child Sweater: Approximate Yardage	Adult Sweater: Approximate Yardage
2 sts/in.	300–750 yd.	850–1,500 yd.
3 sts/in.	350–850 yd.	925–1,750 yd.
4 sts/in.	450–1,000 yd.	1,200–2,000 yd.
5 sts/in.	550–1,100 yd.	1,400–2,300 yd.
6 sts/in.	700–1,500 yd.	1,650–3,000 yd.

NOTES ON THE SAMPLES

The women's pullover is worked in GGH/Muench *Aspen* (Colors #19 and #26, 50% merino wool/50% acrylic, 63yd./50g ball, 3 sts per inch). It is worked using a wide band of 2x3 ribbed edging with a stripe of a contrast color, and the body is worked in reverse stockinette stitch. It has a cropped length, a round collar with a turtleneck (which is simply 2x3 rib worked for several inches), and rounded armhole shaping.

The child's cardigan is knit in GGH/Muench *Savanna* (Colors #17, #5, and #13, 43% alpaca/23% linen/19% wool/15% nylon, 88 yd./50g ball, 4 sts per inch). It has multiple edgings. The edging along the bottom is a hem in a contrast color. The sleeve cuffs are worked in a contrast color 2x2 rib with a third color stripe. The button bands are worked in seed stitch with a garter stitch accent along the pick-up row. The neckband is worked in 1x1 rib, also with a garter stitch accent along the pick-up row. There is an easy Fair Isle band above the hem. The neck and armhole use round shaping.

CONTINUED ON NEXT PAGE

Edging Stitch Patterns

You usually want to include an edging to ensure a neat fit for your sweater. Ribbings and hems also keep the edges from stretching and flaring. You might want to knit your edging in needles one or two sizes smaller than those used for the sweater body to guarantee a firm edge.

1X1 RIBBED EDGING (EVEN NO. OF STS)

This edging, worked on an even number of stitches, is the most common choice for vests and sweaters and is easy to do.

1 Row 1: *K1, p1; rep from * to end of row.

2 Rep row 1 to desired length.

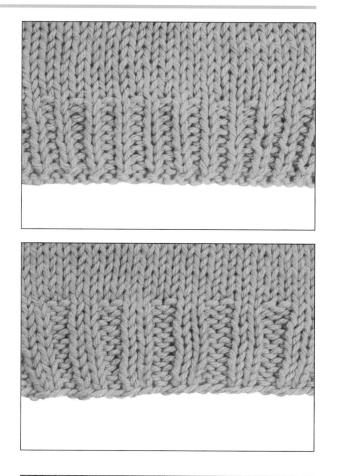

2X2 RIBBED EDGING (EVEN NO. OF STS)

This edging creates a nice elastic trim. For a multiple of 4 sts, work as follows:

1 Row 1: *K2, p2; rep from * to end of row.

2 Rep row 1 to desired length.

For a multiple of 4 sts plus 2, work as follows:

1 Row 1: K2, *p2, k2; rep from * to end of row.

2 Row 2: P2, *k2, p2; rep from * to end of row.

3 Rep rows 1 and 2 to desired length.

> **Note:** *You can make a ribbed edging using virtually any number of stitches. For example, the adult sweater shown in this chapter uses a 3x2 ribbed edging. Creating a unique edging is a powerful design technique.*

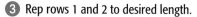

ROLLED EDGING (ANY NO. OF STS)

To make this easy edging tidy, use needles one size smaller than the needles used for the body of the sweater.

1 Row 1 (RS): Knit.

2 Row 2 (WS): Purl.

3 Rep rows 1 and 2 for approx 1 inch.

> **Note:** *If you are using this edging for the bands around the neck or cardigan fronts and you have picked up stitches from the RS, begin edging with row 2.*

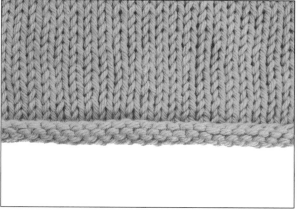

GARTER STITCH EDGING (ANY NO. OF STS)

To make this flat edging firm, use needles one size smaller than the needles used for the body of the sweater.

① Row 1 (RS): Knit.

② Rep row 1 to desired length.

SEED STITCH EDGING (ANY NO. OF STS)

Seed stitch has a tendency to work up in a looser gauge than stockinette stitch, so use needles one size smaller than the needles used for the body of the sweater. For an even number of sts, work as follows:

① Row 1 (RS): *K1, p1; rep from * to end of row.

② Row 2 (WS): *P1, k1; rep from * to end of row.

③ Rep rows 1 and 2 to desired length.

For an odd number of sts, work as follows:

① Row 1 (RS): K1, *p1, k1; rep from * to end of row.

② Rep row 1 to desired length.

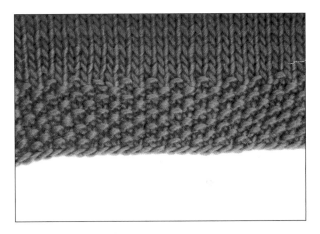

TURNED HEM (ANY NO. OF STS)

This edging is nice if you don't want the hem of your sweater to pull in. For steps 1–4 of this edging, use needles one size smaller than the needles used for the body of the sweater.

① Row 1 (RS): Knit.

② Row 2 (WS): Purl.

③ Rep rows 1 and 2 for approx 1 inch.

④ Next row (RS): Purl across row to form folding ridge.

> **Note:** *For a picot hem, work the folding ridge as an eyelet row by repeating k2tog, yo across, ending k1 if necessary.*

⑤ Change to larger needles to beg working body of vest.

> **Note:** *Measure from the folding ridge when pattern specifies to measure from the beginning.*

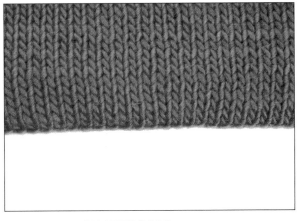

CONTINUED ON NEXT PAGE

How to Make the Sweaters

The instructions for the baby/child version and the adult version of the sweaters are presented together. The back is worked the same for both the pullover and the cardigan. You work the sweater from the hem to where the armhole begins, perform the initial bind-off at the beginning of the armhole—except for the straight armhole version—and then go to the armhole shaping style you have chosen. Next, you make the sleeve that corresponds to the armhole shape.

Make Back

Follow the instructions for the back in your size under "All Styles" where indicated, and then for your armhole style where indicated. For example, if you're making the sweater with the angled armhole, cast on for the back as directed for your size under "All Styles," and when you're ready to begin the armhole shaping, skip ahead to the section "Angled Armhole Shaping."

CAST ON BACK: ALL STYLES

1. CO sts for your size and gauge according to Table 2.

   Note: *If you want to work an edging that requires a different number of sts than that specified for your size and gauge in Table 2, you can cast on 1 or 2 fewer sts and work the edging to one row before the end. Increase back to the stitch count specified in Table 2 on the last edging row.*

2. Choose one of the edgings from pages 166–167 and work for desired length, ending with a WS row.

3. Beg with a knit row, work in St st until back measures 6½ (7, 8, 9, 10) inches from CO edge for baby/child back or 11 (12, 13, 13½, 14, 15) inches from CO edge for adult back, ending with a WS row.

4. Go to the appropriate instructions under "Shape Back Armhole," on the next page.

Table 2. Cast On for Sweater Back		
	No. of Sts to CO	
Gauge	**Baby/Child**	**Adult**
2 sts/in.	22 (24, 28, 30, 32) sts	36 (38, 40, 44, 48, 52) sts
3 sts/in.	33 (36, 42, 45, 48) sts	54 (57, 60, 66, 72, 78) sts
4 sts/in.	44 (48, 56, 60, 64) sts	72 (76, 80, 88, 96, 104) sts
5 sts/in.	55 (60, 70, 75, 80) sts	90 (95, 100, 110, 120, 130) sts
6 sts/in.	66 (72, 84, 90, 96) sts	108 (114, 120, 132, 144, 156) sts

SHAPE BACK ARMHOLE

At this point, you need to choose which armhole shaping to use. To work a square or rounded armhole, go to "Sweater with Square or Rounded Armhole Back: Initial Armhole Shaping," below. To work a straight armhole, go to "Sweater with Straight Armhole Back: Armhole Shaping," below, and to work an angled armhole, go to "Sweater with Angled Armhole Back: Armhole Shaping," page 170.

Sweater with Square or Rounded Armhole Back: Initial Armhole Shaping

1 Beg armhole shaping (RS): Beg next 2 rows, BO the number of sts specified for your size and gauge in Table 3. You should have rem the number of sts indicated for your size and gauge in Table 4.

2 Go to either "Sweater with Square Armhole Back: Armhole Shaping," page 170, or "Sweater with Rounded Armhole Back: Armhole Shaping," page 171, depending on which armhole you're working.

Table 3. Sweater Back, Square or Rounded Armhole: Begin Armhole Shaping		
No. of Sts to BO Beg Next 2 Rows		
Gauge	**Baby/Child**	**Adult**
2 sts/in.	2 sts	3 (3, 3, 3, 3, 4) sts
3 sts/in.	3 sts	4 (4, 4, 5, 5, 6) sts
4 sts/in.	4 sts	6 (6, 6, 7, 7, 8) sts
5 sts/in.	5 sts	7 (7, 7, 8, 8, 9) sts
6 sts/in.	6 sts	9 (9, 9, 10, 10, 10) sts

Table 4. Sweater Back, Square or Rounded Armhole: Stitches Remaining After Initial Armhole Bind-off		
No. of St After BO for Armhole		
Gauge	**Baby/Child**	**Adult**
2 sts/in.	18 (20, 24, 26, 28) sts	30 (32, 34, 38, 42, 44) sts
3 sts/in.	27 (30, 36, 39, 42) sts	46 (49, 52, 56, 62, 66) sts
4 sts/in.	36 (40, 48, 52, 56) sts	60 (64, 68, 74, 82, 88) sts
5 sts/in.	45 (50, 60, 65, 70) sts	76 (81, 86, 94, 104, 112) sts
6 sts/in.	54 (60, 72, 78, 84) sts	90 (96, 102, 112, 124, 136) sts

Sweater with Straight Armhole Back: Armhole Shaping

The straight armhole is not shaped at all. It's just a continuation of the sweater body and results in drop shoulders.

1 Continue working without shaping until back measures 12 (13, 14½, 16, 17½) inches from CO edge for baby/child back or 19½ (21, 22½, 23½, 24½, 26) inches from CO edge for adult back, ending with a WS row.

2 Go to "Sweater with Straight Armhole Back: Shoulder Shaping," page 172.

CONTINUED ON NEXT PAGE

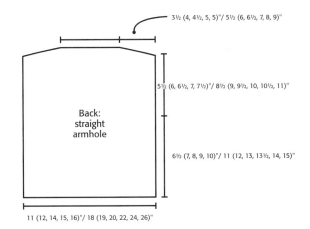

3½ (4, 4½, 5, 5)"/ 5½ (6, 6½, 7, 8, 9)"

5½ (6, 6½, 7, 7½)"/ 8½ (9, 9½, 10, 10½, 11)"

Back: straight armhole

6½ (7, 8, 9, 10)"/ 11 (12, 13, 13½, 14, 15)"

11 (12, 14, 15, 16)"/ 18 (19, 20, 22, 24, 26)"

Sweater with Square Armhole Back: Armhole Shaping

The only shaping for the square armhole is the initial bind-off you performed previously.

1 Continue working without further shaping until back measures 12 (13, 14½, 16, 17½) inches from CO edge for baby/child back or 19½ (21, 22½, 23½, 24½, 26) inches from CO edge for adult back, ending with a WS row.

2 Go to "Sweater with Square or Angled Armhole Back: Shoulder Shaping," page 173.

Sweater with Angled Armhole Back: Armhole Shaping

The angled armhole is set in the same amount as the square armhole, but the indentation is gradual rather than perpendicular.

1 Beg next row (RS), dec 1 st each end every RS row the number of times specified for your size and gauge in Table 5. You should have rem the number of sts indicated for your size and gauge in Table 6.

2 Continue working without further shaping until back measures 12 (13, 14½, 16, 17½) inches from CO edge for baby/child back or 19½ (21, 22½, 23½, 24½, 26) inches from CO edge for adult back, ending with a WS row.

3 Go to "Sweater with Square or Angled Armhole Back: Shoulder Shaping," page 173.

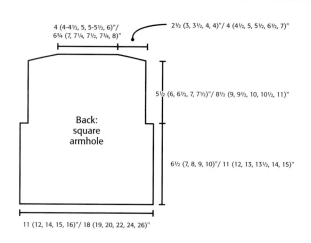

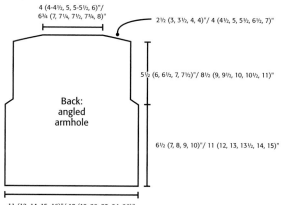

Table 5. Sweater Back, Angled Armhole: Armhole Shaping

No. of Times to Dec 1 St Each End Every RS Row

Gauge	Baby/Child	Adult
2 sts/in.	2 times	3 (3, 3, 3, 3, 4) times
3 sts/in.	3 times	4 (4, 4, 5, 5, 6) times
4 sts/in.	4 times	6 (6, 6, 7, 7, 8) times
5 sts/in.	5 times	7 (7, 7, 8, 8, 9) times
6 sts/in.	6 times	9 (9, 9, 10, 10, 10) times

Table 6. Sweater Back, Angled Armhole: Stitches Remaining After Armhole Shaping

No. of Sts After Angled Armhole Shaping

Gauge	Baby/Child	Adult
2 sts/in.	18 (20, 24, 26, 28) sts	30 (32, 34, 38, 42, 44) sts
3 sts/in.	27 (30, 36, 39, 42) sts	46 (49, 52, 56, 62, 66) sts
4 sts/in.	36 (40, 48, 52, 56) sts	60 (64, 68, 74, 82, 88) sts
5 sts/in.	45 (50, 60, 65, 70) sts	76 (81, 86, 94, 104, 112) sts
6 sts/in.	54 (60, 72, 78, 84) sts	90 (96, 102, 112, 124, 136) sts

Sweater with Rounded Armhole Back: Armhole Shaping

The rounded armhole is the most tailored of the choices, resulting in a shorter shoulder. After the initial bind-off that you performed previously, you decrease over a series of rows to create a curve.

1 Beg next row (RS), dec 1 st each end every RS row the number of times specified for your size and gauge in Table 7. You should have rem the number of sts specified for your size and gauge in Table 8.

2 Continue without further shaping until armhole measures 5½ (6, 6½, 7, 7½) inches for baby/child version or 8½ (9, 9½, 10, 10½, 11) inches for adult version, ending with a WS row.

3 Go to "Sweater with Rounded Armhole Back: Shoulder Shaping," page 174.

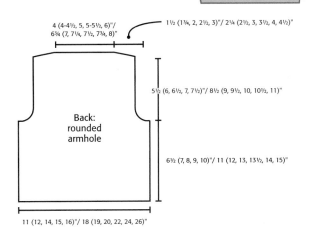

4 (4-4½, 5, 5-5½, 6)"/ 6¾ (7, 7¼, 7½, 7¾, 8)"

1½ (1¾, 2, 2½, 3)"/ 2¼ (2½, 3, 3½, 4, 4½)"

5½ (6, 6½, 7, 7½)"/ 8½ (9, 9½, 10, 10½, 11)"

Back: rounded armhole

6½ (7, 8, 9, 10)"/ 11 (12, 13, 13½, 14, 15)"

11 (12, 14, 15, 16)"/ 18 (19, 20, 22, 24, 26)"

Table 7. Sweater Back, Rounded Armhole: Armhole Shaping		
No. of Times to Dec 1 St Each End Every RS Row		
Gauge	**Baby/Child**	**Adult**
2 sts/in.	2 (2, 3, 3, 2) times	3 (4, 4, 4, 5, 5) times
3 sts/in.	3 (4, 5, 4, 3) times	6 (6, 6, 7, 7, 8) times
4 sts/in.	4 (5, 6, 5, 4) times	7 (8, 7, 8, 10, 10) times
5 sts/in.	5 (6, 7, 6, 5) times	9 (10, 10, 11, 13, 13) times
6 sts/in.	6 (7, 9, 7, 6) times	11 (12, 11, 12, 15, 17) times

Table 8. Sweater Back, Rounded Armhole: Stitches Remaining After Armhole Shaping		
No. of Sts After Rounded Armhole Shaping		
Gauge	**Baby/Child**	**Adult**
2 sts/in.	14 (16, 18, 20, 24) sts	24 (24, 26, 30, 32, 34) sts
3 sts/in.	21 (22, 26, 31, 36) sts	34 (37, 40, 42, 48, 50) sts
4 sts/in.	28 (30, 36, 42, 48) sts	46 (48, 54, 58, 62, 68) sts
5 sts/in.	35 (38, 46, 53, 60) sts	58 (61, 66, 72, 78, 86) sts
6 sts/in.	42 (46, 54, 64, 72) sts	68 (72, 80, 88, 94, 102) sts

CONTINUED ON NEXT PAGE

SHAPE BACK SHOULDERS

You shape a shoulder by binding off half the stitches over the first row and the remaining stitches over the next row. This results in a gentle slope that hugs the shoulder nicely. Be sure to shape the shoulder according to your armhole style, as the armhole shaping results in different stitch counts.

Sweater with Straight Armhole Back: Shoulder Shaping

1 Beg shoulder shaping (RS): Beg next 2 rows, BO the number of sts specified for your size and gauge in Table 9.

2 Beg next 2 rows, BO the number of sts specified for your size and gauge in Table 10.

3 Cut yarn and put rem neck sts onto holder or spare needle for later. Table 11 shows how many sts this should be for your size and gauge.

4 Go to instructions for desired front style under "Make Front," page 174.

Table 9. Sweater Back, Straight Armhole: Begin Shoulder Shaping

No. of Sts to BO Beg Next 2 Rows

Gauge	Baby/Child	Adult
2 sts/in.	4 (4, 5, 5, 5) sts	6 (6, 7, 7, 8, 9) sts
3 sts/in.	5 (6, 7, 7, 8) sts	9 (9, 10, 11, 12, 14) sts
4 sts/in.	7 (8, 9, 10, 10) sts	11 (12, 13, 15, 17, 18) sts
5 sts/in.	9 (10, 11, 12, 13) sts	14 (15, 16, 18, 21, 23) sts
6 sts/in.	11 (11, 14, 14, 15) sts	17 (18, 19, 22, 25, 27) sts

Table 10. Sweater Back, Straight Armhole: Finish Shoulder Shaping

No. of Sts to BO Beg Next 2 Rows

Gauge	Baby/Child	Adult
2 sts/in.	3 (4, 4, 5, 5) sts	5 (6, 6, 7, 8, 9) sts
3 sts/in.	5 (6, 6, 7, 7) sts	8 (9, 9, 11, 12, 13) sts
4 sts/in.	7 (7, 9, 9, 10) sts	11 (12, 12, 14, 16, 18) sts
5 sts/in.	8 (9, 11, 11, 12) sts	14 (15, 16, 18, 20, 22) sts
6 sts/in.	10 (11, 13, 14, 15) sts	17 (18, 19, 21, 24, 27) sts

Table 11. Sweater Back, Straight Armhole: Neck Stitches Remaining After Shoulder Shaping

No. of Neck Sts on Holder After Shoulder Shaping

Gauge	Baby/Child	Adult
2 sts/in.	8 (8, 10, 10, 12) sts	14 (14, 14, 16, 16, 16) sts
3 sts/in.	13 (12, 16, 17, 18) sts	20 (21, 22, 22, 24, 24) sts
4 sts/in.	16 (18, 20, 22, 24) sts	28 (28, 30, 30, 30, 32) sts
5 sts/in.	21 (22, 26, 29, 30) sts	34 (35, 36, 38, 38, 40) sts
6 sts/in.	24 (28, 30, 34, 36) sts	40 (42, 44, 46, 46, 48) sts

Sweater with Square or Angled Armhole Back: Shoulder Shaping

1 Beg shoulder shaping (RS): Beg next 2 rows, BO the number of sts specified for your size and gauge in Table 12.

2 Beg next 2 rows, BO the number of sts specified for your size and gauge in Table 13.

3 Cut yarn and put rem neck sts onto holder or spare needle for later. Table 14 shows how many sts this should be for your size and gauge.

4 Go to instructions for desired front style under "Make Front," page 174.

Table 12. Sweater Back, Square or Angled Armhole: Begin Shoulder Shaping		
No. of Sts to BO Beg Next 2 Rows		
Gauge	**Baby/Child**	**Adult**
2 sts/in.	3 (3, 4, 4, 4) sts	4 (5, 5, 6, 7, 7) sts
3 sts/in.	4 (5, 5, 6, 6) sts	7 (7, 8, 9, 10, 11) sts
4 sts/in.	5 (6, 7, 8, 8) sts	8 (9, 10, 11, 13, 14) sts
5 sts/in.	6 (7, 9, 9, 10) sts	11 (12, 13, 14, 17, 18) sts
6 sts/in.	8 (8, 11, 11, 12) sts	13 (14, 15, 17, 20, 22) sts

Table 13. Sweater Back, Square or Angled Armhole: Finish Shoulder Shaping		
No. of Sts to BO Beg Next 2 Rows		
Gauge	**Baby/Child**	**Adult**
2 sts/in.	2 (3, 3, 4, 4) sts	4 (4, 5, 5, 6, 7) sts
3 sts/in.	3 (4, 5, 5, 6) sts	6 (7, 7, 8, 9, 10) sts
4 sts/in.	5 (5, 7, 7, 8) sts	8 (9, 9, 11, 13, 14) sts
5 sts/in.	6 (7, 8, 9, 10) sts	10 (11, 12, 14, 16, 18) sts
6 sts/in.	7 (8, 10, 11, 12) sts	12 (14, 14, 16, 19, 22) sts

Table 14. Sweater Back, Square or Angled Armhole: Neck Stitches Remaining After Shoulder Shaping		
No. of Neck Sts on Holder After Shoulder Shaping		
Gauge	**Baby/Child**	**Adult**
2 sts/in.	8 (8, 10, 10, 12) sts	14 (14, 14, 16, 16, 16) sts
3 sts/in.	13 (12, 16, 17, 18) sts	20 (21, 22, 22, 24, 24) sts
4 sts/in.	16 (18, 20, 22, 24) sts	28 (28, 30, 30, 30, 32) sts
5 sts/in.	21 (22, 26, 29, 30) sts	34 (35, 36, 38, 38, 40) sts
6 sts/in.	24 (28, 30, 34, 36) sts	40 (42, 44, 46, 46, 48) sts

CONTINUED ON NEXT PAGE

Sweater with Rounded Armhole Back: Shoulder Shaping

1 Beg shoulder shaping (RS): Beg next 2 rows, BO the number of sts specified for your size and gauge in Table 15.

2 Beg next 2 rows, BO the number of sts specified for your size and gauge in Table 16.

3 Cut yarn and put rem neck sts on holder or spare needle for later. Table 17 shows how many sts this should be for your size and gauge.

4 Go to instructions for desired front style under "Make Front," below.

Table 15. Sweater Back, Rounded Armhole: Begin Shoulder Shaping		
No. of Sts to BO Beg Next 2 Rows		
Gauge	**Baby/Child**	**Adult**
2 sts/in.	2 (2, 2, 3, 3) sts	3 (3, 3, 4, 4, 5) sts
3 sts/in.	2 (3, 3, 4, 5) sts	4 (4, 5, 5, 6, 7) sts
4 sts/in.	3 (3, 4, 5, 6) sts	5 (5, 6, 7, 8, 9) sts
5 sts/in.	4 (4, 5, 6, 8) sts	6 (7, 8, 9, 10, 12) sts
6 sts/in.	5 (5, 6, 8, 9) sts	7 (8, 9, 11, 12, 14) sts

Table 16. Sweater Back, Rounded Armhole: Finish Shoulder Shaping		
No. of Sts to BO Beg Next 2 Rows		
Gauge	**Baby/Child**	**Adult**
2 sts/in.	1 (2, 2, 2, 3) sts	2 (2, 3, 3, 4, 4) sts
3 sts/in.	2 (2, 2, 3, 4) sts	3 (4, 4, 5, 6, 6) sts
4 sts/in.	3 (3, 4, 5, 6) sts	4 (5, 6, 7, 8, 9) sts
5 sts/in.	3 (4, 5, 6, 7) sts	6 (6, 7, 8, 10, 11) sts
6 sts/in.	4 (4, 6, 7, 9) sts	7 (7, 9, 10, 12, 13) sts

Table 17. Sweater Back, Rounded Armhole: Neck Stitches Remaining After Shoulder Shaping		
No. of Neck Sts on Holder After Shoulder Shaping		
Gauge	**Baby/Child**	**Adult**
2 sts/in.	8 (8, 10, 10, 12) sts	14 (14, 14, 16, 16, 16) sts
3 sts/in.	13 (12, 16, 17, 18) sts	20 (21, 22, 22, 24, 24) sts
4 sts/in.	16 (18, 20, 22, 24) sts	28 (28, 30, 30, 30, 32) sts
5 sts/in.	21 (22, 26, 29, 30) sts	34 (35, 36, 38, 38, 40) sts
6 sts/in.	24 (28, 30, 34, 36) sts	40 (42, 44, 46, 46, 48) sts

Make Front

You have a few choices for the sweater front: a pullover with a round neck, a pullover with a v-neck, a cardigan with a round neck, or a cardigan with a v-neck—all with any of the four armhole styles presented for the back. Be sure to match your front to the back in terms of measurements, armhole style, and shoulder shaping.

MAKE ROUND-NECK PULLOVER FRONT

The front lower body and armhole shaping of the round-neck pullover and the v-neck pullover are worked the same as the back up to where the neck shaping begins. Then you go to the appropriate set of instructions for neck shaping and shoulder shaping.

1 Work as for back, including armhole shaping, until front measures 10 (11, 12½, 13½, 15) inches from CO edge for baby/child version or 17½ (19, 20½, 21, 22, 23) inches from CO edge for adult version, ending with a RS row.

2 Go to round-neck shaping for your armhole style under "Shape Round-Neck Pullover Front," on the next page.

SHAPE ROUND-NECK PULLOVER FRONT

At this point, you have to go to the correct directions for your armhole style. You work the round neck by putting one set of shoulder stitches onto a holder while working the other side. After the first side of the neck and the corresponding shoulder are complete, you shape the other side of the neck.

Pullover with Straight Armhole Front: Round-Neck Shaping

1. Shape right neck and shoulder (WS): Work across the number of sts specified for your size and gauge in Table 18.

2. Put rem (unworked) sts onto holder or spare needle. Table 19 shows how many sts this should be for your size and gauge.

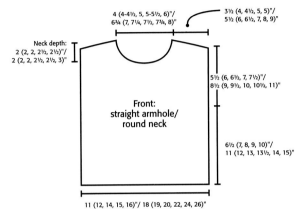

4 (4-4½, 5, 5-5½, 6)"/
6¾ (7, 7¼, 7½, 7¾, 8)"

3½ (4, 4½, 5, 5)"/
5½ (6, 6½, 7, 8, 9)"

Neck depth:
2 (2, 2, 2½, 2½)"/
2 (2, 2, 2½, 2½, 3)"

5½ (6, 6½, 7, 7½)"/
8½ (9, 9½, 10, 10½, 11)"

Front:
straight armhole/
round neck

6½ (7, 8, 9, 10)"/
11 (12, 13, 13½, 14, 15)"

11 (12, 14, 15, 16)"/ 18 (19, 20, 22, 24, 26)"

Table 18. Pullover Front, Straight Armhole and Round Neck: Begin Neck Shaping		
No. of Sts to Work Across		
Gauge	Baby/Child	Adult
2 sts/in.	10 (11, 12, 13, 13) sts	15 (16, 16, 18, 20, 21) sts
3 sts/in.	15 (16, 18, 19, 19) sts	22 (23, 24, 27, 29, 32) sts
4 sts/in.	20 (21, 24, 25, 26) sts	29 (31, 32, 36, 40, 43) sts
5 sts/in.	24 (26, 30, 31, 32) sts	37 (39, 41, 45, 50, 54) sts
6 sts/in.	29 (31, 36, 37, 39) sts	44 (46, 48, 54, 59, 64) sts

Table 19. Pullover Front, Straight Armhole and Round Neck: Left Shoulder Stitches on Holder		
No. of Unworked Sts on Holder for Left Shoulder		
Gauge	Baby/Child	Adult
2 sts/in.	12 (13, 16, 17, 19) sts	21 (22, 24, 26, 28, 31) sts
3 sts/in.	18 (20, 24, 26, 29) sts	32 (34, 36, 39, 43, 46) sts
4 sts/in.	24 (27, 32, 35, 38) sts	43 (45, 48, 52, 56, 61) sts
5 sts/in.	31 (34, 40, 44, 48) sts	53 (56, 59, 65, 70, 76) sts
6 sts/in.	37 (41, 48, 53, 57) sts	64 (68, 72, 78, 85, 92) sts

CONTINUED ON NEXT PAGE

③ Turn, and working right shoulder sts only, dec 1 st at neck edge every row the number of times specified for your size and gauge in Table 20.

④ Dec 1 st at neck edge every other row the number of times specified for your size and gauge in Table 21. You should have rem the number of sts specified for your size and gauge in Table 22.

Table 20. Pullover Front, Straight Armhole and Round Neck: Begin Right Neck Shaping

No. of Rows to Dec 1 St at Neck Edge Every Row

Gauge	Baby/Child	Adult
2 sts/in.	All sizes: 2 rows	All sizes: 2 rows
3 sts/in.	2 (1, 2, 2, 1) rows	All sizes: 3 rows
4 sts/in.	All sizes: 2 rows	All sizes: 4 rows
5 sts/in.	All sizes: 3 rows	All sizes: 5 rows
6 sts/in.	3 (4, 4, 4, 4) rows	All sizes: 6 rows

Table 21. Pullover Front, Straight Armhole and Round Neck: Finish Right Neck Shaping

No. of Times to Dec 1 St at Neck Edge Every Other Row

Gauge	Baby/Child	Adult
2 sts/in.	All sizes: 1 time	2 (2, 1, 2, 2, 1) times
3 sts/in.	3 (3, 4, 4, 3) times	All sizes: 2 times
4 sts/in.	4 (4, 4, 4, 4) times	All sizes: 3 times
5 sts/in.	All sizes: 2 times	All sizes: 4 times
6 sts/in.	All sizes: 3 times	4 (4, 4, 5, 4, 4) times

Table 22. Pullover Front, Straight Armhole and Round Neck: Shoulder Stitches Remaining After Neck Shaping

No. of Sts After Shaping Right Neck

Gauge	Baby/Child	Adult
2 sts/in.	7 (8, 9, 10, 10) sts	11 (12, 13, 14, 16, 18) sts
3 sts/in.	10 (12, 13, 14, 15) sts	17 (18, 19, 22, 24, 27) sts
4 sts/in.	14 (15, 18, 19, 20) sts	22 (24, 25, 29, 33, 36) sts
5 sts/in.	17 (19, 22, 23, 25) sts	28 (30, 32, 36, 41, 45) sts
6 sts/in.	21 (22, 27, 28, 30) sts	34 (36, 38, 43, 49, 54) sts

⑤ AT THE SAME TIME, when front measures 12 (13, 14½, 16, 17½) inches from beg for baby/child version or 19½ (21, 22½, 23½, 24½, 26) inches from beg for adult version, ending with a RS row, beg shaping shoulders. Beg next row (WS), BO the number of sts specified for your size and gauge in Table 23.

⑥ Next row (RS): Knit.

⑦ Next row (WS): BO rem shoulder sts. Table 24 shows how many sts this should be for your size and gauge.

⑧ Shape left neck and shoulder: Slip onto a holder the number of center neck sts indicated for your size and gauge in Table 25.

⑨ Slip rem sts onto your needle.

⑩ Beg with a RS row, rejoin yarn and work 1 row.

⑪ Shape left neck and shoulder as for right neck and shoulder, reversing sides.

⑫ Go to "Make Sleeves," page 198.

Table 23. Pullover Front, Straight Armhole and Round Neck: Begin Shoulder Shaping

No. of Sts to BO Beg This Row

Gauge	Baby/Child	Adult
2 sts/in.	4 (4, 5, 5, 5) sts	6 (6, 7, 7, 8, 9) sts
3 sts/in.	5 (6, 7, 7, 8) sts	9 (9, 10, 11, 12, 14) sts
4 sts/in.	7 (8, 9, 10, 10) sts	11 (12, 13, 15, 17, 18) sts
5 sts/in.	9 (10, 11, 12, 13) sts	14 (15, 16, 18, 21, 23) sts
6 sts/in.	11 (11, 14, 14, 15) sts	17 (18, 19, 22, 25, 27) sts

Table 24. Pullover Front, Straight Armhole and Round Neck: Finish Shoulder Shaping

No. of Sts to BO for Shoulder

Gauge	Baby/Child	Adult
2 sts/in.	3 (4, 4, 5, 5) sts	5 (6, 6, 7, 8, 9) sts
3 sts/in.	5 (6, 6, 7, 7) sts	8 (9, 9, 11, 12, 13) sts
4 sts/in.	7 (7, 9, 9, 10) sts	11 (12, 12, 14, 16, 18) sts
5 sts/in.	8 (9, 11, 11, 12) sts	14 (15, 16, 18, 20, 22) sts
6 sts/in.	10 (11, 13, 14, 15) sts	33 (18, 19, 21, 24, 27) sts

Table 25. Pullover Front, Straight Armhole and Round Neck: Center Neck Stitches on Holder

No. of Sts on Holder After Shaping Right Neck

Gauge	Baby/Child	Adult
2 sts/in.	2 (2, 4, 4, 6) sts	6 (6, 8, 8, 8, 10) sts
3 sts/in.	3 (4, 6, 7, 10) sts	10 (11, 12, 12, 14, 14) sts
4 sts/in.	4 (6, 8, 10, 12) sts	14 (14, 16, 16, 16, 18) sts
5 sts/in.	7 (8, 10, 13, 16) sts	16 (17, 18, 20, 20, 22) sts
6 sts/in.	8 (10, 12, 16, 18) sts	20 (22, 24, 24, 26, 28) sts

CONTINUED ON NEXT PAGE

Pullover with Square or Angled Armhole Front: Round-Neck Shaping

1 Shape right neck and shoulder: Work across the number of sts specified for your size and gauge in Table 26.

2 Turn and put rem (unworked) sts onto holder or spare needle. Table 27 shows how many sts this should be for your size and gauge.

3 Working right shoulder sts only, dec 1 st at neck edge every row for the number of rows specified for your size and gauge in Table 28.

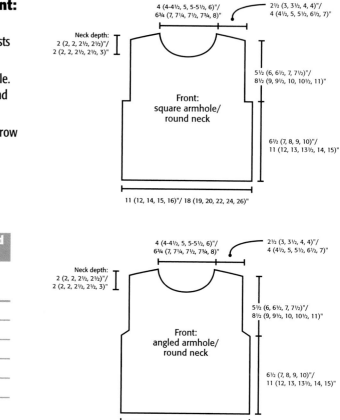

Front: square armhole/round neck

Neck depth: 2 (2, 2, 2½, 2½)"/ 2 (2, 2, 2½, 2½, 3)"

4 (4-4½, 5, 5-5½, 6)"/ 6¾ (7, 7¼, 7½, 7¾, 8)"

2½ (3, 3½, 4, 4)"/ 4 (4½, 5, 5½, 6½, 7)"

5½ (6, 6½, 7, 7½)"/ 8½ (9, 9½, 10, 10½, 11)"

6½ (7, 8, 9, 10)"/ 11 (12, 13, 13½, 14, 15)"

11 (12, 14, 15, 16)"/ 18 (19, 20, 22, 24, 26)"

Front: angled armhole/round neck

Neck depth: 2 (2, 2, 2½, 2½)"/ 2 (2, 2, 2½, 2½, 3)"

4 (4-4½, 5, 5-5½, 6)"/ 6¾ (7, 7¼, 7½, 7¾, 8)"

2½ (3, 3½, 4, 4)"/ 4 (4½, 5, 5½, 6½, 7)"

5½ (6, 6½, 7, 7½)"/ 8½ (9, 9½, 10, 10½, 11)"

6½ (7, 8, 9, 10)"/ 11 (12, 13, 13½, 14, 15)"

11 (12, 14, 15, 16)"/ 18 (19, 20, 22, 24, 26)"

Table 26. Pullover Front, Square or Angled Armhole and Round Neck: Begin Neck Shaping

No. of Sts to Work Across

Gauge	Baby/Child	Adult
2 sts/in.	8 (9, 10, 11, 11) sts	12 (13, 13, 15, 17, 17) sts
3 sts/in.	12 (13, 15, 16, 16) sts	18 (19, 20, 22, 24, 26) sts
4 sts/in.	16 (17, 20, 21, 22) sts	23 (25, 26, 29, 33, 35) sts
5 sts/in.	19 (21, 25, 26, 27) sts	30 (32, 34, 37, 42, 45) sts
6 sts/in.	23 (25, 30, 31, 33) sts	35 (37, 39, 44, 49, 54) sts

Table 27. Pullover Front, Square or Angled Armhole and Round Neck: Left Shoulder Stitches on Holder

No. of Sts on Holder for Left Shoulder

Gauge	Baby/Child	Adult
2 sts/in.	10 (11, 14, 15, 17) sts	18 (19, 21, 23, 25, 27) sts
3 sts/in.	15 (17, 19, 23, 26) sts	28 (30, 32, 34, 38, 40) sts
4 sts/in.	20 (23, 28, 31, 34) sts	37 (39, 42, 45, 49, 53) sts
5 sts/in.	26 (29, 35, 39, 43) sts	46 (49, 52, 57, 62, 67) sts
6 sts/in.	31 (35, 42, 47, 51) sts	55 (59, 63, 68, 75, 82) sts

Table 28. Pullover Front, Square or Angled Armhole and Round Neck: Begin Right Neck Shaping

No. of Rows to Dec 1 St at Neck Edge Every Row

Gauge	Baby/Child	Adult
2 sts/in.	2 (2, 2, 2, 2) rows	All sizes: 2 rows
3 sts/in.	3 (2, 3, 3, 2) rows	All sizes: 3 rows
4 sts/in.	3 (3, 3, 3, 3) rows	All sizes: 4 rows
5 sts/in.	4 (4, 4, 4, 4) rows	All sizes: 5 rows
6 sts/in.	4 (5, 5, 5, 5) rows	All sizes: 6 rows

4 Dec 1 st at neck edge every other row the number of times specified for your size and gauge in Table 29. You should have rem the number of sts specified for your size and gauge in Table 30.

Table 29. Pullover Front, Square or Angled Armhole and Round Neck: Finish Right Neck Shaping

	No. of Times to Dec 1 St at Neck Edge Every Other Row	
Gauge	**Baby/Child**	**Adult**
2 sts/in.	All sizes: 1 time	2 (2, 1, 2, 2, 1) times
3 sts/in.	3 (3, 4, 4, 3) times	All sizes: 2 times
4 sts/in.	4 (4, 4, 4, 4) times	All sizes: 3 times
5 sts/in.	All sizes: 2 times	All sizes: 4 times
6 sts/in.	All sizes: 3 times	4 (4, 4, 5, 4, 4) times

Table 30. Pullover Front, Square or Angled Armhole and Round Neck: Shoulder Stitches Remaining After Neck Shaping

	No. of Sts After Shaping Right Neck	
Gauge	**Baby/Child**	**Adult**
2 sts/in.	5 (6, 7, 8, 8) sts	8 (9, 10, 11, 13, 14) sts
3 sts/in.	7 (9, 10, 11, 12) sts	13 (14, 15, 17, 19, 21) sts
4 sts/in.	10 (11, 12, 15, 16) sts	16 (18, 19, 22, 26, 28) sts
5 sts/in.	12 (14, 17, 18, 20) sts	21 (23, 25, 28, 33, 36) sts
6 sts/in.	15 (16, 21, 22, 24) sts	25 (28, 29, 33, 39, 44) sts

CONTINUED ON NEXT PAGE

5 AT THE SAME TIME, when armhole measures 5½ (6, 6½, 7, 7½) inches for baby/child version or 8½ (9, 9½, 10, 10½, 11) inches for adult version, ending with a RS row, beg shaping shoulders. Beg next row (WS), BO the number of sts specified for your size and gauge in Table 31.

6 Next row (RS): Knit.

7 Next row (WS): BO rem shoulder sts. Table 32 shows how many sts this should be for your size and gauge.

8 Shape left neck and shoulder: Slip onto a holder for later the number of center neck sts indicated for your size and gauge in Table 33.

9 Slip rem sts onto your needle.

10 Beg with a RS row, rejoin yarn and work 1 row.

11 Shape left neck and shoulder as right neck and shoulder, reversing sides.

12 Go to "Make Sleeves," page 198.

Table 31. Pullover Front, Square or Angled Armhole and Round Neck: Begin Shoulder Shaping

No. of Sts to BO Beg This Row

Gauge	Baby/Child	Adult
2 sts/in.	3 (3, 4, 4, 4) sts	4 (5, 5, 6, 7, 7) sts
3 sts/in.	4 (5, 5, 6, 6) sts	7 (7, 8, 9, 10, 11) sts
4 sts/in.	5 (6, 7, 8, 8) sts	8 (9, 10, 11, 13, 14) sts
5 sts/in.	6 (7, 9, 9, 10) sts	11 (12, 13, 14, 17, 18) sts
6 sts/in.	8 (8, 11, 11, 12) sts	13 (14, 15, 17, 20, 22) sts

Table 32. Pullover Front, Square or Angled Armhole and Round Neck: Finish Shoulder Shaping

No. of Sts to BO for Shoulder

Gauge	Baby/Child	Adult
2 sts/in.	2 (3, 3, 4, 4) sts	4 (4, 5, 5, 6, 7) sts
3 sts/in.	3 (4, 5, 5, 6) sts	6 (7, 7, 8, 9, 10) sts
4 sts/in.	5 (5, 7, 7, 8) sts	8 (9, 10, 11, 13, 14) sts
5 sts/in.	6 (7, 8, 9, 10) sts	10 (11, 12, 14, 16, 18) sts
6 sts/in.	7 (8, 10, 11, 12) sts	12 (14, 14, 16, 19, 22) sts

Table 33. Pullover Front, Square or Angled Armhole and Round Neck: Center Neck Stitches on Holder

No. of Sts on Holder After Shaping Right Neck

Gauge	Baby/Child	Adult
2 sts/in.	2 (2, 4, 4, 6) sts	6 (6, 8, 8, 8, 10) sts
3 sts/in.	3 (4, 6, 7, 10) sts	10 (11, 12, 12, 14, 14) sts
4 sts/in.	4 (6, 8, 10, 12) sts	14 (14, 16, 16, 16, 18) sts
5 sts/in.	7 (8, 10, 13, 16) sts	16 (17, 18, 20, 20, 22) sts
6 sts/in.	8 (10, 12, 16, 18) sts	20 (22, 24, 24, 26, 28) sts

Pullover with Rounded Armhole Front: Round-Neck Shaping

1 Shape right neck and shoulder: Work across the number of sts specified for your size and gauge in Table 34.

2 Turn and put rem (unworked) sts onto holder or spare needle. Table 35 shows how many sts this should be for your size and gauge.

3 Working right shoulder sts only, dec 1 st at neck edge every row for the number of rows specified for your size and gauge in Table 36.

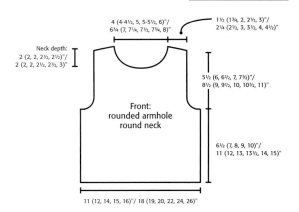

4 (4-4½, 5, 5-5½, 6)"/ 6¾ (7, 7¼, 7½, 7¾, 8)"

1½ (1¾, 2, 2½, 3)"/ 2¼ (2½, 3, 3½, 4, 4½)"

Neck depth: 2 (2, 2, 2½, 2½)"/ 2 (2, 2, 2½, 2½, 3)"

5½ (6, 6½, 7, 7½)"/ 8½ (9, 9½, 10, 10½, 11)"

Front: rounded armhole round neck

6½ (7, 8, 9, 10)"/ 11 (12, 13, 13½, 14, 15)"

11 (12, 14, 15, 16)"/ 18 (19, 20, 22, 24, 26)"

Table 34. Pullover Front, Rounded Armhole and Round Neck: Begin Neck Shaping

No. of Sts to Work Across

Gauge	Baby/Child	Adult
2 sts/in.	6 (7, 7, 8, 9) sts	9 (9, 9, 11, 12, 12) sts
3 sts/in.	9 (9, 10, 12, 13) sts	12 (13, 14, 15, 17, 18) sts
4 sts/in.	12 (12, 14, 16, 18) sts	16 (17, 19, 21, 23, 25) sts
5 sts/in.	14 (15, 18, 20, 22) sts	21 (22, 24, 26, 29, 32) sts
6 sts/in.	17 (18, 21, 24, 27) sts	24 (25, 28, 32, 34, 37) sts

Table 35. Pullover Front, Rounded Armhole and Round Neck: Left Shoulder Stitches on Holder

No. of Sts on Holder for Left Shoulder

Gauge	Baby/Child	Adult
2 sts/in.	8 (9, 11, 12, 15) sts	15 (15, 17, 19, 20, 22) sts
3 sts/in.	12 (13, 16, 19, 23) sts	22 (24, 26, 27, 31, 32) sts
4 sts/in.	16 (18, 22, 26, 30) sts	30 (31, 35, 37, 39, 43) sts
5 sts/in.	21 (23, 28, 33, 38) sts	37 (39, 42, 46, 49, 54) sts
6 sts/in.	25 (28, 33, 40, 45) sts	44 (47, 52, 56, 60, 65) sts

Table 36. Pullover Front, Rounded Armhole and Round Neck: Right Neck Shaping

No. of Rows to Dec 1 St at Neck Edge Every Row

Gauge	Baby/Child	Adult
2 sts/in.	2 (2, 2, 2, 2) rows	All sizes: 2 rows
3 sts/in.	3 (2, 3, 3, 2) rows	All sizes: 3 rows
4 sts/in.	3 (3, 3, 3, 3) rows	All sizes: 4 rows
5 sts/in.	4 (4, 4, 4, 4) rows	All sizes: 5 rows
6 sts/in.	4 (5, 5, 5, 5) rows	All sizes: 6 rows

CONTINUED ON NEXT PAGE

4 Dec 1 st at neck edge every other row the number of times specified for your size and gauge in Table 37. You should have rem the number of sts specified for your size and gauge in Table 38.

5 AT THE SAME TIME, when armhole measures 5½ (6, 6½, 7, 7½) inches for baby/child version or 8½ (9, 9½, 10, 10½, 11) inches for adult version, ending with a RS row, beg shaping shoulders. Beg next row (WS), BO the number of sts specified for your size and gauge in Table 39.

6 Next row (RS): Knit.

Table 37. Pullover Front, Rounded Armhole and Round Neck: Right Neck Shaping

No. of Times to Dec 1 St at Neck Edge Every Other Row

Gauge	Baby/Child	Adult
2 sts/in.	All sizes: 1 time	2 (2, 1, 2, 2, 1) times
3 sts/in.	3 (3, 4, 4, 3) times	All sizes: 2 times
4 sts/in.	4 (4, 4, 4, 4) times	All sizes: 3 times
5 sts/in.	All sizes: 2 times	All sizes: 4 times
6 sts/in.	All sizes: 3 times	4 (4, 4, 5, 4, 4) times

Table 38. Pullover Front, Rounded Armhole and Round Neck: Shoulder Stitches Remaining After Neck Shaping

No. of Sts After Right Neck Shaping

Gauge	Baby/Child	Adult
2 sts/in.	3 (4, 4, 5, 6) sts	5 (5, 6, 7, 8, 9) sts
3 sts/in.	4 (5, 5, 7, 9) sts	7 (8, 9, 10, 12, 13) sts
4 sts/in.	6 (6, 8, 10, 12) sts	9 (10, 12, 14, 16, 18) sts
5 sts/in.	7 (8, 10, 12, 15) sts	12 (13, 15, 17, 20, 23) sts
6 sts/in.	9 (9, 12, 15, 18) sts	14 (15, 18, 21, 24, 27) sts

Table 39. Pullover Front, Rounded Armhole and Round Neck: Begin Shoulder Shaping

No. of Sts to BO Beg This Row

Gauge	Baby/Child	Adult
2 sts/in.	2 (2, 2, 3, 3) sts	3 (3, 3, 4, 4, 5) sts
3 sts/in.	2 (3, 3, 4, 5) sts	4 (4, 5, 5, 6, 7) sts
4 sts/in.	3 (3, 4, 5, 6) sts	5 (5, 6, 7, 8, 9) sts
5 sts/in.	4 (4, 5, 6, 8) sts	6 (7, 8, 9, 10, 12) sts
6 sts/in.	5 (5, 6, 8, 9) sts	7 (8, 9, 11, 12, 14) sts

7. Next row (WS): BO rem shoulder sts. Table 40 shows how many sts this should be for your size and gauge.

8. Shape left neck and shoulder: Slip onto a holder for later the number of center neck sts indicated for your size and gauge in Table 41.

9. Slip rem sts onto your needle.

10. Beg with a RS row, rejoin yarn and work 1 row.

11. Shape left neck and shoulder as right neck and shoulder, reversing sides.

12. Go to "Make Sleeves," page 198.

Table 40. Pullover Front, Rounded Armhole and Round Neck: Finish Shoulder Shaping		
No. of Sts to BO for Shoulder		
Gauge	*Baby/Child*	*Adult*
2 sts/in.	1 (2, 2, 2, 3) sts	2 (2, 3, 3, 4, 4) sts
3 sts/in.	2 (2, 2, 3, 4) sts	3 (4, 4, 5, 6, 6) sts
4 sts/in.	3 (3, 4, 5, 6) sts	4 (5, 6, 7, 8, 9) sts
5 sts/in.	3 (4, 5, 6, 7) sts	6 (6, 7, 8, 10, 11) sts
6 sts/in.	4 (4, 6, 7, 9) sts	7 (7, 9, 10, 12, 13) sts

Table 41. Pullover Front, Rounded Armhole and Round Neck: Center Neck Stitches on Holder		
No. of Sts on Holder After Shaping Right Neck		
Gauge	*Baby/Child*	*Adult*
2 sts/in.	2 (2, 4, 4, 6) sts	6 (6, 8, 8, 8, 10) sts
3 sts/in.	3 (4, 6, 7, 10) sts	10 (11, 12, 12, 14, 14) sts
4 sts/in.	4 (6, 8, 10, 12) sts	14 (14, 16, 16, 16, 18) sts
5 sts/in.	7 (8, 10, 13, 16) sts	16 (17, 18, 20, 20, 22) sts
6 sts/in.	8 (10, 12, 16, 18) sts	20 (22, 24, 24, 26, 28) sts

MAKE V-NECK PULLOVER FRONT

The front lower body of the v-neck pullover is worked the same as the front lower body of the round-neck pullover. After you finish the lower body and have worked the armhole up to the point indicated for your size in the instructions that follow, you go to the appropriate set of instructions under "Shape Pullover V-Neck Front," page 184. Then you shape the v-neck—and the remainder of the armhole—starting with the left side. When you complete the left shoulder, you move on to the right neck and shoulder.

CONTINUED ON NEXT PAGE

1 Work as for back, including armhole shaping, until front measures 8 (8½, 9½, 10½, 11½) inches from CO edge for baby/child version or 13½ (14½, 15½, 16, 16½, 17½) inches from CO edge for adult version, ending with a WS row.

2 If you are working on an odd number of sts, work to the center st and put the center st onto a safety pin or holder. If you are working on an even number of sts, work halfway across row, m1. Put this new st onto a safety pin or holder.

3 Put rem unworked right shoulder sts onto another holder or spare needle.

4 Turn and work left shoulder sts only.

5 Next row (WS): Purl.

6 Go to v-neck shaping instructions for your armhole style under "Shape Pullover V-Neck Front," below.

SHAPE PULLOVER V-NECK FRONT

At this point, you have to go to the correct directions for your armhole style. You work the v-neck by putting one set of shoulder stitches onto a holder while the other side is worked. When the first side of the neck and the corresponding shoulder are complete, you shape the other side.

Pullover with Straight Armhole Front: V-Neck Shaping

1 Beg v-neck shaping: Dec 1 st at neck edge by k2tog at end of every RS row until you have rem the number of sts indicated for your size and gauge in Table 42.

2 Continue without further shaping until front measures same as back at beg shoulder shaping, ending with a WS row.

3 Next row (RS)—Beg shoulder shaping: BO beg this row the number of sts specified for your size and gauge in Table 43.

4 Next row (WS): Purl.

5 Next row (RS): BO rem shoulder sts. Table 44 shows how many sts this should be for your size and gauge.

6 Put right shoulder sts back onto needle, leaving center st on holder for later. Finish right neck and shoulder as left, reversing shaping and shaping right v-neck by beg every RS with ssk.

7 Go to "Make Sleeves," page 198.

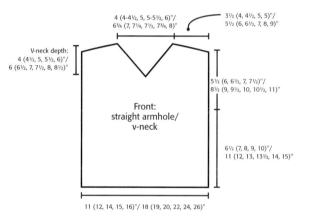

4 (4-4½, 5, 5-5½, 6)"/
6¾ (7, 7¼, 7½, 7¾, 8)"

3½ (4, 4½, 5, 5)"/
5½ (6, 6½, 7, 8, 9)"

V-neck depth:
4 (4½, 5, 5½, 6)"/
6 (6½, 7, 7½, 8, 8½)"

5½ (6, 6½, 7, 7½)"/
8½ (9, 9½, 10, 10½, 11)"

Front:
straight armhole/
v-neck

6½ (7, 8, 9, 10)"/
11 (12, 13, 13½, 14, 15)"

11 (12, 14, 15, 16)"/ 18 (19, 20, 22, 24, 26)"

Table 42. Pullover Front, Straight Armhole and V-Neck: Shoulder Stitches Remaining After Left Neck Shaping

No. of Sts After Armhole and Left V-Neck Shaping

Gauge	Baby/Child	Adult
2 sts/in.	7 (8, 9, 10, 10) sts	11 (12, 13, 14, 16, 18) sts
3 sts/in.	10 (12, 13, 14, 15) sts	17 (18, 19, 22, 24, 27) sts
4 sts/in.	14 (15, 18, 19, 20) sts	22 (24, 25, 29, 33, 36) sts
5 sts/in.	17 919, 22, 23, 25) sts	28 (30, 32, 36, 41, 45) sts
6 sts/in.	21 (22, 27, 28, 30) sts	34 (36, 38, 43, 49, 54) sts

Table 43. Pullover Front, Straight Armhole and V-Neck: Begin Shoulder Shaping

No. of Sts to BO Beg This Row

Gauge	Baby/Child	Adult
2 sts/in.	4 (4, 5, 5, 5) sts	6 (6, 7, 7, 8, 9) sts
3 sts/in.	5 (6, 7, 7, 8) sts	9 (9, 10, 11, 12, 14) sts
4 sts/in.	7 (8, 9, 10, 10) sts	11 (12, 13, 15, 17, 18) sts
5 sts/in.	9 (10, 11, 12, 13) sts	14 (15, 16, 18, 21, 23) sts
6 sts/in.	11 (11, 14, 14, 15) sts	17 (18, 19, 22, 25, 27) sts

Table 44. Pullover Front, Straight Armhole and V-Neck: Finish Shoulder Shaping

No. of Sts to BO for Shoulder

Gauge	Baby/Child	Adult
2 sts/in.	3 (4, 4, 5, 5) sts	5 (6, 6, 7, 8, 9) sts
3 sts/in.	5 (6, 6, 7, 7) sts	8 (9, 9, 11, 12, 13) sts
4 sts/in.	7 (7, 9, 9, 10) sts	11 (12, 12, 14, 16, 18) sts
5 sts/in.	8 (9, 11, 11, 12) sts	14 (15, 16, 18, 20, 22) sts
6 sts/in.	10 (11, 13, 14, 15) sts	33 (18, 19, 21, 24, 27) sts

CONTINUED ON NEXT PAGE

Pullover with Square or Angled Armhole Front: V-Neck Shaping

1 If armhole shaping is not completed already, continue to shape armhole as established.

2 AT THE SAME TIME, beg v-neck shaping: Dec 1 st at neck edge by k2tog at end of every RS row until you have rem the number of sts indicated for your size and gauge in Table 45.

3 Continue without further shaping until front measures same as back at beg shoulder shaping, ending with a WS row.

4 Next row (RS)—Beg shoulder shaping: BO beg this row the number of sts specified for your size and gauge in Table 46.

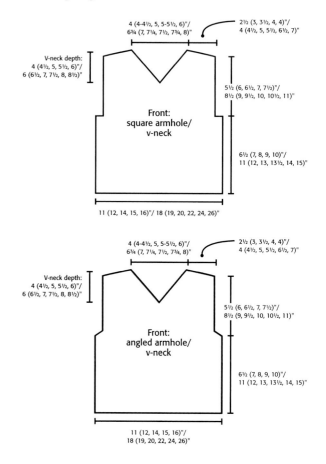

Table 45. Pullover Front, Square or Angled Armhole and V-Neck: Shoulder Stitches Remaining After Left Neck Shaping

No. of Sts After Armhole and Left V-Neck Shaping

Gauge	Baby/Child	Adult
2 sts/in.	5 (6, 7, 8, 8) sts	8 (9, 10, 11, 13, 14) sts
3 sts/in.	7 (9, 10, 11, 12) sts	13 (14, 15, 17, 19, 21) sts
4 sts/in.	10 (11, 12, 15, 16) sts	16 (18, 19, 22, 26, 28) sts
5 sts/in.	12 (14, 17, 18, 20) sts	21 (23, 25, 28, 33, 36) sts
6 sts/in.	15 (16, 21, 22, 24) sts	25 (28, 29, 33, 39, 44) sts

Table 46. Pullover Front, Square or Angled Armhole and V-Neck: Begin Shoulder Shaping

No. of Sts to BO Beg This Row

Gauge	Baby/Child	Adult
2 sts/in.	3 (3, 4, 4, 4) sts	4 (5, 5, 6, 7, 7) sts
3 sts/in.	4 (5, 5, 6, 6) sts	7 (7, 8, 9, 10, 11) sts
4 sts/in.	5 (6, 7, 8, 8) sts	8 (9, 10, 11, 13, 14) sts
5 sts/in.	6 (7, 9, 9, 10) sts	11 (12, 13, 14, 17, 18) sts
6 sts/in.	8 (8, 11, 11, 12) sts	13 (14, 15, 17, 20, 22) sts

⑤ Next row (WS): Purl.

⑥ Next row (RS): BO rem shoulder sts. Table 47 shows how many sts this should be for your size and gauge.

⑦ Put right shoulder sts back onto needle, leaving center st on holder for later. Finish right armhole and shoulder as left, reversing shaping and shaping right v-neck by beg every RS row with ssk.

⑧ Go to "Make Sleeves," page 198.

Table 47. Pullover Front, Square or Angled Armhole and V-Neck: Finish Shoulder Shaping

No. of Sts to BO for Shoulder

Gauge	Baby/Child	Adult
2 sts/in.	2 (3, 3, 4, 4) sts	4 (4, 5, 5, 6, 7) sts
3 sts/in.	3 (4, 5, 5, 6) sts	6 (7, 7, 8, 9, 10) sts
4 sts/in.	5 (5, 7, 7, 8) sts	8 (9, 10, 11, 13, 14) sts
5 sts/in.	6 (7, 8, 9, 10) sts	10 (11, 12, 14, 16, 18) sts
6 sts/in.	7 (8, 10, 11, 12) sts	12 (14, 14, 16, 19, 22) sts

Pullover with Rounded Armhole Front: V-Neck Shaping

① If armhole shaping is not completed already, continue to shape armhole as established.

② AT THE SAME TIME, beg v-neck shaping: Dec 1 st at neck edge by k2tog at end of every RS row until you have rem the number of sts indicated for your size and gauge in Table 48.

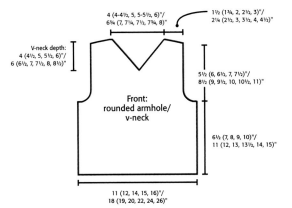

4 (4-4½, 5, 5-5½, 6)"/
6¾ (7, 7¼, 7½, 7¾, 8)"

1½ (1¾, 2, 2½, 3)"/
2¼ (2½, 3, 3½, 4, 4½)"

V-neck depth:
4 (4½, 5, 5½, 6)"/
6 (6½, 7, 7½, 8, 8½)"

5½ (6, 6½, 7, 7½)"/
8½ (9, 9½, 10, 10½, 11)"

Front:
rounded armhole/
v-neck

6½ (7, 8, 9, 10)"/
11 (12, 13, 13½, 14, 15)"

11 (12, 14, 15, 16)"/
18 (19, 20, 22, 24, 26)"

Table 48. Pullover Front, Rounded Armhole and V-Neck: Shoulder Stitches Remaining After Left Neck Shaping

No. of Sts After Armhole and Left V-Neck Shaping

Gauge	Baby/Child	Adult
2 sts/in.	3 (4, 4, 5, 6) sts	5 (5, 6, 7, 8, 9) sts
3 sts/in.	4 (5, 5, 7, 9) sts	7 (8, 9, 10, 12, 13) sts
4 sts/in.	6 (6, 8, 10, 12) sts	9 (10, 12, 14, 16, 18) sts
5 sts/in.	7 (8, 10, 12, 15) sts	12 (13, 15, 17, 20, 23) sts
6 sts/in.	9 (9, 12, 15, 18) sts	14 (15, 18, 21, 24, 27) sts

CONTINUED ON NEXT PAGE

③ Continue without further shaping until front measures same as back at beg shoulder shaping, ending with a WS row.

④ Next row (RS)—Beg shoulder shaping: BO beg this row the number of sts specified for your size and gauge in Table 49.

⑤ Next row (WS): Purl.

⑥ Next row (RS): BO rem shoulder sts. Table 50 shows how many sts this should be for your size and gauge.

⑦ Put right shoulder sts back onto needle, leaving center st on holder for later. Finish armhole and shoulder as left, reversing shaping and shaping right v-neck by beg every RS with ssk.

⑧ Go to "Make Sleeves," page 198.

Table 49. Pullover Front, Rounded Armhole and V-Neck: Begin Shoulder Shaping		
No. of Sts to BO Beg This Row		
Gauge	**Baby/Child**	**Adult**
2 sts/in.	2 (2, 2, 3, 3) sts	3 (3, 3, 4, 4, 5) sts
3 sts/in.	2 (3, 3, 4, 5) sts	4 (4, 5, 5, 6, 7) sts
4 sts/in.	3 (3, 4, 5, 6) sts	5 (5, 6, 7, 8, 9) sts
5 sts/in.	4 (4, 5, 6, 8) sts	6 (7, 8, 9, 10, 12) sts
6 sts/in.	5 (5, 6, 8, 9) sts	7 (8, 9, 11, 12, 14) sts

Table 50. Pullover Front, Rounded Armhole and V-Neck: Finish Shoulder Shaping		
No. of Sts to BO for Shoulder		
Gauge	**Baby/Child**	**Adult**
2 sts/in.	1 (2, 2, 2, 3) sts	2 (2, 3, 3, 4, 4) sts
3 sts/in.	2 (2, 2, 3, 4) sts	3 (4, 4, 5, 6, 6) sts
4 sts/in.	3 (3, 4, 5, 6) sts	4 (5, 6, 7, 8, 9) sts
5 sts/in.	3 (4, 5, 6, 7) sts	6 (6, 7, 8, 10, 11) sts
6 sts/in.	4 (4, 6, 7, 9) sts	7 (7, 9, 10, 12, 13) sts

MAKE CARDIGAN LEFT FRONT

Regardless of the sleeve style you've chosen, you start the cardigan the same way: with the left front lower body. Then you shape the armhole as desired, working up to the point where the neck shaping begins. Then you shape either the v-neck or the round neck, and finish up with the shoulder shaping.

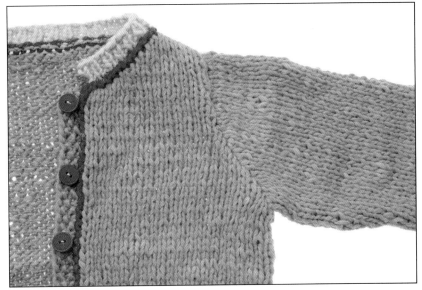

1 CO sts for your size and gauge according to Table 51.

Note: *If you want to work an edging that requires a different number of sts than that specified for your size and gauge in Table 51, you can cast on 1 or 2 fewer sts and work the edging to one row before the end. Increase back to the stitch count specified in Table 51 on the last edging row.*

2 Work edging to same length as back edging, then cont in St st until left front measures 6½ (7, 8, 9, 10) inches from CO edge for baby/child version or 11 (12, 13, 13½, 14, 15) inches from CO edge for adult version, ending with a WS row.

3 Go to "Shape Cardigan Left Front," page 190.

Table 51. Cast on for Cardigan Left Front		
No. of Sts to CO		
Gauge	**Baby/Child**	**Adult**
2 sts/in.	11 (12, 14, 15, 16) sts	18 (19, 20, 22, 24, 26) sts
3 sts/in.	16 (18, 21, 22, 24) sts	27 (28, 30, 33, 36, 39) sts
4 sts/in.	22 (24, 26, 30, 32) sts	36 (38, 40, 44, 48, 52) sts
5 sts/in.	27 (30, 35, 37, 40) sts	45 (47, 50, 55, 60, 65) sts
6 sts/in.	33 (36, 42, 45, 48) sts	54 (57, 60, 66, 72, 78) sts

CONTINUED ON NEXT PAGE

SHAPE CARDIGAN LEFT FRONT

At this point, you need to go to the appropriate directions for your chosen armhole style. To work a square or rounded armhole, go to "Cardigan with Square or Rounded Armhole Left Front: Initial Shaping," below. To work a straight armhole, go to "Cardigan with Straight Armhole Left Front: Round-Neck Shaping," on the next page, and to work an angled armhole, go to "Cardigan with Angled Armhole Left Front: Round-Neck Shaping," page 194.

Cardigan with Square or Rounded Armhole Left Front: Initial Shaping

1. Next row (RS): BO beg this row the number of sts indicated for your size and gauge in Table 52. You should have rem the number of sts indicated for your size and gauge in Table 53.

2. Next row (WS): Purl.

3. Depending on which armhole and neck style you're working, go to either "Cardigan with Square Armhole Left Front: Round-Neck Shaping," page 193, "Cardigan with Rounded Armhole Left Front: Round-Neck Shaping," page 195, or "Cardigan with Any Armhole Style Left Front: V-Neck Shaping," page 197.

Table 52. Cardigan Front, Square or Rounded Armhole: Begin Armhole Shaping

No. of Sts to BO Beg This Row

Gauge	Baby/Child	Adult
2 sts/in.	2 sts	3 (3, 3, 3, 3, 4) sts
3 sts/in.	3 sts	4 (4, 4, 5, 5, 6) sts
4 sts/in.	4 sts	6 (6, 6, 7, 7, 8) sts
5 sts/in.	5 sts	7 (7, 7, 8, 8, 9) sts
6 sts/in.	6 sts	9 (9, 9, 10, 10, 10) sts

Table 53. Cardigan Front, Square or Rounded Armhole: Stitches Remaining After Initial Armhole Shaping

No. of Sts After BO for Armhole

Gauge	Baby/Child	Adult
2 sts/in.	9 (10, 12, 13, 14) sts	15 (16, 17, 19, 21, 22) sts
3 sts/in.	13 (15, 18, 19, 21) sts	23 (24, 26, 28, 31, 33) sts
4 sts/in.	18 (20, 22, 26, 28) sts	30 (32, 34, 37, 41, 44) sts
5 sts/in.	22 (25, 30, 32, 35) sts	38 (40, 43, 47, 52, 56) sts
6 sts/in.	27 (30, 36, 39, 42) sts	45 (48, 51, 56, 62, 68) sts

Cardigan with Straight Armhole Left Front: Round-Neck Shaping

1. Continue working without any shaping until left front measures 10 (11, 12½, 13½, 15) inches from CO edge for baby/child version or 17½ (19, 20½, 21, 22, 23) inches from CO edge for adult version, ending with a RS row.

2. Next row (WS)—Beg neck shaping: BO beg this row the number of sts indicated for your size and gauge in Table 54.

3. Dec 1 st at neck edge every row for the number of rows specified for your size and gauge in Table 55.

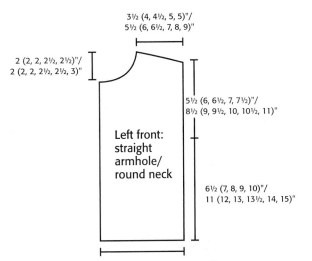

3½ (4, 4½, 5, 5)"/
5½ (6, 6½, 7, 8, 9)"

2 (2, 2, 2½, 2½)"/
2 (2, 2, 2½, 2½, 3)"

5½ (6, 6½, 7, 7½)"/
8½ (9, 9½, 10, 10½, 11)"

Left front: straight armhole/ round neck

6½ (7, 8, 9, 10)"/
11 (12, 13, 13½, 14, 15)"

5½ (6, 7, 7½, 8)"/ 9 (9½, 10, 11, 12, 13)"

Table 54. Cardigan Front, Straight Armhole and Round Neck: Begin Neck Shaping

No. of Sts to BO Beg This Row

Gauge	Baby/Child	Adult
2 sts/in.	1 (1, 2, 2, 3) sts	3 (3, 4, 4, 4, 5) sts
3 sts/in.	1 (2, 3, 3, 5) sts	5 (5, 6, 6, 7, 7) sts
4 sts/in.	2 (3, 4, 5, 6) sts	7 (7, 8, 8, 8, 9) sts
5 sts/in.	3 (4, 5, 6, 8) sts	8 (8, 9, 10, 10, 11) sts
6 sts/in.	4 (5, 6, 8, 9) sts	10 (11, 12, 12, 13, 14) sts

Table 55. Cardigan Front, Straight Armhole and Round Neck: Neck Shaping

No. of Rows to Dec 1 St at Neck Edge Every Row

Gauge	Baby/Child	Adult
2 sts/in.	All sizes: 2 rows	All sizes: 2 rows
3 sts/in.	3 (2, 3, 3, 2) rows	All sizes: 3 rows
4 sts/in.	All sizes: 3 rows	All sizes: 4 rows
5 sts/in.	All sizes: 4 rows	All sizes: 5 rows
6 sts/in.	4 (5, 5, 5, 5) rows	All sizes: 6 rows

CONTINUED ON NEXT PAGE

4 Dec 1 st at neck edge every other row the number of times indicated for your size and gauge in Table 56. You should have rem the number of sts specified for your size and gauge in Table 57.

5 AT THE SAME TIME, when left front measures 12 (13, 14½, 16, 17½) inches from beg for baby/child version or 19½ (21, 22½, 23½, 24½, 26) inches from beg for adult version, ending with a WS row, beg shaping shoulders. Beg next row (RS), BO the number of sts specified for your size and gauge in Table 58.

6 Next row (WS): Purl.

7 Next row (RS): BO rem shoulder sts. Table 59 shows how many sts this should be for your size and gauge.

8 Go to "Make Cardigan Right Front," page 197.

Table 56. Cardigan Front, Straight Armhole and Round Neck: Finish Neck Shaping

No. of Times to Dec 1 St at Neck Edge Every Other Row

Gauge	Baby/Child	Adult
2 sts/in.	All sizes: 1 time	2 (2, 1, 2, 2, 1) times
3 sts/in.	3 (3, 4, 4, 3) times	All sizes: 2 times
4 sts/in.	4 (4, 4, 4, 4) times	All sizes: 3 times
5 sts/in.	All sizes: 2 times	All sizes: 4 times
6 sts/in.	All sizes: 3 times	4 (4, 4, 5, 4, 4) times

Table 57. Cardigan Front, Straight Armhole and Round Neck: Shoulder Stitches Remaining After Neck Shaping

No. of Sts After Shaping Neck

Gauge	Baby/Child	Adult
2 sts/in.	7 (8, 9, 10, 10) sts	11 (12, 13, 14, 16, 18) sts
3 sts/in.	10 (12, 13, 14, 15) sts	17 (18, 19, 22, 24, 27) sts
4 sts/in.	14 (15, 18, 19, 20) sts	22 (24, 25, 29, 33, 36) sts
5 sts/in.	17 (19, 22, 23, 25) sts	28 (30, 32, 36, 41, 45) sts
6 sts/in.	21 (22, 27, 28, 30) sts	34 (36, 38, 43, 49, 54) sts

Table 58. Cardigan Front, Straight Armhole and Round Neck: Begin Shoulder Shaping

No. of Sts to BO Beg This Row

Gauge	Baby/Child	Adult
2 sts/in.	4 (4, 5, 5, 5) sts	6 (6, 7, 7, 8, 9) sts
3 sts/in.	5 (6, 7, 7, 8) sts	9 (9, 10, 11, 12, 14) sts
4 sts/in.	7 (8, 9, 10, 10) sts	11 (12, 13, 15, 17, 18) sts
5 sts/in.	9 (10, 11, 12, 13) sts	14 (15, 16, 18, 21, 23) sts
6 sts/in.	11 (11, 14, 14, 15) sts	17 (18, 19, 22, 25, 27) sts

Table 59. Cardigan Front, Straight Armhole and Round Neck: Finish Shoulder Shaping

No. of Sts to BO for Shoulder

Gauge	Baby/Child	Adult
2 sts/in.	3 (4, 4, 5, 5) sts	5 (6, 6, 7, 8, 9) sts
3 sts/in.	5 (6, 6, 7, 7) sts	8 (9, 9, 11, 12, 13) sts
4 sts/in.	7 (7, 9, 9, 10) sts	11 (12, 12, 14, 16, 18) sts
5 sts/in.	8 (9, 11, 11, 12) sts	14 (15, 16, 18, 20, 22) sts
6 sts/in.	10 (11, 13, 14, 15) sts	33 (18, 19, 21, 24, 27) sts

Cardigan with Square Armhole Left Front: Round-Neck Shaping

1. Continue working without further shaping until left front measures 10 (11, 12½, 13½, 15) inches from CO edge for baby/child version or 17½ (19, 20½, 21, 22, 23) inches from CO edge for adult version, ending with a RS row.

2. Shape round neck as for straight armhole (pages 191–192). You should have rem the number of sts specified for your size and gauge in Table 60.

3. AT THE SAME TIME, when armhole measures 5½ (6, 6½, 7, 7½) inches for baby/child version or 8½ (9, 9½, 10, 10½, 11) inches for adult version, ending with a WS row, beg shaping shoulder. Beg next row (RS), BO the number of sts specified for your size and gauge in Table 61.

4. Next row (WS): Purl.

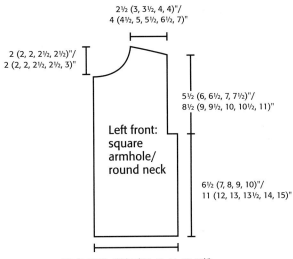

2½ (3, 3½, 4, 4)"/
4 (4½, 5, 5½, 6½, 7)"

2 (2, 2, 2½, 2½)"/
2 (2, 2, 2½, 2½, 3)"

5½ (6, 6½, 7, 7½)"/
8½ (9, 9½, 10, 10½, 11)"

Left front: square armhole/ round neck

6½ (7, 8, 9, 10)"/
11 (12, 13, 13½, 14, 15)"

5½ (6, 7, 7½, 8)"/ 9 (9½, 10, 11, 12, 13)"

Table 60. Cardigan Front, Square Armhole and Round Neck: Shoulder Stitches Remaining After Neck Shaping

No. of Sts After Neck Shaping

Gauge	Baby/Child	Adult
2 sts/in.	5 (6, 7, 8, 8) sts	8 (9, 10, 11, 13, 14) sts
3 sts/in.	7 (9, 10, 11, 12) sts	13 (14, 15, 17, 19, 21) sts
4 sts/in.	10 (11, 12, 15, 16) sts	16 (18, 19, 22, 26, 28) sts
5 sts/in.	12 (14, 17, 18, 20) sts	21 (23, 25, 28, 33, 36) sts
6 sts/in.	15 (16, 21, 22, 24) sts	25 (28, 29, 33, 39, 44) sts

Table 61. Cardigan Front, Square Armhole and Round Neck: Begin Shoulder Shaping

No. of Sts to BO Beg This Row

Gauge	Baby/Child	Adult
2 sts/in.	3 (3, 4, 4, 4) sts	4 (5, 5, 6, 7, 7) sts
3 sts/in.	4 (5, 5, 6, 6) sts	7 (7, 8, 9, 10, 11) sts
4 sts/in.	5 (6, 7, 8, 8) sts	8 (9, 10, 11, 13, 14) sts
5 sts/in.	6 (7, 9, 9, 10) sts	11 (12, 13, 14, 17, 18) sts
6 sts/in.	8 (8, 11, 11, 12) sts	13 (14, 15, 17, 20, 22) sts

CONTINUED ON NEXT PAGE

5 Next row (RS): BO rem shoulder sts. Table 62 shows how many sts this should be for your size and gauge.

6 Go to "Make Cardigan Right Front," page 197.

Table 62. Cardigan Front, Square Armhole and Round Neck: Finish Shoulder Shaping

No. of Sts to BO for Shoulder

Gauge	Baby/Child	Adult
2 sts/in.	2 (3, 3, 4, 4) sts	4 (4, 5, 5, 6, 7) sts
3 sts/in.	3 (4, 5, 5, 6) sts	6 (7, 7, 8, 9, 10) sts
4 sts/in.	5 (5, 7, 7, 8) sts	8 (9, 10, 11, 13, 14) sts
5 sts/in.	6 (7, 8, 9, 10) sts	10 (11, 12, 14, 16, 18) sts
6 sts/in.	7 (8, 10, 11, 12) sts	12 (14, 14, 16, 19, 22) sts

Cardigan with Angled Armhole Left Front: Round-Neck Shaping

1 Next row (RS)—Shape armhole: Dec 1 st beg every RS row the number of times specified for your size and gauge in Table 63. You should have rem the number of sts indicated for your size and gauge in Table 64.

Table 63. Cardigan Front, Angled Armhole: Armhole Shaping

No. of Times to Dec 1 St Beg Every RS Row

Gauge	Baby/Child	Adult
2 sts/in.	2 times	3 (3, 3, 3, 3, 4) times
3 sts/in.	3 times	4 (4, 4, 5, 5, 6) times
4 sts/in.	4 times	6 (6, 6, 7, 7, 8) times
5 sts/in.	5 times	7 (7, 7, 8, 8, 9) times
6 sts/in.	6 times	9 (9, 9, 10, 10, 10) times

Table 64. Cardigan Front, Angled Armhole: Stitches Remaining After Armhole Shaping

No. of Sts After Angled Armhole Shaping

Gauge	Baby/Child	Adult
2 sts/in.	9 (10, 12, 13, 14) sts	15 (16, 17, 19, 21, 22) sts
3 sts/in.	13 (15, 18, 19, 21) sts	23 (24, 26, 28, 31, 33) sts
4 sts/in.	18 (20, 22, 26, 28) sts	30 (32, 34, 37, 41, 44) sts
5 sts/in.	22 (25, 30, 32, 35) sts	38 (40, 43, 47, 52, 56) sts
6 sts/in.	27 (30, 36, 39, 42) sts	45 (48, 51, 56, 62, 68) sts

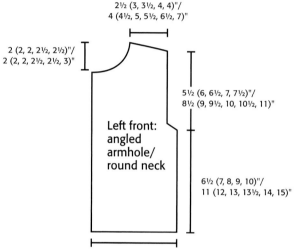

2½ (3, 3½, 4, 4)"/
4 (4½, 5, 5½, 6½, 7)"

2 (2, 2, 2½, 2½)"/
2 (2, 2, 2½, 2½, 3)"

5½ (6, 6½, 7, 7½)"/
8½ (9, 9½, 10, 10½, 11)"

Left front: angled armhole/ round neck

6½ (7, 8, 9, 10)"/
11 (12, 13, 13½, 14, 15)"

5½ (6, 7, 7½, 8)"/ 9 (9½, 10, 11, 12, 13)"

2 Continue working without any shaping until left front measures 10 (11, 12½, 13½, 15) inches from CO edge for baby/child version or 17½ (19, 20½, 21, 22, 23) inches from CO edge for adult version, ending with a RS row.

3 Shape round neck as for straight armhole style (pages 191–192). AT THE SAME TIME, when armhole measures 5½ (6, 6½, 7, 7½) inches for baby/child version or 8½ (9, 9½, 10, 10½, 11) inches for adult version, ending with a WS row, shape shoulder as for square armhole style (pages 193–194).

4 Go to "Make Cardigan Right Front," page 197.

Cardigan with Rounded Armhole Left Front: Round-Neck Shaping

1 Next row (RS)–Shape armhole: Dec 1 st beg every RS row the number of times indicated for your size and gauge in Table 65.

2 Work without further shaping until left front measures 10 (11, 12½, 13½, 15) inches from CO edge for baby/child version or 17½ (19, 20½, 21, 22, 23) inches from CO edge for adult version, ending with a RS row.

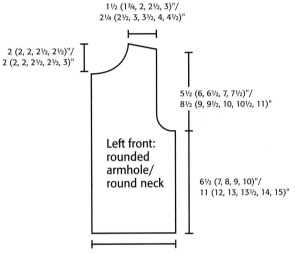

1½ (1¾, 2, 2½, 3)"/
2¼ (2½, 3, 3½, 4, 4½)"

2 (2, 2, 2½, 2½)"/
2 (2, 2, 2½, 2½, 3)"

5½ (6, 6½, 7, 7½)"/
8½ (9, 9½, 10, 10½, 11)"

Left front: rounded armhole/round neck

6½ (7, 8, 9, 10)"/
11 (12, 13, 13½, 14, 15)"

5½ (6, 7, 7½, 8)"/ 9 (9½, 10, 11, 12, 13)"

Table 65. Cardigan Front, Rounded Armhole and Round Neck: Armhole Shaping

No. of Times to Dec 1 St Beg Every RS Row

Gauge	Baby/Child	Adult
2 sts/in.	2 (2, 3, 3, 2) times	3 (4, 4, 4, 5, 5) times
3 sts/in.	3 (4, 5, 4, 3) times	6 (6, 6, 7, 7, 8) times
4 sts/in.	4 (5, 6, 5, 4) times	7 (8, 7, 8, 10, 10) times
5 sts/in.	5 (6, 7, 6, 5) times	9 (10, 10, 11, 13, 13) times
6 sts/in.	6 (7, 9, 7, 6) times	11 (12, 11, 12, 15, 17) times

CONTINUED ON NEXT PAGE

③ Shape round neck as for straight armhole (pages 191–192). You should have rem the number of sts specified for your size and gauge in Table 66.

④ AT THE SAME TIME, when armhole measures 5½ (6, 6½, 7, 7½) inches for baby/child version or 8½ (9, 9½, 10, 10½, 11) inches for adult version, ending with a WS row, beg shoulder shaping. Next row (RS): BO beg this row the number of sts indicated for your size and gauge in Table 67.

⑤ Next row (WS): Purl.

⑥ Next row (RS): BO rem sts. Table 68 shows how many sts this should be for your size and gauge.

⑦ Go to "Make Cardigan Right Front," on the next page.

Table 66. Cardigan Front, Rounded Armhole and Round Neck: Shoulder Stitches Remaining After Neck and Armhole Shaping

Gauge	No. of Sts After Neck and Armhole Shaping	
	Baby/Child	Adult
2 sts/in.	3 (4, 4, 5, 6) sts	5 (5, 6, 7, 8, 9) sts
3 sts/in.	4 (5, 5, 7, 9) sts	7 (8, 9, 10, 12, 13) sts
4 sts/in.	6 (6, 8, 10, 12) sts	9 (10, 12, 14, 16, 18) sts
5 sts/in.	7 (8, 10, 12, 15) sts	12 (13, 15, 17, 20, 23) sts
6 sts/in.	9 (9, 12, 15, 18) sts	14 (15, 18, 21, 24, 27) sts

Table 67. Cardigan Front, Rounded Armhole and Round Neck: Begin Shoulder Shaping

Gauge	No. of Sts to BO Beg Next RS Row	
	Baby/Child	Adult
2 sts/in.	2 (2, 2, 3, 3) sts	3 (3, 3, 4, 4, 5) sts
3 sts/in.	2 (3, 3, 4, 5) sts	4 (4, 5, 5, 6, 7) sts
4 sts/in.	3 (3, 4, 5, 6) sts	5 (5, 6, 7, 8, 9) sts
5 sts/in.	4 (4, 5, 6, 8) sts	6 (7, 8, 9, 10, 12) sts
6 sts/in.	5 (5, 6, 8, 9) sts	7 (8, 9, 11, 12, 14) sts

Table 68. Cardigan Front, Rounded Armhole and Round Neck: Finish Shoulder Shaping

Gauge	No. of Sts to BO	
	Baby/Child	Adult
2 sts/in.	1 (2, 2, 2, 3) sts	2 (2, 3, 3, 4, 4) sts
3 sts/in.	2 (2, 2, 3, 4) sts	3 (4, 4, 5, 6, 6) sts
4 sts/in.	3 (3, 4, 5, 6) sts	4 (5, 6, 7, 8, 9) sts
5 sts/in.	3 (4, 5, 6, 7) sts	6 (6, 7, 8, 10, 11) sts
6 sts/in.	4 (4, 6, 7, 9) sts	7 (7, 9, 10, 12, 13) sts

Cardigan with Any Armhole Style Left Front: V-Neck Shaping

1 Work as for cardigan round-neck left front, including the appropriate armhole shaping.

2 AT THE SAME TIME, when front measures 8 (8½, 9½, 10½, 11½) inches from beg for baby/child version or 13½ (14½, 15½, 16, 16½, 17½) inches from beg for adult version, ending with a WS row, beg v-neck shaping: Dec 1 st at neck edge by k2tog at end of every RS row until you have rem the number of shoulder sts indicated for your size, gauge, and armhole style as for round neck cardigan.

3 Continue working until armhole measures 5½ (6, 6½, 7, 7½) inches for baby/child version or 8½ (9, 9½, 10, 10½, 11) inches for adult version, ending with a WS row; shape shoulders as indicated for your size, gauge, and armhole style as for round neck cardigan.

4 Go to "Make Cardigan Right Front," below.

MAKE CARDIGAN RIGHT FRONT

1 Work as for left front, reversing armhole, neck, and shoulder shaping to other side.

2 Go to "Make Sleeves," page 198.

CONTINUED ON NEXT PAGE

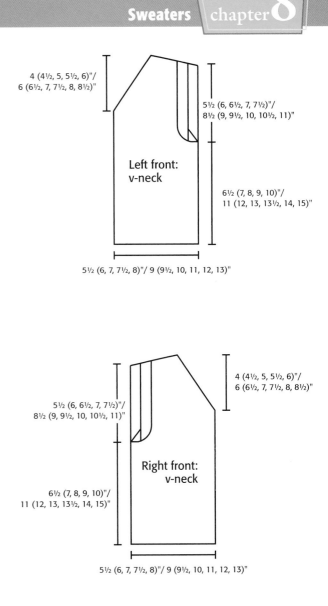

4 (4½, 5, 5½, 6)"/
6 (6½, 7, 7½, 8, 8½)"

5½ (6, 6½, 7, 7½)"/
8½ (9, 9½, 10, 10½, 11)"

Left front:
v-neck

6½ (7, 8, 9, 10)"/
11 (12, 13, 13½, 14, 15)"

5½ (6, 7, 7½, 8)"/ 9 (9½, 10, 11, 12, 13)"

4 (4½, 5, 5½, 6)"/
6 (6½, 7, 7½, 8, 8½)"

5½ (6, 6½, 7, 7½)"/
8½ (9, 9½, 10, 10½, 11)"

Right front:
v-neck

6½ (7, 8, 9, 10)"/
11 (12, 13, 13½, 14, 15)"

5½ (6, 7, 7½, 8)"/ 9 (9½, 10, 11, 12, 13)"

Make Sleeves

You make two identical sleeves. Be sure to follow the instructions for the shaping style you used for the body of the sweater.

CAST ON: ALL STYLES

① CO sts for your size and gauge according to Table 69.

> **Note:** *If you want to work an edging that requires a different number of sts than that specified for your size and gauge in Table 69, you can cast on 1 or 2 fewer sts and work the edging to one row before the end. Increase back to the stitch count specified in Table 69 on the last edging row.*

② Work in desired edging for 1 (1½, 1½, 2, 2) inches for baby/child version or 2½ (2½, 3, 3, 3½, 3½) inches for adult version, ending with a WS row.

③ Go to shaping instructions for your armhole/sleeve style under "Shape Sleeve," below.

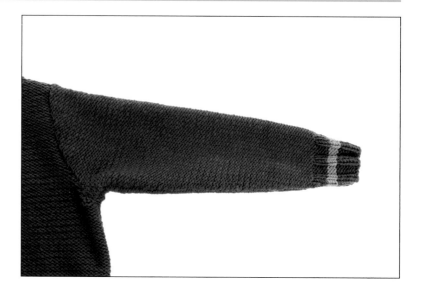

Table 69. Cast On for Sleeves		
No. of Sts to CO		
Gauge	**Baby/Child**	**Adult**
2 sts/in.	12 (14, 16, 18, 20) sts	20 (22, 22, 24, 24, 26) sts
3 sts/in.	18 (21, 24, 27, 30) sts	30 (33, 33, 36, 36, 39) sts
4 sts/in.	24 (28, 32, 36, 40) sts	40 (44, 44, 48, 48, 52) sts
5 sts/in.	30 (35, 40, 45, 50) sts	50 (55, 55, 60, 60, 65) sts
6 sts/in.	36 (42, 48, 54, 60) sts	60 (66, 66, 72, 72, 78) sts

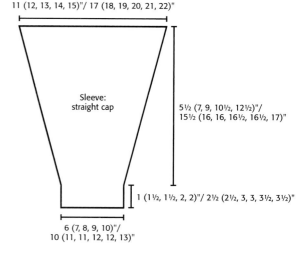

11 (12, 13, 14, 15)"/ 17 (18, 19, 20, 21, 22)"

Sleeve: straight cap

5½ (7, 9, 10½, 12½)"/ 15½ (16, 16, 16½, 16½, 17)"

1 (1½, 1½, 2, 2)"/ 2½ (2½, 3, 3, 3½, 3½)"

6 (7, 8, 9, 10)"/ 10 (11, 11, 12, 12, 13)"

SHAPE SLEEVE

The straight, square, and angled armhole sleeves are all shaped the same from the end of the cuff to the beginning of the cap. For any of these styles, you follow the directions under "Straight, Square, and Angled Armhole Sleeve Shaping," which start on the next page. The sleeve shaping between the cuff and cap is different for the rounded armhole, so if you're using that style, you need to skip ahead to "Rounded Armhole Sleeve Shaping," page 202.

Straight, Square, and Angled Armhole Sleeve Shaping

1 Next row: Inc 1 st each end.

2 Inc 1 st each end every RS row the number of times indicated for your size, stitch gauge, and row gauge in column 3 or column 4 of Table 70. If the number is 0, skip ahead to the next step.

Note: Refer to your gauge swatch to determine your row gauge. If the row gauge you are achieving is not listed for your stitch gauge, choose the closest one from your stitch gauge. Don't use the instructions for any other stitch gauge, even if the row gauge matches yours, or the math will be off.

3 Inc 1 st each end every 4th row (that is, work 3 non-inc rows after each inc row) the number of times indicated for your size, stitch gauge, and row gauge in column 5 or column 6 of Table 70.

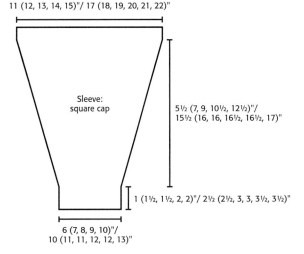

11 (12, 13, 14, 15)"/ 17 (18, 19, 20, 21, 22)"

Sleeve: square cap

5½ (7, 9, 10½, 12½)"/ 15½ (16, 16, 16½, 16½, 17)"

1 (1½, 1½, 2, 2)"/ 2½ (2½, 3, 3, 3½, 3½)"

6 (7, 8, 9, 10)"/ 10 (11, 11, 12, 12, 13)"

Stitch Gauge	Row Gauge	Inc 1 St Each End Every RS Row (Step 2) Baby/Child	Adult	Inc 1 St Each End Every Other RS Row (Step 3) Baby/Child	Adult
2 sts/in.	2½ rows/in.	2 (1, 0, 0, 0) times	All sizes: 0 times	2 (3, 3, 1, 0) times	0 (0, 2, 2, 5, 4) times
2 sts/in.	3 rows/in.	All sizes: 0 times	All sizes: 0 times	4 (2, 0, 0, 0) times	0 (0, 0, 0, 0, 0) times
3 sts/in.	4 rows/in.	4 (0, 0, 0, 0) times	All sizes: 0 times	3 (7, 3, 0, 0) times	0 (0, 1, 1, 7, 5) times
3 sts/in.	4½ rows/in.	1 (0, 0, 0, 0) times	All sizes: 0 times	6 (5, 0, 0, 0) times	0 (0, 0, 0, 2, 1) times
4 sts/in.	5 rows/in.	5 (2, 0, 0, 0) times	All sizes: 0 times	4 (7, 7, 2, 0) times	1 (0, 7, 4, 11, 9) times
4 sts/in.	5½ rows/in.	4 (0, 0, 0, 0) times	All sizes: 0 times	5 (9, 3, 0, 0) times	0 (0, 3, 0, 8, 7) times
5 sts/in.	6 rows/in.	9 (3, 0, 0, 0) times	All sizes: 0 times	3 (9, 10, 5, 0) times	5 (5, 10, 9, 17, 18) times
5 sts/in.	7 rows/in.	6 (0, 0, 0, 0) times	All sizes: 0 times	6 (12, 5, 0, 0) times	0 (0, 3, 0, 10, 10) times
6 sts/in.	7½ rows/in.	8 (3, 0, 0, 0) times	All sizes: 0 times	6 (11, 9, 3, 0) times	3 (0, 11, 10, 18, 17) times
6 sts/in.	8 rows/in.	7 (1, 0, 0, 0) times	All sizes: 0 times	7 (13, 8, 1, 0) times	0 (0, 8, 3, 13, 12) times

Table 70. Sleeve, Straight, Square, or Angled Cap: Sleeve Shaping

CONTINUED ON NEXT PAGE

4 Inc 1 st each end every 6th row (that is, work 5 non-inc rows after each inc row) the number of times indicated for your size, stitch gauge, and row gauge in Table 71.

5 Inc 1 st each end every 8th row (that is, work 7 non-inc rows after each inc row) the number of times indicated for your size, stitch gauge, and row gauge in Table 72.

You should now have rem the number of sts indicated for your size and gauge in Table 73.

6 Go to the instructions for the sleeve cap shaping that matches your armhole style, under "Make Sleeve Cap," page 205.

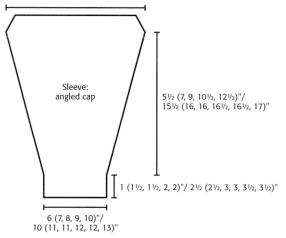

11 (12, 13, 14, 15)"/ 17 (18, 19, 20, 21, 22)"

Sleeve: angled cap

5½ (7, 9, 10½, 12½)"/ 15½ (16, 16, 16½, 16½, 17)"

1 (1½, 1½, 2, 2)"/ 2½ (2½, 3, 3, 3½, 3½)"

6 (7, 8, 9, 10)"/ 10 (11, 11, 12, 12, 13)"

Table 71. Sleeve, Straight, Square, or Angled Cap: Sleeve Shaping (Step 4)			
		No. of Times to Inc 1 St Each End Every 6th Row	
Stitch Gauge	**Row Gauge**	**Baby/Child**	**Adult**
2 sts/in.	2½ rows/in.	0 (0, 1, 3, 3) times	6 (5, 5, 5, 3, 4) times
2 sts/in.	3 rows/in.	0 (2, 4, 2, 0) times	2 (1, 5, 5, 8, 8) times
3 sts/in.	4 rows/in.	0 (0, 4, 7, 3) times	10 (9, 10, 10, 6, 8) times
3 sts/in.	4½ rows/in.	0 (2, 7, 4, 0) times	6 (6, 9, 9, 11, 12) times
4 sts/in.	5 rows/in.	0 (0, 1, 7, 6) times	12 (13, 8, 11, 6, 8) times
4 sts/in.	5½ rows/in.	0 (0, 6, 8, 2) times	10 (10, 11, 15, 8, 9) times
5 sts/in.	6 rows/in.	0 (0, 2, 7, 12) times	12 (11, 9, 10, 5, 5) times
5 sts/in.	7 rows/in.	0 (0, 7, 12, 5) times	15 (15, 16, 19, 11, 12) times
6 sts/in.	7½ rows/in.	0 (0, 5, 11, 10) times	16 (20, 12, 12, 6, 6) times
6 sts/in.	8 rows/in.	0 (0, 6, 13, 7) times	19 (18, 13, 20, 12, 13) times

Table 72. Sleeve, Straight, Square, or Angled Cap: Sleeve Shaping (Step 5)

No. of Times to Inc 1 St Each End Every 8th Row

Stitch Gauge	Row Gauge	Baby/Child	Adult
2 sts/in.	2½ rows/in.	0 (0, 0, 0, 1) times	0 (1, 0, 0, 0, 0) times
2 sts/in.	3 rows/in.	0 (0, 0, 2, 4) times	4 (5, 2, 2, 0, 0) times
3 sts/in.	4 rows/in.	0 (0, 0, 0, 4) times	0 (1, 0, 0, 0, 0) times
3 sts/in.	4½ rows/in.	0 (0, 0, 3, 7) times	4 (4, 2, 2, 0, 0) times
4 sts/in.	5 rows/in.	0 (0, 1, 0, 3) times	All sizes: 0 times
4 sts/in.	5½ rows/in.	0 (0, 0, 1, 7) times	3 (3, 1, 0, 1, 1) times
5 sts/in.	6 rows/in.	All sizes: 0 times	0 (1, 0, 0, 0, 0) times
5 sts/in.	7 rows/in.	0 (0, 0, 0, 7) times	2 (2, 0, 0, 1, 1) times
6 sts/in.	7½ rows/in.	0 (0, 0, 0, 4) times	1 (0, 0, 1, 2, 3) times
6 sts/in.	8 rows/in.	0 (0, 0, 0, 7) times	1 (1, 2, 0, 1, 1) times

Table 73. Sleeve, Straight, Square, or Angled Cap: Stitches Remaining After Shaping Sides

No. of Sts After Shaping Sides

Gauge	Baby/Child	Adult
2 sts/in.	22 (24, 26, 28, 30) sts	34 (36, 38, 40, 42, 44) sts
3 sts/in.	34 (37, 40, 43, 46) sts	52 (55, 57, 60, 64, 67) sts
4 sts/in.	44 (48, 52, 56, 60) sts	68 (72, 76, 80, 84, 88) sts
5 sts/in.	56 (61, 66, 71, 76) sts	86 (91, 95, 100, 106, 111) sts
6 sts/in.	66 (72, 78, 84, 90) sts	102 (108, 114, 120, 126, 132) sts

CONTINUED ON NEXT PAGE

Rounded Armhole Sleeve Shaping

The shaping for this sleeve is different from the shaping for the other sleeves only because the stitch count needed to begin the sleeve cap is smaller. The actual side shaping looks the same as for the other sleeves; it's just drawn out differently over the rows that make up the length.

1 Next row (RS): Inc 1 st each end.

2 Inc 1 st each end every 4th row (that is, work 3 non-inc rows after each inc row) the number of times indicated for your size, stitch gauge, and row gauge in Table 74. If the number is 0, skip ahead to the next step.

Note: Refer to your gauge swatch to determine your row gauge. If the row gauge you are achieving is not listed for your stitch gauge, choose the closest one from your stitch gauge. Don't use the instructions for any other stitch gauge, even if the row gauge matches yours, or the math will be off.

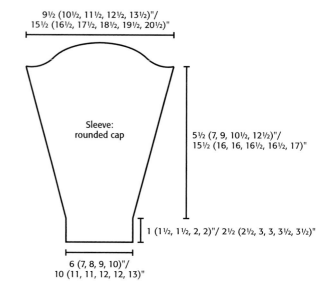

9½ (10½, 11½, 12½, 13½)"/
15½ (16½, 17½, 18½, 19½, 20½)"

Sleeve: rounded cap

5½ (7, 9, 10½, 12½)"/
15½ (16, 16, 16½, 16½, 17)"

1 (1½, 1½, 2, 2)"/ 2½ (2½, 3, 3, 3½, 3½)"

6 (7, 8, 9, 10)"/
10 (11, 11, 12, 12, 13)"

		No. of Times to Inc 1 St Each End Every 4th Row	
Stitch Gauge	**Row Gauge**	**Baby/Child**	**Adult**
2 sts/in.	2½ rows/in.	3 (1, 1, 0, 0) times	0 (0, 0, 0, 1, 0) times
2 sts/in.	3 rows/in.	1 (0, 0, 0, 0) times	0 (0, 0, 0, 0, 0) times
3 sts/in.	4 rows/in.	1 (0, 0, 0, 0) times	0 (0, 0, 0, 0, 0) times
3 sts/in.	4½ rows/in.	All sizes: 0 times	All sizes: 0 times
4 sts/in.	5 rows/in.	5 (2, 0, 0, 0) times	0 (0, 0, 0, 2, 2) times
4 sts/in.	5½ rows/in.	4 (0, 0, 0, 0) times	0 (0, 0, 0, 0, 0) times
5 sts/in.	6 rows/in.	8 (3, 0, 0, 0) times	0 (0, 0, 0, 6, 6) times
5 sts/in.	7 rows/in.	6 (0, 0, 0, 0) times	0 (0, 0, 0, 0, 0) times
6 sts/in.	7½ rows/in.	10 (5, 0, 0, 0) times	2 (0, 0, 0, 9, 8) times
6 sts/in.	8 rows/in.	9 (3, 0, 0, 0) times	0 (0, 0, 0, 0, 0) times

Table 74. Sleeve, Rounded Cap: Sleeve Shaping (Step 2)

③ Inc 1 st each end every 6th row (that is, work 5 non-inc rows after each inc row) the number of times indicated for your size, stitch gauge, and row gauge in Table 75.

④ Inc 1 st each end every 8th row (that is, work 7 non-inc rows after each inc row) the number of times indicated for your size, stitch gauge, and row gauge in Table 76.

Table 75. Sleeve, Rounded Cap: Sleeve Shaping (Step 3)

		No. of Times to Inc 1 St Each End Every 6th Row	
Stitch Gauge	Row Gauge	Baby/Child	Adult
2 sts/in.	2½ rows/in.	0 (2, 0, 1, 0) times	1 (0, 5, 5, 6, 7) times
2 sts/in.	3 rows/in.	2 (3, 0, 0, 0) times	0 (0, 0, 0, 4, 3) times
3 sts/in.	4 rows/in.	3 (2, 0, 0, 0) times	2 (0, 4, 4, 7, 7) times
3 sts/in.	4½ rows/in.	4 (0, 0, 0, 0) times	0 (0, 0, 0, 4, 4) times
4 sts/in.	5 rows/in.	1 (4, 4, 0, 0) times	2 (0, 9, 9, 12, 11) times
4 sts/in.	5½ rows/in.	2 (6, 0, 0, 0) times	0 (0, 5, 5, 10, 10) times
5 sts/in.	6 rows/in.	0 (5, 6, 2, 0) times	7 (5, 12, 11, 12, 11) times
5 sts/in.	7 rows/in.	2 (8, 1, 0, 0) times	2 (2, 6, 5, 14, 14) times
6 sts/in.	7½ rows/in.	0 (5, 7, 2, 0) times	2 (6, 17, 16, 9, 8) times
6 sts/in.	8 rows/in.	1 (7, 5, 0, 0) times	6 (0, 14, 13, 22, 21) times

Table 76. Sleeve, Rounded Cap: Sleeve Shaping (Step 4)

		No. of Times to Inc 1 St Each End Every 8th Row	
Stitch Gauge	Row Gauge	Baby/Child	Adult
2 sts/in.	2½ rows/in.	0 (0, 2, 2, 1) times	4 (5, 0, 0, 0, 0) times
2 sts/in.	3 rows/in.	0 (0, 3, 1, 0) times	2 (3, 6, 6, 3, 4) times
3 sts/in.	4 rows/in.	0 (2, 2, 4, 0) times	0 (3, 5, 5, 3, 2) times
3 sts/in.	4½ rows/in.	0 (4, 0, 1, 0) times	0 (0, 9, 9, 6, 5) times
4 sts/in.	5 rows/in.	0 (0, 2, 6, 0) times	8 (10, 2, 2, 0, 0) times
4 sts/in.	5½ rows/in.	0 (0, 6, 2, 0) times	8 (8, 6, 6, 4, 3) times
5 sts/in.	6 rows/in.	0 (0, 2, 6, 4) times	5 (8, 3, 4, 0, 0) times
5 sts/in.	7 rows/in.	0 (0, 7, 4, 0) times	8 (5, 8, 9, 4, 3) times
6 sts/in.	7½ rows/in.	0 (0, 3, 8, 5) times	12 (9, 1, 2, 4, 6) times
6 sts/in.	8 rows/in.	0 (0, 5, 10, 2) times	7 (16, 4, 4, 0, 0) times

CONTINUED ON NEXT PAGE

5 Inc 1 st each end every 10th row (that is, work 9 non-inc rows after each inc row) the number of times indicated for your size, stitch gauge, and row gauge in Table 77. You should now have rem the number of sts indicated for your size and gauge in Table 78.

6 Cont without further shaping until sleeve measures 6½ (8½, 10½, 12½, 14½) inches from CO edge for baby/child version or 18 (18½, 19, 19½, 20, 20½) inches from CO edge for adult version, ending with a WS row.

7 Beg next 2 rows, BO the number of sts specified for your size and gauge in Table 79.

8 Go to "Rounded Armhole Sleeve Cap," page 206.

Table 77. Sleeve, Rounded Cap: Sleeve Shaping (Step 5)

		No. of Times to Inc 1 St Each End Every 10th Row	
Stitch Gauge	Row Gauge	Baby/Child	Adult
2 sts/in.	2½ rows/in.	0 (0, 0, 0, 2) times	0 (0, 1, 1, 0, 0) times
2 sts/in.	3 rows/in.	0 (0, 0, 2, 3) times	3 (2, 0, 0, 0, 0) times
3 sts/in.	4 rows/in.	0 (0, 2, 1, 5) times	5 (4, 0, 0, 0, 1) times
3 sts/in.	4½ rows/in.	0 (0, 4, 4, 5) times	7 (7, 0, 0, 0, 1) times
4 sts/in.	5 rows/in.	0 (0, 0, 0, 6) times	0 (0, 1, 1, 0, 1) times
4 sts/in.	5½ rows/in.	0 (0, 0, 4, 6) times	2 (2, 1, 1, 0, 1) times
5 sts/in.	6 rows/in.	0 (0, 0, 0, 4) times	1 (0, 0, 0, 0, 1) times
5 sts/in.	7 rows/in.	0 (0, 0, 4, 8) times	3 (6, 1, 1, 0, 1) times
6 sts/in.	7½ rows/in.	0 (0, 0, 0, 5) times	0 (1, 1, 1, 0, 0) times
6 sts/in.	8 rows/in.	0 (0, 0, 0, 8) times	3 (0, 1, 2, 0, 1) times

Table 78. Sleeve, Rounded Cap: Stitches Remaining After Shaping Sides

	No. of Sts After Shaping Sides	
Gauge	Baby/Child	Adult
2 sts/in.	20 (22, 24, 26, 28) sts	32 (34, 36, 38, 40, 42) sts
3 sts/in.	28 (31, 34, 39, 42) sts	46 (49 53, 56, 58, 61) sts
4 sts/in.	38 (42, 46, 50, 54) sts	62 (66, 70, 74, 78, 82) sts
5 sts/in.	48 (53, 58, 63, 68) sts	78 (83, 87, 92, 98, 103) sts
6 sts/in.	58 (64, 70, 76, 82) sts	94 (100, 106, 112, 118, 124) sts

Table 79. Sleeve, Rounded Cap: Prepare for Cap Shaping

	No. of Sts to BO Beg Next 2 Rows	
Gauge	Baby/Child	Adult
2 sts/in.	All sizes: 2 sts	3 (3, 3, 3, 3, 4) sts
3 sts/in.	All sizes: 3 sts	4 (4, 4, 5, 5, 6) sts
4 sts/in.	All sizes: 4 sts	6 (6, 6, 7, 7, 8) sts
5 sts/in.	All sizes: 5 sts	7 (7, 7, 8, 8, 9) sts
6 sts/in.	All sizes: 6 sts	9 (9, 9, 10, 10, 10) sts

MAKE SLEEVE CAP

The way you work the sleeve depends on the type of armhole you're using. The sleeve cap for the straight armhole is the easiest: You just bind off when the sleeve is the proper length. The square armhole requires about an inch of straight edge along the sides at the top of the sleeve, so that it can be set into the square hole. The angled armhole and the rounded armhole call for sleeve caps that fit into the form created by the armhole shaping.

Straight Armhole Sleeve Cap

1. Cont without further shaping until sleeve measures 6½ (8½, 10½, 12½, 14½) inches from CO edge for baby/child version or 18 (18½, 19, 19½, 20, 20½) inches from CO edge for adult version.

2. BO sts.

3. Go to "Block: All Sweaters," page 206.

Square Armhole Sleeve Cap

1. Cont without further shaping until sleeve measures at least 6½ (8½, 10½, 12½, 14½) inches from CO edge for baby/child version or 18 (18½, 19, 19½, 20, 20½) inches from CO edge for adult version AND you have 1 inch of knitting beyond the last inc row.

2. BO sts.

3. Go to "Block: All Sweaters," page 206.

Angled Armhole Sleeve Cap

1. Cont without further shaping until sleeve measures 6½ (8½, 10½, 12½, 14½) inches from CO edge for baby/child version or 18 (18½, 19, 19½, 20, 20½) inches from CO edge for adult version, ending with a WS row.

2. Beg next row (RS), dec 1 st each end every RS row the number of times specified for your size and gauge in Table 80. You should have rem the number of sts indicated for your size and gauge in Table 81.

3. BO sts.

4. Go to "Block: All Sweaters," page 206.

Table 80. Angled Sleeve Cap: Shaping		
No. of Times to Dec 1 St Each End Every RS Row		
Gauge	**Baby/Child**	**Adult**
2 sts/in.	2 times	3 (3, 3, 3, 3, 4) times
3 sts/in.	3 times	4 (4, 4, 5, 5, 6) times
4 sts/in.	4 times	6 (6, 6, 7, 7, 8) times
5 sts/in.	5 times	7 (7, 7, 8, 8, 9) times
6 sts/in.	6 times	9 (9, 9, 10, 10, 10) times

Table 81. Angled Sleeve Cap: Stitches Remaining After Shaping		
No. of Sts After Shaping Angled Sleeve Cap		
Gauge	**Baby/Child**	**Adult**
2 sts/in.	18 (20, 22, 24, 26) sts	28 (30, 32, 34, 36, 40) sts
3 sts/in.	28 (31, 34, 37, 40) sts	44 (47, 49, 50, 54, 55) sts
4 sts/in.	36 (40, 44, 48, 52) sts	56 (60, 64, 66, 70, 72) sts
5 sts/in.	46 (51, 56, 61, 66) sts	72 (77, 81, 84, 90, 93) sts
6 sts/in.	54 (60, 66, 72, 78) sts	84 (90, 94, 100, 106, 112) sts

CONTINUED ON NEXT PAGE

Rounded Armhole Sleeve Cap

1 Beg next row (RS), dec 1 st each end every RS row the number of times specified for your size and gauge in Table 82. You should have rem the number of sts specified for your size and gauge in Table 83.

2 Beg next row, dec 1 st each end *every* row until you have rem the number of sts specified for your size and gauge in Table 84.

3 BO sts.

4 Go to "Block: All Sweaters," below.

Table 82. Rounded Sleeve Cap: Shaping

No. of Times to Dec 1 St Each End Every RS Row

Gauge	Baby/Child	Adult
2 sts/in.	2 (2, 3, 3, 2) times	3 (4, 4, 4, 5, 5) times
3 sts/in.	3 (4, 5, 4, 3) times	6 (6, 6, 7, 7, 8) times
4 sts/in.	4 (5, 6, 5, 4) times	7 (8, 7, 8, 10, 10) times
5 sts/in.	5 (6, 7, 6, 5) times	9 (10, 10, 11, 13, 13) times
6 sts/in.	6 (7, 9, 7, 6) times	11 (12, 11, 12, 15, 17) times

Table 83. Rounded Sleeve Cap: Stitches Remaining After Initial Shaping

No. of Sts After Initial Rounded Armhole Shaping

Gauge	Baby/Child	Adult
2 sts/in.	12 (14, 14, 16, 20) sts	20 (20, 22, 24, 24, 24) sts
3 sts/in.	16 (17, 19, 25, 30) sts	26 (29, 33, 32, 34, 33) sts
4 sts/in.	22 (24, 26, 32, 38) sts	36 (38, 44, 44, 44, 46) sts
5 sts/in.	28 (31, 34, 41, 48) sts	46 (49, 53, 54, 56, 59) sts
6 sts/in.	34 (38, 40, 50, 58) sts	54 (58, 66, 68, 68, 70) sts

Table 84. Rounded Sleeve Cap: Stitches Remaining After Final Shaping

No. of Sts After Final Rounded Armhole Shaping

Gauge	Baby/Child	Adult
2 sts/in.	6 (6, 8, 8, 10) sts	10 (10, 10, 12, 12, 12) sts
3 sts/in.	10 (9, 11, 13, 15) sts	14 (15, 15, 16, 18, 19) sts
4 sts/in.	12 (12, 14, 16, 18) sts	18 (20, 20, 22, 24, 26) sts
5 sts/in.	16 (17, 17, 21, 22) sts	22 (25, 25, 26, 30, 31) sts
6 sts/in.	18 (18, 20, 24, 28) sts	28 (30, 30, 32, 36, 38) sts

Block: All Sweaters

1 Weave in loose ends.

2 Block sweater pieces to measurements, if yarn's care instructions allow.

3 Go to the neckband instructions for your sweater style under "Make Neckband," on the next page.

Make Neckband

You can work the neckband in a number of ways. One option is to sew both shoulder seams and then pick up stitches and work the neckband in the round. Another way is to sew one shoulder seam and then pick up stitches and work the neckband in rows, sewing the neckband seam later. These are just a couple of approaches, however; you can also pick up stitches and then knit a collar, or you can work a decorative edging. (See Appendix A for more on knit collars and decorative edgings.)

Note: *When picking up stitches along a vertical or shaped edge, remember that row height is less than stitch width: Pick up approximately 3 stitches every 4 rows or 4 stitches every 5 rows. Also, if you are working an edging that requires a certain multiple of sts, be sure to work that in when picking up sts. For more information on picking up stitches, see pages 262–263.*

ROUND-NECK PULLOVER NECKBAND

You work this edging back and forth in rows, using a short circular needle or double-pointed needles one size smaller than the needles used for the sweater body.

1 Sew right shoulder seam and steam, if yarn's care instructions allow. (For information on seams, see pages 163 and 253–256.)

2 With RS facing, use short circ needle or dpns to pick up and k sts evenly down left front neck to holder, k across the center neck sts from holder, pick up and k the same number of sts up the right front neck to shoulder seam as picked up for left front neck, and k across the back neck sts from holder.

3 Work in edging of your choice to desired length.

4 BO in patt.

5 Sew left shoulder seam, including neckband.

6 Go to "Attach Sleeves: All Sweaters," page 210.

V-NECK PULLOVER NECKBAND

You work this edging in rounds, using a short circular needle or double-pointed needles one size smaller than the needles used for the sweater body.

1 Sew both shoulder seams and steam, if yarn's care instructions allow. (For information on seams, see pages 163 and 253–256.)

2 With RS facing, use a short circ needle to pick up and k sts evenly down left front neck to v-neck center, k the center st from holder and mark it with a split-ring marker, pick up and k the same number of sts up right front neck to shoulder seam as picked up for left front neck, and k across the back neck sts from holder.

3 Place marker for beg of rnd, join rnd, and work in chosen edging, shaping center v-neck as foll.

4 Rnd 1: Work patt to within 2 sts of center st, k2tog, k center st, ssk, work in patt to end of rnd.

5 Rnd 2: Work edging patt without shaping.

6 Rep rnds 1 and 2 to desired length, ending with rnd 2.

7 BO in patt, working the dec at center v-neck as in previous rnds.

8 Go to "Attach Sleeves: All Sweaters," page 210.

CONTINUED ON NEXT PAGE

ROUND-NECK CARDIGAN: NECKBAND AND BUTTON BANDS

You work the neck edging first, using a circular needle so as to be able to comfortably pick up stitches around the front and back neck. Even though it's on a circular needle, you work it back and forth in rows. When the neckband is done, you work the button bands on either straight or circular needles.

1. Sew both shoulder seams and steam, if yarn's care instructions allow. (For information on seams, see pages 163 and 253–256.)

2. With RS facing and starting at beg right neck shaping, use circ needle one size smaller than the needles used for the sweater body to pick up and k sts up the right neck to shoulder seam, k across the back neck sts from holder, and pick up and k the same number of sts down left front neck as picked up for right neck.

3. Work in edging of your choice to desired length.

4. BO in patt.

5. Place markers (pm) for buttons (on left front for females and right front for males): Pm ½ inch up from hem, pm ½ inch down from beg neck shaping, and place 3 or 5 more markers, evenly spaced between these two.

6. With RS facing and beg at right front hem, use circ needle one size smaller than the needles used for the sweater body to pick up and k sts evenly up right front to beg neck shaping.

7. If working buttonholes on this band, work in edging of your choice for 1 or 2 rows, and go to step 8. If not, work in edging patt of your choice to desired length and skip ahead to step 10.

8. Next row (buttonhole row): Work in edging patt but work buttonholes opposite markers this row. (See pages 260–261 for buttonhole styles and techniques.)

9. Cont in patt to desired length.

10. BO in patt.

11. Work left front button band/buttonhole band as for right front band, only pick up sts with RS facing beg at left front neck edge. (Work buttonholes on this band if the sweater is for a male.)

12. Go to "Attach Sleeves: All Sweaters," page 210.

V-NECK CARDIGAN NECKBAND AND BUTTON BANDS

It's easy to work the button bands and neckband as one continuous band when your cardigan has a v-neck. You work this edging using a long circular needle so as to be able to comfortably pick up stitches all the way around the fronts and the neck opening. Even though it's on a circular needle, you work it back and forth in rows. (See pages 262–263 for more on picking up stitches.)

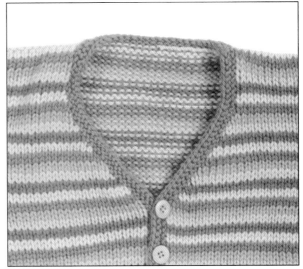

1 Sew both shoulder seams and steam, if yarn's care instructions allow. (For information on seams, see pages 163 and 253–256.)

2 Place markers (pm) for buttons (on left front for females and right front for males): Pm ½ inch up from hem, pm ½ inch down from beg neck shaping, and place 3 or 5 more markers, evenly spaced between these two.

3 With RS facing and beg at right front hem, use circ needle one size smaller than the needles used for the sweater body to pick up and k sts evenly up right front to shoulder seam, k across the back neck sts from holder, and pick up and k the same number of sts down left front to hem as picked up for right front.

4 Work in edging of your choice for 1 or 2 rows.

5 Next row: Work in edging patt but work buttonholes opposite markers this row. (See pages 260–261 for buttonhole techniques.)

6 Cont in patt to desired length.

7 BO in patt.

8 Go to "Attach Sleeves: All Sweaters," page 210.

CONTINUED ON NEXT PAGE

Attach Sleeves: All Sweaters

This chapter covers many different ways to shape armholes and sleeve caps, but all the sleeves are attached in a similar manner. After blocking all pieces, working the edging on the neck, and joining and pressing shoulder seams, you can attach the sleeves.

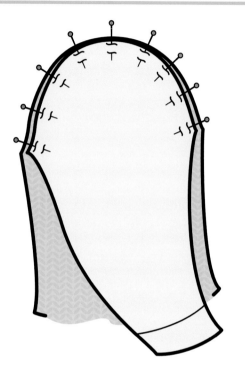

1. Find the center of the sleeve cap by folding the sleeve in half lengthwise and then mark the center with a pin.

2. Pin the center of the sleeve cap to the shoulder seam, with the RS facing each other, and then pin the rest of the sleeve cap to the armhole, lining up the sleeve cap shaping with the corresponding armhole shaping.

3. Sew the sleeve in place at shoulder. (For information on seams, see pages 163 and 253–256.)

Finish: All Sweaters

1. Weave in rem loose ends.

2. Before sewing side and sleeve seams, lightly steam shoulder and armhole seams to neaten, if yarn's care instructions allow.

3. Sew side and sleeve seams. (For information on seams, see pages 163 and 253–256.)

4. Lightly steam seams to neaten, taking care not to mash or stretch out ribbings.

5. For cardigan, sew buttons opposite buttonholes. Reinforce buttonholes, if necessary. (See page 261 for instructions.)

This women's coat uses the master pattern as a starting point and then takes off in a different direction. The body has been lengthened and the sleeves made roomier. A raglan arm-hole and raglan sleeve shaping have been substituted for the other styles.

Specifications

SIZES

S (M, L)

Finished chest measurements when buttoned: 44 (48, 52) inches

MATERIALS

11 (12, 13) hanks Plymouth Yarn *Baby Alpaca Grande* (Color #2569, 100% baby alpaca, 110 yd./100g hank, 3.5 sts per inch)

1 pair size 10 (6mm) straight needles, or size needed to obtain gauge

Size 9 circular needle to work collar

Size F crochet hook

Tapestry needle

2 stitch holders

Row counter

5 buttons

GAUGE

14 stitches and 18 rows to 4 inches over stockinette stitch on size 10 needles

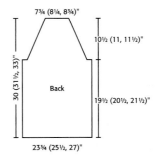

Back

7¾ (8¼, 8¾)"

10½ (11, 11½)"

30 (31½, 33)"

19½ (20½, 21½)"

23¾ (25½, 27)"

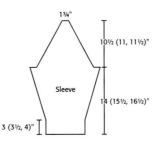

Sleeve

1¾"

10½ (11, 11½)"

14 (15½, 16½)"

3 (3½, 4)"

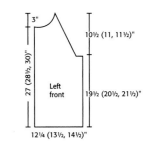

Left front

3"

10½ (11, 11½)"

27 (28½, 30)"

19½ (20½, 21½)"

12¼ (13½, 14½)"

CONTINUED ON NEXT PAGE

PATTERN STITCH

Moss Stitch

Rows 1 and 4 (RS): K1, *p1, k1; rep from * to end of row.

Rows 2 and 3 (WS): P1, *k1, p1; rep from * to end of row.

Rep rows 1–4 for moss stitch.

How to Make the Women's Coat

MAKE BACK

1. CO 83 (89, 95) sts.

2. Work in moss st for 4 inches, ending with a WS row.

3. Beg with a knit row, work in St st until back measures 19½ (20½, 21½) inches from CO edge, ending with a WS row.

4. Shape raglan armholes: BO 4 sts beg next 2 rows–75 (81, 87) sts.

5. Next row (RS): K1, sl1, k1, psso, k to last 3 sts, k2tog, k1–73 (79, 85) sts.

6. Next row (WS): P1, p2tog, p to last 3 sts, p2tog, p1–71 (77, 83) sts.

7. Rep last 2 rows 0 (1, 2) times–71 (73, 75) sts.

8. Next row (RS): K1, sl1, k1, psso, k to last 3 sts, k2tog, k1–69 (71, 73) sts.

9. Next row (WS): Purl.

10. Rep last 2 rows 21 times, ending with a WS row–27 (29, 31) sts.

11. Cut yarn, leaving a 6-inch tail, and place rem neck sts on holder for later.

12. Go to "Make Left Front," below.

MAKE LEFT FRONT

1. CO 43 (47, 51) sts.

2. Work moss st edging as for back, ending with a WS row.

3. Beg with a knit row, work in St st until left front measures 19½ (20½, 21½) inches from CO edge, ending with a WS row.

4. Shape raglan armhole (RS): BO 4 sts, k to end of row–39 (43, 47) sts.

5. Next row: Purl.

6. Next row (RS): K1, sl1, k1, psso, k to end of row–38 (42, 46) sts.

7. Next row: Purl to last 3 sts, p2tog, p1–37 (41, 45) sts.

8. Rep last 2 rows 0 (1, 2) times to 37 (39, 41) sts.

9. Next row (RS): K1, sl1, k1, psso, k to end of row–36 (38, 40) sts.

10 Next row (WS): Purl.

11 Next row (RS): K1, sl1, k1, psso, k to end of row—35 (37, 39) sts.

12 Rep last 2 rows 13 times, ending with a RS row—22 (24, 26) sts.

13 Beg neck shaping (WS): BO 6 (7, 8) sts beg this row, purl to end of row—16 (17, 18) sts.

14 Continue to shape raglan armhole, dec 1 st as established every RS row. AT THE SAME TIME, dec 1 st at neck edge *every* row 6 (7, 8) times—7 (6, 6) sts.

15 Cont shaping armhole only every RS row to 4 sts, ending with a WS row.

16 Next row (RS): K2tog twice—2 sts.

17 BO purlwise.

18 Go to "Make Right Front," below.

MAKE RIGHT FRONT

1 Work as for left front, reversing armhole and neck shaping to other side.

2 Go to "Make Sleeves," below.

MAKE SLEEVES

1 CO 51 (55, 59) sts.

2 Work moss st for 3 (3½, 4) inches, ending with a WS row.

3 Shape sleeves: Inc 1 st each end this row, then every 12th (14th, 14th) row 3 times—59 (63, 67) sts.

4 Work without further shaping until sleeve measures 14 (15½, 16½) inches from CO edge, ending with a WS row.

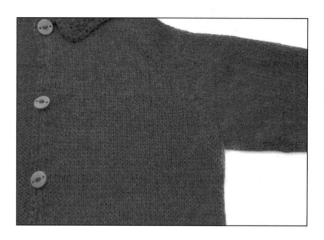

5 Shape raglan armholes: BO 4 sts beg next 2 rows—51 (55, 59) sts.

6 Next row (RS): K1, sl1, k1, psso, k to last 3 sts, k2tog, k1—49 (53, 57) sts.

7 Next row (WS): P1, p2tog, p to last 3 sts, p2tog, p1—47 (51, 55) sts.

8 Rep last 2 rows 0 (1, 2) times—47 sts.

9 Next row (RS): K1, sl1, k1, psso, k to last 3 sts, k2tog, k1—45 sts.

10 Next row (WS): Purl.

11 Rep last 2 rows 20 times, ending with a WS row—5 sts.

12 Next row (RS): K1, K3tog, k1—3 sts.

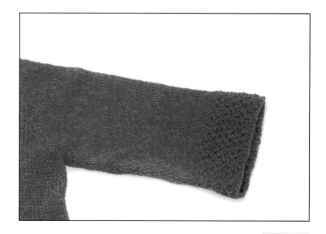

CONTINUED ON NEXT PAGE

⑬ Next row (WS): Purl.

⑭ BO knitwise.

⑮ Rep steps 1–14 for the second sleeve.

⑯ Go to "Make Pockets," below.

MAKE POCKETS

① CO 23 sts.

② Work in St st until pocket measures 6 inches from CO edge.

③ BO loosely.

④ Work crochet edging around sides and bottom of pocket: With RS facing, work 2 rows sc from top corner to opposite top corner, leaving the top pocket edge to roll, working 3 sc at each lower corner the first row, then 2 sc into the center stitch at each pocket corner the second row. (For crochet instructions, see page 272.)

⑤ Cut yarn, pull through last loop, and secure.

⑥ Weave in ends and tidy the crochet join.

⑦ Lightly steam pockets to block if your yarn's care instructions allow.

⑧ Rep steps 1–7 for the second pocket.

⑨ Go to "Block Coat," below.

BLOCK COAT

① Weave in loose ends, except those that can be used to sew seams.

② Block all pieces to measurements, if yarn's care instructions allow, taking care not to mash edgings.

③ Go to "Work Collar," below.

WORK COLLAR

① Neatly pin together the four raglan seams from beg armhole shaping to neck. Sew raglan seams. (For information on seams, see pages 163 and 253–256.)

② With WS facing and beg at left front neck edge, pick up and k21 (22, 23) sts along neck shaping, across left front and back raglan seam to back neck sts, k27 (29, 31) sts from holder for back neck, pick up and k21 (22, 23) sts across right back and front raglan seams and down right front neck shaping to edge—69 (73, 77) sts.

③ Beg with row 2, work in moss st until collar measures 4½ (4¾, 5) inches from picked-up row.

④ BO loosely in patt.

⑤ Go to "Finish Coat," on the next page.

FINISH COAT

1. Sew sleeve seams and side seams. (For information on seams, see pages 163 and 253–256.)

   Note: *You can leave an opening slit at the side seams 3 inches up from cast-on edge at hem, if desired.*

2. Lightly steam seams, if yarn's care instructions allow.

3. Sew pockets to fronts, with lower edges 4 inches up from hem and pocket sides 1 inch in from side seams, following the instructions on page 214.

4. Work left front edging: With RS facing and beg at neck edge, use crochet hook to work one row of sc down to hem. Ch1, turn, and work another row of sc back up to neck edge.

5. Cut yarn, leaving a 6-inch tail, pull through last loop, and secure.

6. Place markers (pm) for button loops on right front ½ inch down from neck edge, 7 inches up from CO edge at hem, and 3 more evenly spaced between.

7. Work right front edging: With RS facing and beg at lower-right front edge, use crochet hook to *sc up to within ½ inch of next marker, ch for 1 inch, insert hook back into right front 1 inch from beg of ch so that it lies flush with edge; rep from * 4 times, sc1 at neck edge. Ch1, turn, and work sc along edge and loops back down to hem.

8. Cut yarn, leaving a 6-inch tail, pull through last loop, and secure.

9. Work 2 rows of sc around collar ends and BO edge, sc3 at corners in the 1st row and sc2 into center sc at corners in the 2nd row.

10. Cut yarn, leaving a 6-inch tail, pull through last loop, and secure.

11. Weave in rem ends.

12. Steam crochet edgings, if your yarn's care instructions allow.

13. Sew buttons opposite button loops.

Altering the Master Patterns

Even though the master patterns provided in the previous pages cover numerous sizes, gauges, and styles, you will most likely want to make further adjustments to suit your own personal design sense. You can add color, adjust the length, work in a new stitch pattern, and even change the body shape. You can use the master patterns as stepping-stones to designing your own knits.

Why not adjust a master pattern to make it your own? You can change the edgings or the main stitch pattern to achieve the look you're going for, and you can add embroidery or crochet. With a little planning, you can also add collars or pockets, or you can lengthen or shorten the original design.

EMBELLISHMENTS

There are infinite ways to liven up plain knitting. Adding fringe, pompoms, or tassels to edges is a fast and easy way to decorate a plain sweater or hat. Or substitute a ruffle or crochet edging for the ribbing on mittens, socks, or a sweater. Embroidery of simple motifs, words, or initials can alter the feel of a garment, bag, or blanket entirely. See Appendix A for more ideas on how to embellish your knitting.

KNIT-ON ADDITIONS

Consider altering a sweater by adding a collar. You can pick up stitches around the neckline and knit the collar directly onto the sweater, or you can knit the collar as a separate piece and sew it on later. Another easy change you can make to a master pattern is to add pockets. You can sew patch pockets directly onto a sweater, vest, bag, or scarf; or you can work inset pockets into your knitting. For more on adding pockets, see pages 264–265.

MAKING IT LONGER

You can easily make a pullover—either vest or sweater—into a tunic; and it is simple to make a cardigan into a jacket or coat. It is not difficult to add length to your knitting, as long as the change occurs over an unshaped, or straight, area. To add length to a pattern, you simply knit more rows. To lengthen a sweater or vest that has armhole shaping, you knit more rows over the area below the armhole only, so as not to alter the armhole measurement. Of course, adding length requires more yarn, so purchase accordingly. Adding length *and* changing the shaping requires more work and planning, however. See pages 224–225 for help on adjusting the body shape.

MAKING IT SHORTER

Shortening a scarf is simple: You knit fewer rows. The same basic principle applies to making a sweater or vest shorter—as long as the body below the armholes is the same width from hem to armhole. You can easily make the sweaters and vests from the master patterns into crop tops or shrug-like sweaters by knitting fewer rows below the armhole. For a very cropped look, try knitting the body half or one-third the length specified for the sweater.

MAKING IT NARROWER OR WIDER

People come in all shapes and sizes, and often measurement charts and knitting pattern sizes do not suit the person for whom you're knitting. For example, a tall, thin person may fit best into a sweater with a small circumference and long length. Likewise, a petite person may need a small size in terms of length but not in terms of width. One simple way to make these types of adjustments is to work the circumference as for a smaller or larger size and add or subtract length in unshaped areas—like the body below the armhole, or the cuff of the sleeve.

Most of the sweaters and vests in Chapters 7 and 8 are knit in stockinette stitch, but you can substitute another stitch pattern in a sweater or vest—or any other knit item—to add interest.

MAKING A STITCH PATTERN SWATCH

These three swatches are all made from the same yarn and using the same needles, over 20 stitches and 30 rows, but with different stitch patterns. You can see how varied the sizes of the final results are. That's why it's important to knit up a swatch in the stitch pattern you want to integrate into a master pattern. In some cases, the gauge may be just slightly off and easily remedied by blocking to measurements.

In other cases, the difference will be so pronounced that you'll have to rewrite the pattern entirely or follow the instructions—stitch-count-wise, not vertical-measurement-wise—for one of the other gauges or sizes presented in the master pattern. To do this, you would cast on and work the shaping according to the other gauge or size that suits the gauge for your swatch but follow the lengthwise instructions for your size.

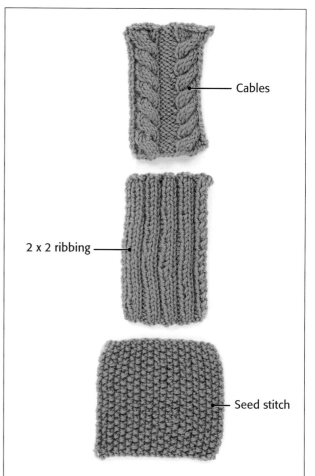

Cables

2 x 2 ribbing

Seed stitch

INCORPORATING STITCH PATTERNS

To substitute a stitch pattern for plain stockinette stitch without rewriting the pattern or doing a lot of calculating, you can choose a stitch pattern that works to exactly the same gauge as specified in the pattern. It is also easiest to incorporate a stitch pattern with a repeat that divides evenly into the initial stitch count. For example, diagonal rib has a 4-stitch repeat, so it should be worked over a stitch count that is divisible by 4 (for example, 24, 28, 32, 36, and so on).

The simplest approach is to find a stitch pattern that suits the stitch count specified in the pattern. To center a cable or stitch pattern made up of an odd number of stitches, you start with an odd number of stitches so that the cable is truly centered. In this case, if the cast-on number is even and the edging requires an even number, you cast on and work the edging as written, increasing 1 stitch in the center of the last edging row. Just remember that you will have an extra neck stitch when you get to that point.

MAKING ADJUSTMENTS

If your stitch pattern gauge is close to the gauge of the item you want to make—off by $\frac{1}{4}$ stitch per inch, for example—you can probably go ahead and knit it, knowing that you will have to fudge it to the measurements when pinning and blocking later. (However, this type of adjustment may not work well with inelastic yarns or novelty yarns that cannot be blocked.) Don't go ahead and knit it if the final width is going to be more than $1\frac{1}{2}$ to 2 inches off. Blocking can only go so far.

If your stitch pattern results in a gauge that is more than 1 stitch per inch different from that specified in the pattern, you will have to either rewrite the pattern yourself or follow the master pattern instructions for one of the other sizes or gauges. For example, if you're using a yarn that usually knits to 3 stitches per inch in stockinette stitch, and you're getting 4 stitches per inch with your stitch pattern, you can follow the pattern for 4 stitches per inch in your size. Or, if you're getting $4\frac{1}{2}$ stitches per inch, and the pattern is written for 2, 3, 4, 5, and 6 stitches per inch, choose the stitch count from any of the gauges that results in the correct finished circumference measurements when divided by $4\frac{1}{2}$. Just remember to follow the schematic's vertical measurements to get the length right.

One of the most enjoyable aspects of knitting is choosing the colors—standing in the yarn shop, holding one ball of yarn next to another to see how they work together. One way to add interest to a plain stockinette stitch garment is to work it in more than one color. Here are some ideas about adding color. (For more on working with color, see page 286.)

COLOR BLOCK

Knitting the different parts of a sweater in assorted colors—also called color block—is the easiest way to vary the color within one garment. Babies' and children's sweaters often employ this technique. Another way to color block is to knit the edgings in different colors.

HORIZONTAL STRIPES

It's easy to add horizontal stripes to any of the master patterns since doing so does not affect the gauge or how the shaping is worked. You have to calculate what approximate percentage of your work will be in the accent color and buy yarn accordingly. Adding horizontal stripes is also a great way to use up stash yarns of the same gauge.

FAIR ISLE PATTERNS

If you want to work in a Fair Isle pattern, you should knit a gauge swatch in the color pattern and see how it compares to the gauge of yarn that weight in the master pattern. Some knitters go up one needle size to work Fair Isle patterns, to compensate for the tighter gauge. This may be all you need to do to match the desired gauge. However, you might need to follow the instructions—in terms of stitch count, not vertical measurements—for one of the other gauges presented.

It is easiest to apply a Fair Isle pattern that has a repeat that fits into your stitch count. But you can still make other Fair Isle patterns work, by casting on 1 or 2 stitches more or less to accommodate it or to center it. Be sure to take these extra/fewer stitches into account when reworking the shaping.

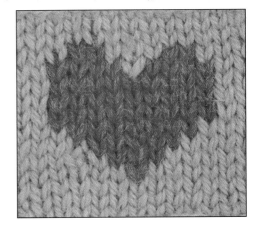

INTARSIA MOTIFS

Adding intarsia motifs is another way to enhance a master pattern. You can chart a schematic on graph paper and map out where you want to place the motifs on each knit piece. You can scatter numerous motifs throughout a garment or simply center one on the front of a sweater or vest or on the back of a mitten or glove.

You should chart out the placement of each individual motif so that it is centered properly, both horizontally and vertically. In addition, you need to be careful not to knit motifs too tightly so as to change the overall size of your final garment.

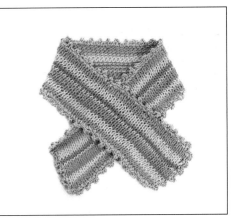

COLOR EMBELLISHMENTS

If you finish knitting a project, and it's not as interesting as you'd hoped it would be, you can spruce it up by adding some color after the fact. You can completely change the look of your handknits by adding colorful embroidery, crochet trims, pompoms or tassels, buttons, handknit flowers, or other accents. Sometimes a simple whipstitched edge in contrast yarn is all you need to transform a dull sweater. Embellishing in this way is a great way to use up leftover yarn, too.

You may want to change the body shape of a particular sweater design. There are a few ways to achieve this, some more complicated than others. Choose the option that best suits your sweater design and skill level.

CALCULATING A-LINE SHAPING

Width and length were added to the body of the vest master pattern to create the A-line shape of the tunic shown here. For this adjustment, you calculate how many more stitches are needed for the added circumference at the hem and at what interval, row-wise, the shaping decreases should occur.

Let's say you want to make the hem 6 inches larger *in total circumference* than the pattern calls for, and you want to add 10 inches to the body length below the armholes. If you're working the sweater body in two pieces—a back and a front—you divide the extra circumference by 2 and add that amount of width to each piece at the hem. If you're working the sweater body as a cardigan in three pieces, you add half that amount to the sweater back and one-quarter of that width to each front piece. In our example, we're adding 6 inches of circumference to a two-piece garment, so we add 3 inches of width to the hem of each the back and the front. Here's how it works:

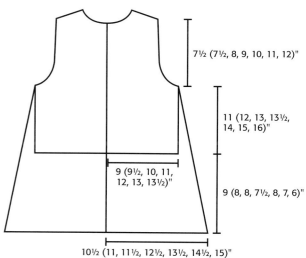

7½ (7½, 8, 9, 10, 11, 12)"

11 (12, 13, 13½, 14, 15, 16)"

9 (9½, 10, 11, 12, 13, 13½)"

9 (8, 8, 7½, 8, 7, 6)"

10½ (11, 11½, 12½, 13½, 14½, 15)"

1. Multiply your stitch gauge by 3 to determine how many more stitches to cast on. If the result is an odd number, round up to the nearest even number. For example, if your gauge is 5 stitches per inch, multiply 5 by 3 and round up to 16 stitches.

2. Add the number from step 1 to the cast-on number in the pattern to determine how many stitches to cast on for the new width. For example, if your pattern says to cast on 90 stitches for the back or front, add 16 to 90 and cast on 106 stitches for the wider hem.

3. To calculate the 10-inch length adjustment, multiply your row gauge by 10 to determine how many additional rows you need to knit. For example, if your gauge is 6 rows per inch, add an additional 60 rows.

4. Multiply the original body length (from cast-on edge to armhole, as written on the schematic) by your row gauge to determine how many rows make up the original length. For example, if the original body length from cast-on edge to armhole is 11 inches and your gauge is 6 rows per inch, you need 66 rows for the original length.

5. Add the result from step 3 to the result from step 4 to determine the total number of rows to knit for the new length, from cast-on edge to armhole. For example, adding the 60 rows from step 3 to the 66 rows from step 4 equals a total of 126 rows to achieve the new length.

6 Because 2 stitches are decreased every decrease row, divide the number you achieved in step 1 by 2 to determine the number of decrease rows to work over the tapered section between the cast-on edge and armhole. For example, the number of extra stitches in step 1 is 16. So divide 16 by 2 to determine the number of decrease rows—which in this case is 8. The goal is to decrease gradually over the tapered section the same number of extra cast-on stitches, so that you'll have the original cast-on number when you begin the armhole shaping.

7 Divide the number from step 5 by the number from step 6. The result equals the number of rows to work between decrease rows so that the decrease rows are spread out evenly from hem to armhole. For example, if you divide 126 by 8, you get a number slightly less than 16, so you work decreases about every 15 or 16 rows.

Note: *If you're beginning the shaping after the edging at the hem, subtract that length in rows from the result in step 5.*

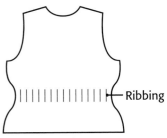
Ribbing

EASY WAIST SHAPING

A quick and easy way to give a sweater a more flattering silhouette is to work some ribbing at the waistline. For this approach, omit ribbing at the hem and work an edge that doesn't gather, like seed stitch or garter stitch. Work up to just before where the waist falls and then work in ribbing for 1½ to 3 inches.

Easy waist shaping

TAILORED WAIST SHAPING

You can work a tailored waistline into the body of a sweater by using a series of gradual decreases from the cast-on edge to the waist, followed by the same number of gradual increases from the waist to the armhole. The general rule is to decrease 4 inches *total* for a tailored waist: Decrease 2 inches worth of stitches on the back and 2 inches on the front. (For a cardigan, decrease 2 inches on the back and 1 inch on each side edge of the front pieces.)

To work such a waist, you cast on according to the master pattern and work a nongathering edging for about an inch. Then you begin decreasing as determined by the following calculations:

1 Calculate for your gauge how many stitches you need to decrease for the back: 2 (inches) × Stitch gauge. (For example, if your stitch gauge is 4 stitches per inch, you decrease 8 stitches for the waist.)

2 The stitches are decreased at each end of the decrease rows, so divide the result in step 1 by 2 to determine how many decrease rows to work to the waist. For this example, 8 divided by 2 is 4, so you work 4 decrease rows.

3 Subtract 1 inch from the body length from cast-on edge to armhole. (The actual waist after the decreases and before the increases is worked even for about 1 inch.) So, if the body length is 11 inches, the result for this step is 10.

4 Multiply the result from step 3 by your row gauge and divide that result by 2 to determine how many rows to work for the body sections above and below the 1 inch of waist. For example, your result in step 3 is 10. If your gauge is 6 rows per inch, the total body length less the 1 inch of waist takes 60 rows. Therefore, you need 30 rows below and above the waist.

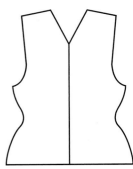
Tailored waist shaping

5 Divide the result from step 4 by the result from step 2 to determine how many rows should be worked between decrease/increase rows. For example, 30 divided by 4 is 7.5, so you need to work decreases about every 7 or 8 rows.

After you work the waist even for about an inch, you work the same number of increase rows as decrease rows—at the same interval—up to the armhole. You should finish with the same number of stitches that you started with.

Adjusting sleeve length and shape is not as clear-cut as simply adding length to straight knitting. However, when you understand how to calculate length and width based on your row and stitch gauge, you can work out a new length or shape without too much trouble.

Adjusting Sleeve Length

One way to lengthen a sleeve is to simply knit a longer cuff. By the same token, knitting a shorter cuff, or omitting the cuff altogether, is an easy way to shorten a sleeve.

To add length to a sleeve above the cuff, you use your row gauge to determine how many additional rows are needed to reach the desired length and then work those additional rows, evenly spaced, between increase rows. To subtract length above the cuff, you use your row gauge to determine how many rows need to be eliminated to reach the desired length and then omit those rows periodically between increase rows.

For substantially shorter sleeves, such as three-quarter-length sleeves, you need to cast on more stitches at the cuff to accommodate the larger circumference of the forearm. An easy way to work a three-quarter sleeve from the master pattern is to subtract the length you want from the master pattern's sleeve length and

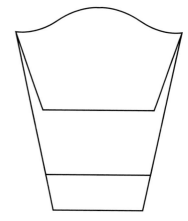

then begin at that point in the pattern, casting on the number of stitches that are expressed at that point in the instructions. (For example, if the original sleeve begins with a cast-on number of 44 at the cuff, and after working and shaping for 4 or 5 inches—which is about where three-quarter-length sleeves would begin—the stitch count is 50, you would begin your three-quarter sleeves by casting on 50 stitches.) That way, you don't have to rewrite the shaping instructions.

Adjusting Sleeve Shape

The sweater master pattern sleeves are shaped traditionally, gradually widening from the cuff up to the cap. You can change this in a number of ways, such as by creating fashionable kimono or bell-shaped sleeves.

KIMONO SLEEVE

One easy way to alter both the length *and* the shape of a sleeve is to make a straight sleeve like the one shown here. This produces a very full, kimono-like sleeve, which can be attractive on a women's coat or casual weekend sweater.

To make this adjustment, you go to the sleeve instructions in the master pattern and find the number of stitches you're supposed to end up with after performing all the increases before the sleeve cap begins. You cast on that number and work straight to where the cap shaping should begin, for the length desired, and shape the cap as written. It's easy to adjust the length of a kimono sleeve because there is no shaping in that section of the sleeve.

BELL SLEEVE

You can alter a sleeve's shape to create bell sleeves. The key is to not disrupt the length too much and to maintain the sleeve cap's width and shaping so that it will still fit in the armhole. Bell sleeves are often a little longer than standard sleeves, so that they cover the wrist and a portion of the back of the hand.

The best way to calculate the adjustments for a bell sleeve is to draw out the sleeve on graph paper and calculate stitch and row counts, decreases, and increases based on size, stitch gauge, and row gauge. There is no rule or formula because sizes, gauges, and style preferences vary greatly. A very easy way to create a bell sleeve look is to work the kimono sleeve as instructed above, adding a 2-inch ribbing, or an eyelet row and tie, that gathers the sleeve about 2 to 3 inches above the cast-on row for a baby or child or 4 to 6 inches above the cast-on row for an older child or woman.

Another approach to making a nice bell sleeve is to cast on twice as many stitches as the master pattern indicates to cast on. You work a nongathering edging for 1 inch and then decrease gradually—over about 2 to 5 inches of length—back to the cast-on number specified in the master pattern. From here, you make the sleeve as written in the master pattern, except that you decrease the number of rows between increase rows, to compensate for the added length of the bell. For a less pronounced bell, you do the same thing but decrease to a stitch count greater than the cast-on number indicated in the master pattern.

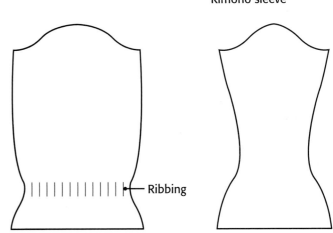

Kimono sleeve

Bell sleeve

Ribbing

chapter 10

Designing Your Own Knits

Are you ready to go a step beyond altering patterns and try your hand at designing your own handknits? You've worked with some of the master patterns and seen how you can adjust a design or pattern to suit your own taste. When you're ready to create from scratch, you can look to this chapter for guidance. Here are some general guidelines to start you on your way to designing your own sweater.

You can find inspiration for new knitting projects everywhere: in nature, at museums, in Persian carpets, or even in old movies. You can also look at knitting books and magazines or even into your own closet for inspiration. When you have an idea of what you want to knit, making sketches can help you solidify your plan.

BOOKS AND MAGAZINES

Most avid knitters collect knitting books and magazines in the same way they accumulate yarn—by the trunk load. Knitting is so popular today that there are countless excellent books to choose from. Stitch pattern reference books provide hundreds of ideas and are a valuable addition to any knitting library. Vintage knitting pattern leaflets and fashion magazines can also inspire; it's fun to start with styles from the past and adapt them for today.

YOUR OWN CLOSET

Consider using your favorite store-bought sweater as a prototype. Take measurements and draw out a schematic. Remember that a difference in yarn thickness and stitch pattern will affect the outcome. What do you like about the sweater—the fit, the color, the stitch pattern, the way it drapes? Experiment with swatches and needle sizes until you find a feel that you like and that will work with that particular style.

MAKE A SKETCH

Sometimes making a rough sketch can help you figure out what you want your item to look like. You can draw versions with or without collars, pockets, or ruffles and make notations on the sketch to indicate buttons, accent colors, or other decorative details. Even though your completed sweater will most likely look very different from your drawing, sketching can help you narrow down the options and figure out what the overall silhouette should be.

It's good to know what style works for you before you embark on an expensive and time-consuming knitting project. If you're knitting for someone else, it's important to determine the right style for that person.

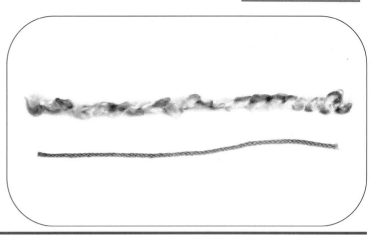

THE RIGHT STYLE FOR YOU

For some knitters, choosing the right style is obvious: They know what suits them and what doesn't. Others find it difficult to choose an appropriate look or cut, and they spend weeks knitting a sweater that they end up giving away because it's the wrong style.

Pictures in books and magazines are tempting, as are the many textures and colors of yarn in a shop. Before you spend a lot of time knitting an expensive sweater, think realistically about what you wear. Look in your closet, if that helps. That hot pink eyelash yarn may look great on the shelf, or the multicolor intarsia sweater might look fun to knit—but would you actually wear something that looks like that? If your closet is filled with neutral-colored clothing and black sweaters, chances are you won't wear these things. Try to design something that you'll love to knit *and* love to wear.

THE RIGHT STYLE FOR OTHERS

Have you ever received a gift from someone that was something they should have given to themselves? Sometimes knitters can get carried away and knit something intended as a gift that suits their own personal taste better than the recipient's taste. It's a shame to let that gift go unappreciated or unworn.

The best bet when knitting something for someone else is to make an accessory such as a scarf, a hat, a bag, or mittens. Babies look great in everything, and a sweater that size works up quickly, so a baby sweater is always a welcome gift. Another option is to ask the person you want to knit for to choose a sweater from one of your books or magazines and then design something based on that.

Designing in Color

One of the many joys of designing handknits is choosing the colors. It's easy to choose one color yarn; but choosing colors that work well together can be challenging. Remember that you'll be spending many hours knitting in this scheme, so you want to choose colors that complement each other *and* that you like—whether they be different shades of one green or high-contrast opposites. Here are a few color concepts to assist you in making color choices.

Choosing Colors That Work Well Together

Sometimes it's hard to choose colors that go well together. You may find yourself drawn to the same color combinations over and over again and decide you need a nudge in a new direction; or perhaps the color combination you would choose is not available in a particular yarn. You can use a color wheel like this one to help you in your choice. To use it, you simply choose a starting color. Then you aim one of the arrows or points of the triangles or rectangles to the starting color and see what colors the color selector recommends. A color wheel might help you find a color combination you never would have thought of on your own.

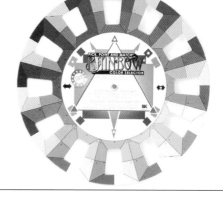

CHOOSING A MONOCHROMATIC COLOR SCHEME

One easy way to select colors that work well together—and you don't need a color wheel for this—is to choose monochromatic colors. A monochromatic scheme uses variations of the same color, like the swatch here, which is a soothing, quiet combination of blue colors.

CHOOSING AN ANALOGOUS COLOR SCHEME

Another easy color option is an analogous color scheme—that is, a scheme made up of three to five adjacent colors on the wheel. The result of this type of combination is generally harmonious and peaceful, as in the swatch shown here. Say, for example, you have one color of yarn you know you want to use, and you would like to choose some colors to go with it. You can match your yarn to its corresponding color on the wheel and then choose yarns that match the adjacent colors on either side.

CHOOSING A COMPLEMENTARY COLOR SCHEME

A complementary color scheme is made up of two colors that are opposites on the color wheel. This high-contrast combination is bold and appealing; however, sometimes bright opposites placed together vibrate so much that they're hard to look at. The swatch here is knit in the complements violet and yellow; blue and orange are also complements, as are red and green.

CONTINUED ON NEXT PAGE

CHOOSING A TRIADIC COLOR SCHEME

The color wheel is made up of 12 color segments. When you choose 3 colors that are equidistant from one another on the wheel, you have selected a triadic color scheme. There are four triadic color schemes: the primary triad, made up of red, yellow, and blue; the secondary triad, made up of orange, green, and violet; and two tertiary triads, one made up of red-orange, yellow-green, and blue-violet and one made up of red-violet, yellow-orange, and blue-green. The primary triadic color scheme conveys a childlike simplicity and can be a little sterile, while secondary and tertiary triadic schemes are rich, subtle, and complex. The swatch shown here is made up of red, yellow, and blue.

CHOOSING A SPLIT COMPLEMENTARY COLOR SCHEME

This swatch is an example of a split complementary color scheme. This type of color scheme is made up of three colors: a starting color and the two colors on either side of its complement. For example, if you had violet yarn and wanted to try a split complementary color combination, you would choose a ball of yellowish green and a ball of orange to go with it because those are the two colors on either side of yellow—violet's complement.

CHOOSING A TETRADIC COLOR SCHEME

Things begin to get complicated when you work with a tetradic color scheme. Usually a daring color statement, a tetradic color scheme is made up of two sets of complementary colors. For example, a tetradic color scheme might be made up of red, green, orange, and blue because red and green are complements, as are orange and blue. Experiment with various amounts of each of these colors, as four competing opposites can be difficult to look at all at once. Note how the swatch here is made up of more orange-red than the other colors.

EXPERIMENTING WITH COLOR

After you've pored over the color wheel, you can knit up test swatches in different color combinations to see how they actually work. This swatch uses the same stitch pattern in three assorted combinations. It's remarkable how dissimilar the same design can look in different color combinations.

Perfecting the Fit

You can design handknits to fit any body type. Creating a perfectly fitting garment isn't as difficult as it might seem. It's mostly a matter of taking accurate measurements, determining ease, and calculating stitch counts based on the measurements. Here we look at how to perfect the fit of a sweater, which is probably the most demanding garment to design.

Taking Body Measurements

To ensure a good fit when designing a sweater—or knitting from a pattern, for that matter—you need to take detailed body measurements. Here's how:

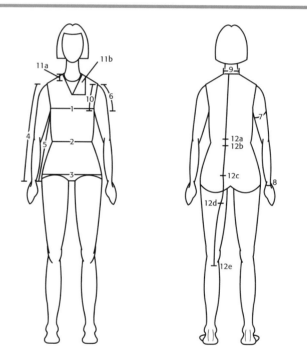

1. Measure the bust or chest by placing the tape measure around the fullest part of the chest, at the underarm.

2. For the waist, measure around the smallest part of the torso.

3. For the hip, measure around the fullest part of the lower torso.

4. Measure for sleeve length by placing the tape measure at the edge of the shoulder and extending down (with arm held straight at side) to the wrist.

5. Measure from the underarm to the wrist to obtain a measurement for where to begin the sleeve cap shaping.

6. If you're designing a short-sleeved sweater, take the same measurements as in steps 4 and 5, only end at the point on the upper arm where you want the sleeve to fall.

7. Measure the circumference of the upper arm.

8. Measure the circumference of the wrist.

9. Measure the circumference of the neck (or the width of the back of the neck).

10. Measure the armhole depth from the top of the shoulder down the front to the base of the underarm.

11. Also take some neck shaping measurements:

    a. For a rounded neck, begin at the neck where the shoulder meets it and measure straight down to where you want the bottom of the rounded part to be.

    b. Do the same for a v-neck.

12 Don't forget to measure the length along the back to best suit your sweater style:

a. For a cropped or shrug-like sweater, measure above the waist.

b. For a short sweater, measure at the waist.

c. For a hip-length sweater, measure at the hip.

d. For a fingertip-length jacket or tunic, measure at the thigh where the fingertips fall.

e. For a long coat, measure anywhere from the knee down.

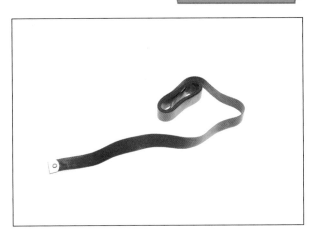

Calculating Ease

Some of your knitted measurements should be a few inches larger than the actual body measurements, or the garment will be too tight. The difference between body measurements and knit measurements is called *ease*.

Things to consider when calculating ease are whether the sweater will be worn over a shirt or other clothing and whether you're aiming toward a tight or tailored fit or a more loose and boxy fit. You can use the table below as a guideline.

What Size to Knit?					
Actual Body Measurement	*Finished Measurements*				
Chest	**Tight Fit**	**Tailored Fit**	**Normal Fit**	**Loose Fit**	**Oversized Fit**
21 in.–22 in.	20 in.	22 in.	24 in.	26 in.	27 in.–28 in.
23 in.–24 in.	22 in.	24 in.	26 in.	28 in.	29 in.–30 in.
25 in.–26 in.	24 in.	26 in.	28 in.	30 in.	31 in.–32 in.
27 in.–28 in.	26 in.	28 in.	30 in.	32 in.	33 in.–34 in.
29 in.–30 in.	28 in.	30 in.	32 in.	34 in.	35 in.–36 in.
31 in.–32 in.	30 in.	32 in.	34 in.	36 in.	37 in.–38 in.
33 in.–34 in.	32 in.	34 in.	36 in.	38 in.	39 in.–40 in.
35 in.–36 in.	34 in.	36 in.	38 in.	40 in.	41 in.–42 in.
37 in.–38 in.	36 in.	38 in.	40 in.	42 in.	43 in.–44 in.
39 in.–40 in.	38 in.	40 in.	42 in.	44 in.	45 in.–46 in.
41 in.–42 in.	40 in.	42 in.	44 in.	46 in.	47 in.–48 in.
43 in.–44 in.	42 in.	44 in.	46 in.	48 in.	49 in.–50 in.
45 in.–46 in.	44 in.	46 in.	48 in.	50 in.	51 in.–52 in.
47 in.–48 in.	46 in.	48 in.	50 in.	52 in.	53 in.–54 in.
49 in.–50 in.	48 in.	50 in.	52 in.	54 in.	55 in.–56 in.

Doing the Math

Most people don't realize how much math goes into a piece of knitting. After you've taken all the necessary measurements and determined the sizing for the item you're designing, you need to sit down with some graph paper, a pencil and an eraser, and a calculator to figure out stitch and row counts. Then you can write out your pattern.

Here we walk through doing the math to design a sweater. You follow basically the same steps to design any other handknit item.

DRAWING A SCHEMATIC

After you calculate your measurements, you should use graph paper to draw a schematic for your sweater's parts (that is, back, front or fronts, and sleeves). You can simply use the lines on the graph paper as a guide for drawing neat and symmetrical pieces, or you can use the squares to represent inches or stitches.

For the sweater back, you need to write down a number of measurements: the width at the cast-on edge, the length to the armhole, the armhole length, the neck width, and the shoulder width. You need to do the same for the front, and also include the neck depth. For the sleeve, you write down the width at the cast-on edge, the length from cast-on edge to cap, and the width of the cap at its widest part. You might want to also write down the length of the ribbing or edging.

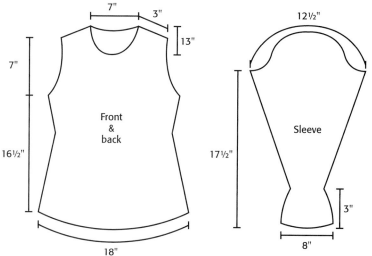

CHECKING YOUR GAUGE

In order to calculate stitch counts and row counts, you need to measure your gauge, as you would for any other knitting project. Using the yarn you've chosen for your sweater and the appropriate needles for that yarn, you knit a 4- or 5-inch gauge swatch in the stitch pattern you plan to use for the sweater. Then you write down your per-inch stitch gauge and your per-inch row gauge.

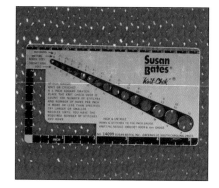

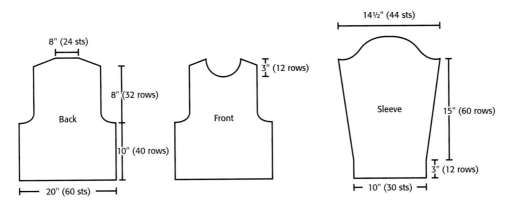

8" (24 sts)

8" (32 rows)

Back

10" (40 rows)

20" (60 sts)

3" (12 rows)

Front

14½" (44 sts)

Sleeve

15" (60 rows)

3" (12 rows)

10" (30 sts)

CALCULATING STITCHES

Starting with the cast-on edge of the back, you multiply the back width by your stitch gauge to determine how many stitches to cast on; for example, if your stitch gauge is 3 sts per inch and the width of the back is 20 inches, you multiply 20 by 3 to come up with 60 stitches to cast on. Then you multiply all the other horizontal measurements by your stitch gauge and jot these stitch counts onto the schematic at their corresponding spots. These numbers will probably need to be adjusted.

Now you adjust the numbers, if necessary, to suit your stitch pattern. Neck and shoulder stitches should add up to the same number of stitches at the width of the sweater after armhole shaping. To calculate armhole shaping, refer to the master pattern and calculate the new numbers based on your stitch gauge.

CALCULATING ROWS

To calculate the number of rows, you multiply all the vertical measurements by your row gauge and write them on the schematic.

Row gauge is used to calculate neck and sleeve shaping. To shape the front neck, you need to end up with the same number of stitches for the front shoulders as for the back shoulders. For a rounded neck, stitches are bound off at the center at the depth of the neck, and then stitches are decreased on each side of the neck until the correct stitch count for the shoulder is reached. The same is true for a v-neck, except that no center stitches are bound off. You calculate how many rows are required for your neck depth to determine the interval of these decreases.

To calculate sleeve shaping, you subtract the number of stitches cast on at the cuff from the number of stitches at the widest point of the cap. (You first adjust either of these numbers, if necessary, so that they are both even or both odd.) Then you divide the result of the subtraction by 2 to determine the number of increases that must be performed to shape the sleeve from above the cuff to the cap, since sleeve shaping involves increasing 1 stitch at each end of every increase row. You take the number of rows that make up this length of sleeve and divide that by the number of increase rows: This tells you approximately at what interval, row-wise, the increases should occur. You should round down and remember that it's easier to perform the shaping on the front side of a piece of knitting.

WRITING YOUR PATTERN

After you calculate the stitch and row counts before and after shaping, you can write out your pattern if that is helpful or necessary. You can start with the instructions from one of the master patterns, substituting your numbers and measurements.

Determining Yarn Yardage

It is difficult to calculate exactly how much yarn you need for a sweater. Certain stitch patterns—such as highly textured stitches and cables—require more yarn than others, and yarn use can vary from knitter to knitter. You can do a fairly accurate estimate by using the method described here; however, it is always advisable to purchase an extra ball or two in the correct dye lot.

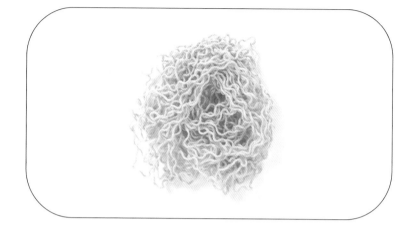

Calculating Yardage

To estimate the yarn needed for a sweater, you need to knit a 4-inch square swatch in the stitch pattern that will be used for the sweater. You also need to calculate the area of each sweater piece, based on your schematic. Here's how you do that:

1. Multiply the width of the back of the sweater by the length and then multiply this number by 2. For example, if your sweater width is 20 inches and length is 23 inches, you multiply 20 by 23 to get 460 square inches for one piece. You multiply 460 by 2 to get 920 square inches total for the back and front.

2. Add the width of the sleeve at the cuff to the width of the sleeve at the cap's widest point; divide the result by 2 and multiply that number by the length of the sleeve. Multiply this new number by 2 to determine the total square inches for both sleeves. For example, if the width of the sleeve at the cuff is 10 inches and the width of the cap is 17 inches, you add 10 to 17 to get 27. Divide 27 by 2 to get 13.5. Multiply 13.5 by the length of the sleeve, 18 inches, and you get 243 square inches for one sleeve. You multiply 243 by 2 to get 486 square inches total for both sleeves.

3. Add together the results from steps 1 and 2. This is approximately the total number of square inches for your sweater. Using the example, if you add 920 to 486, you get 1,406 square inches total for the sweater.

4. Determine the area of your swatch by multiplying the width by the length. Divide the result of step 3 by the area of your swatch. For example, if your swatch is 4 inches square, the area of the swatch is 16 square inches. You divide 1,406 by 16 to get approximately 89.

5. Unravel the swatch and measure how many yards were used to knit it. Let's say it took 17 yards to knit the swatch.

6. Multiply the result from step 4 by the result from step 5 to determine the approximate yardage needed for your sweater. For example, you would multiply 89 by 17 to determine that you need approximately 1,513 yards of yarn for the sweater.

Using Yarn Yardage Charts

The method described on page 240 is good if you have yarn already but you're not sure if it is enough to knit an item. For a more general estimate, you can use the charts on this page as guides to the yardage needed for various items.

Vest: Yarn Weights, Sizes, and Approximate Yardages

Yarn Weight	Baby/Child Finished Chest				Adult Finished Chest			
	24 in.	28 in.	32 in.	36 in.	40 in.	44 in.	48 in.	52 in.
Bulky	200 yd.	300 yd.	400 yd.	500 yd.	600 yd.	700 yd.	800 yd.	900 yd.
Worsted	250 yd.	350 yd.	500 yd.	600 yd.	700 yd.	800 yd.	900 yd.	1,000 yd.
Sport	300 yd.	450 yd.	600 yd.	750 yd.	850 yd.	950 yd.	1,050 yd.	1,150 yd.
Fingering	450 yd.	600 yd.	750 yd.	950 yd.	1,100 yd.	1,250 yd.	1,450 yd.	1,650 yd.

Pullover/Cardigan: Yarn Weights, Sizes, and Approximate Yardages

Yarn Weight	Baby/Child Finished Chest				Adult Finished Chest			
	24 in.	28 in.	32 in.	36 in.	40 in.	44 in.	48 in.	52 in.
Bulky	375 yd.	525 yd.	725 yd.	925 yd.	1,100 yd.	1,300 yd.	1,500 yd.	1,750 yd.
Worsted	500 yd.	700 yd.	1,000 yd.	1,250 yd.	1,400 yd.	1,600 yd.	1,800 yd.	2,000 yd.
Sport	600 yd.	800 yd.	1,100 yd.	1,400 yd.	1,650 yd.	1,900 yd.	2,100 yd.	2,300 yd.
Fingering	750 yd.	1,100 yd.	1,500 yd.	1,750 yd.	2,150 yd.	2,500 yd.	2,750 yd.	3,000 yd.

Hat: Yarn Weights, Sizes, and Approximate Yardages

Yarn Weight	Finished Circumference				
	14 in.	16 in.	18 in.	20 in.	22 in.
Bulky	60 yd.	85 yd.	100 yd.	125 yd.	150 yd.
Worsted	75 yd.	125 yd.	175 yd.	225 yd.	250 yd.
Sport	125 yd.	175 yd.	225 yd.	250 yd.	275 yd.
Fingering	150 yd.	200 yd.	250 yd.	300 yd.	325 yd.

Socks: Yarn Weights, Sizes, and Approximate Yardages

Yarn Weight	Foot Length						
	4 in.	5 in.	6½ in.	8 in.	9½ in.	10½ in.	11½ in.
Bulky	85 yd.	100 yd.	125 yd.	150 yd.	175 yd.	225 yd.	250 yd.
Worsted	125 yd.	175 yd.	225 yd.	250 yd.	300 yd.	350 yd.	400 yd.
Sport	125 yd.	175 yd.	225 yd.	275 yd.	325 yd.	375 yd.	450 yd.
Fingering	150 yd.	200 yd.	250 yd.	325 yd.	400 yd.	475 yd.	550 yd.

appendix A

Techniques and Embellishments

This appendix provides information on basic techniques from casting on to seaming and other finishing techniques, along with add-ons like pockets and collars. It also provides instructions for numerous embellishments, such as pompoms, fringe, and embroidery.

Casting On

Here are two commonly used methods for casting on. Take care not to cast on too tightly, or your edge will have no elasticity. You might want to cast on to a needle a size or two larger than the size you should use for the project; then, when you begin knitting, you switch to the correct size.

Methods

SIMPLE CAST-ON

This method of casting on, also called the backward loop method, is easy and quick, but it does not create a tidy edge.

1 Make a slipknot on one needle. Holding that needle in your right hand and the working yarn in your left, make a loop with the working yarn.

2 Place the loop onto the needle with your left hand and then pull the working yarn to tighten.

3 Repeat steps 1 and 2 until you have the desired number of stitches on the needle.

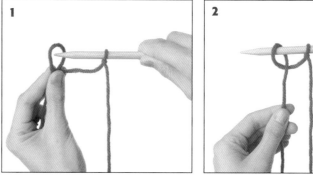

LONG-TAIL CAST-ON

This method is easier than it seems at first, and it provides a neat, elastic edge.

1 Put a slipknot on your needle, leaving a tail that's the equivalent of 1 inch per stitch you plan to cast on, plus a few more inches. (For example, if you plan to cast on 12 stitches, leave a tail that's about 15 inches long.)

2 Hold the yarn with the tail wrapped over your thumb and the working yarn over your forefinger, grasping both ends with your pinky and ring finger in the center of your palm.

③ Lower the needle to create a V while holding the slipknot in place with your right forefinger.

④ Insert the needle up and under the yarn that is looped around the outside of your thumb.

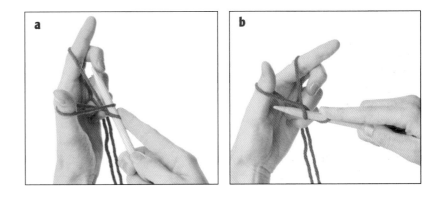

⑤ Move the needle to the right and use it to grab the yarn from the nearest side of your forefinger (a); then pull it through the loop between your thumb and the needle (b).

⑥ Once the yarn is pulled through the loop between your thumb and needle, drop the loops from your thumb and forefinger and pull both ends of the yarn to tighten the stitch on the needle.

You have just cast on 1 stitch.

⑦ Repeat steps 2–6 until you have cast on the desired number of stitches.

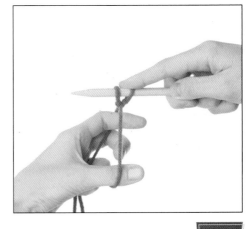

Increasing

There are many types of increases, each with a different appearance or purpose.

Bar Increase

This increase is called a *bar increase* because it creates a visible horizontal bar of yarn where the increase is made. It's also referred to as kfb. You should knit 1 or 2 stitches at the beginning of the row before making a bar increase and 2 or 3 stitches at the end of a row after making a bar increase.

1 Insert the right needle into the next stitch and knit it, except don't bring the old stitch up and off the left needle (a); then insert the right needle into the back of the same stitch and knit it again (b).

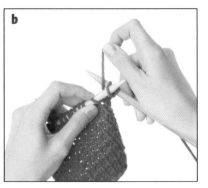

2 Bring the stitch you knit into twice off the left needle.

You have 2 new stitches on the right needle: the one you knit into the front of the stitch and the one you knit into the back of it.

Yarn Over

A yarn over is an increase that is often used for decorative increases and lacy patterns because it makes a hole, or eyelet.

YARN OVER WITH KNIT STITCH

1 To do a yarn over before a knit stitch, bring the working yarn to the front of the needles and lay it over the right needle from front to back.

Laying the yarn over the right needle creates another stitch. On the next row, just knit it or purl as usual.

2 Knit the next stitch.

YARN OVER WITH PURL STITCH

1 To do a yarn over before a purl stitch, bring the working yarn to the front of the needles, wrap it over and under the right needle, and bring it back to the front to be ready to purl.

Laying the yarn over the right needle creates another stitch. On the next row, just knit it or purl as usual.

2 Purl the next stitch.

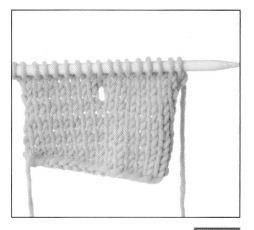

FINISHED INCREASE

After you work a couple rows, you see the hole that the yarn over created.

CONTINUED ON NEXT PAGE

Make One Increase

You can make some increases that are barely visible. One such increase, the make one, involves lifting the horizontal strand between 2 stitches up onto the left needle and knitting it. Here are instructions for both the right-slanting and left-slanting versions.

RIGHT-SLANTING MAKE ONE

1. Before a knit stitch, use the left needle to pick up the horizontal strand (a) *from back to front* between the last stitch worked on the right needle and the next stitch to be worked on the left needle (b).

2. Insert the right needle into the front of the strand and knit it.

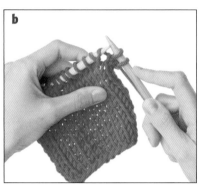

a — Horizontal strand

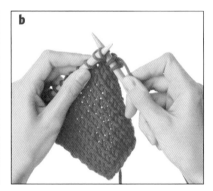

b

LEFT-SLANTING MAKE ONE

1. Before a knit stitch, use the left needle to pick up the horizontal strand *from front to back* between the last stitch worked on the right needle and the next stitch to be worked from the left needle (a).

2. Insert the right needle into the back of the loop and knit it (b).

a

b

FINISHED INCREASE

After you work a few rows, you can see how these increases slant to the right (a) and left (b).

a — Right-slanting make one

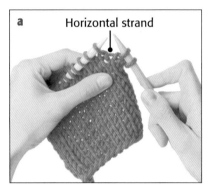

b — Left-slanting make one

Increase Multiple Stitches

The following are a few of the techniques you can use to increase 2 stitches.

DOUBLE BAR INCREASE

This increase is called a double bar increase because you use the bar increase method twice in one row to shape symmetrically. It is usually done over an odd number of stitches, on the front side of a piece of knitting, and in the center of the row of knitting. For a refresher on bar increases, see page 246.

① Knit across to the stitch *before* the center stitch (known as the *axis stitch*) and then work a bar increase.

② Work a second bar increase into the axis stitch. Knit to the end of the row.

Even though the second increase is worked on the axis stitch, the bar appears after it.

DOUBLE YARN OVER INCREASE

The double yarn over increase is similar to the two previous double increases in that you work increases on either side of an axis stitch. For a refresher on basic yarn over stitches, see page 247.

① Knit across to the axis stitch. Perform a yarn over.

② Knit the axis stitch.

③ Perform another yarn over. Knit to the end of the row.

DOUBLE MAKE ONE INCREASE

This increase is similar to the double bar increase in that you increase 1 stitch on either side of an axis stitch, but it is less visible. It is also best worked on the front side of a piece of knitting, over an odd number of stitches. For a refresher on make one increases, see the preceding page.

① Knit across to the axis stitch. Perform a right-slanting make one increase, using the horizontal strand between the last stitch worked and the axis stitch.

② Knit the axis stitch.

③ Perform a left-slanting make one increase, using the horizontal strand between the axis stitch and the next stitch to be worked on the left needle. Knit to the end of the row.

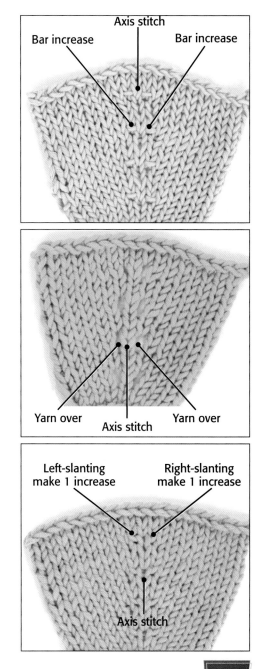

Decreasing

The following decreases are a few of the ones most commonly used. When working decreases in pairs on either end or side of a knitted item, try to use a right-slanting and a left-slanting version.

KNIT 2 TOGETHER/PURL 2 TOGETHER

The two most commonly used decreases are knit 2 together (k2tog) and purl 2 together (p2tog). These decreases both slant somewhat to the right on the front side of a piece of knitting.

1. Insert the right needle into the front of the next 2 stitches on the left needle—as if to knit for k2tog (a) and as if to purl for p2tog (b).

2. Wrap the yarn over the right needle and knit the 2 stitches as 1 stitch for k2tog or purl them together for p2tog.

SLIP, SLIP, KNIT

This almost invisible decrease is worked on the front side of a piece of knitting, and it slants to the left. If you want to shape your knitting on both sides symmetrically, you can begin the row with a slip, slip, knit (ssk) and end the row with a k2tog.

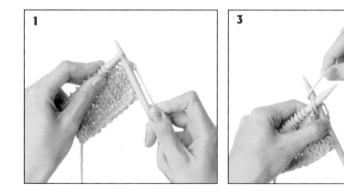

1. Insert the right needle from front to back into the front of the next stitch on the left needle and slip it onto the right needle.

2. Repeat step 1.

   You have slipped 2 stitches from the left needle to the right needle.

3. Insert the left needle into the fronts of both slipped stitches and then knit them as 1 stitch.

SLIP 1, KNIT 1, PASS SLIPPED STITCH OVER

This decrease, worked on the front side of a piece of knitting, slants quite visibly to the left. It is also sometimes referred to as skpo or as slip, knit, pass (skp).

1 Insert the right needle from front to back into the front of the next stitch on the left needle and slip it onto the right needle.

2 Knit the next stitch from the left needle.

3 Insert the left needle into the front of the slipped stitch and bring the slipped stitch over the knit stitch and off the needle.

DOUBLE VERTICAL DECREASE

This double decrease results in symmetrical shaping with a raised vertical stitch in the center. It is worked on the front side of a piece of knitting. It is sometimes called slip 2, knit 1, pass 2 slipped stitches over.

1 Insert the right needle into the next 2 stitches on the left needle as if to knit them together and then slip them off the left needle and onto the right needle.

2 Knit the next stitch from the left needle.

3 Use the left needle to pick up both slipped stitches at the same time and pass them over the knit stitch and off the right needle.

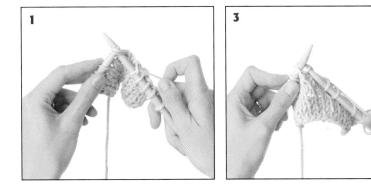

You can see here how the double vertical decrease looks when performed over a progression of rows. The purl rows are worked without decreasing.

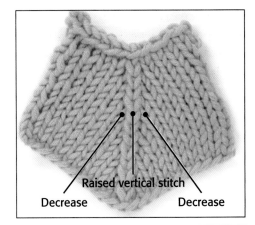

Raised vertical stitch

Decrease   Decrease

Blocking

Blocking is a wonderful fixer of imper-fections. It involves moistening and shaping knitted pieces so that when they dry, they hold the proper shape and size.

You need a large, padded surface, a set of long, rustproof pins, and a measuring tape. When blocking, do not stretch and pin ribbing at cuffs and hems unless the pattern indicates to do so. After ribbing is stretched and blocked, it is no longer elastic.

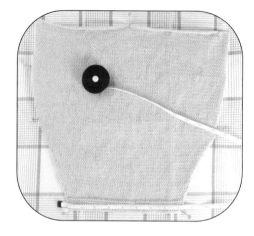

Types of Blocking

WET BLOCKING

Before wet blocking, read your ball band to ensure that washing in water is safe for your yarn. Wet blocking is best for wool blends, some synthetics, and hairy yarns like angora and mohair. It works wonders on textured and cable knits.

1. Lay a knitted piece flat on a padded surface and pin.
2. Measure the knitted piece to see if it has the dimensions that the pattern specifies. Adjust the pins to match the measurements and to make the piece even.
3. Wet the piece thoroughly (excluding ribbing) with a spray bottle.
4. Allow the piece to dry completely and then remove the pins.
5. Repeat steps 1–4 for all pieces of your project.

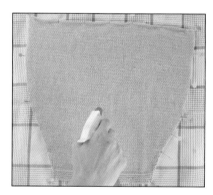

STEAM BLOCKING

You can get fast results blocking using a steam iron or hand steamer. Check that your yarn's care instructions allow applying steam to your yarn and at what tem-perature. Steam blocking is best for wool, cotton, cashmere, and alpaca.

1. Lay a knitted piece flat on a padded surface and pin.
2. Measure the knitted piece to see if it has the dimensions that the pattern specifies. Adjust the pins to match the measurements and to make the piece even.
3. Cover with a light cloth to protect your work from the heat and any potential staining. (You can dampen the cloth with a spray bottle, if desired.) Run the iron lightly above the entire piece, excluding ribbing, taking care not to press or distort the knitting.
4. Allow the piece to dry completely and then remove the pins.
5. Repeat steps 1–4 for all pieces of your project.

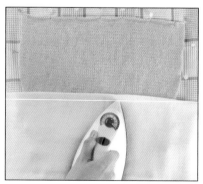

There are numerous ways to sew seams. Some seams are best for shoulders, while others are preferable for vertical seams or certain stitch patterns. See Chapter 8 for more information about how to assemble a sweater and what seam techniques are best for different situations.

A contrast color yarn was used here to sew the seams for illustrative purposes. Be sure to sew your seams with the yarn used to knit the pieces.

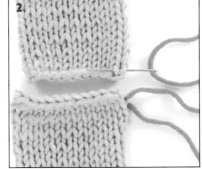

Invisible Horizontal Seam

This seam is an excellent choice for bound-off shoulder seams. It is used to join a horizontal edge to another horizontal edge. When done correctly, the join appears seamless.

① Thread a needle with a long enough strand of yarn to sew the seam and leave a 6-inch tail.

② With right sides facing up, line up the bound-off edges. Insert the needle from back to front through the middle of the first stitch of the lower piece, leaving a 6-inch tail.

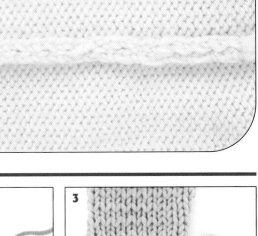

③ Use the needle to pick up the two loops (the V) of the corresponding stitch on the upper piece. Pull the yarn through.

④ Bring the needle across the seam to the next stitch on the lower piece and use it to pick up the loops (the upside-down V), threading it through all the way.

⑤ Repeat steps 3 and 4 across the seam, pulling the yarn lightly—but not too tightly, or it will pucker—every couple stitches to neaten it.

⑥ Weave in the loose ends.

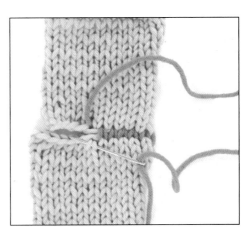

CONTINUED ON NEXT PAGE

Backstitch Seam

You can use this firm seam almost anywhere in constructing a project. You work it with the right sides of the pieces facing each other, so that they are inside out. You should work it about 1 stitch in from the edge.

① Thread a needle with a long enough strand of yarn to sew the seam and leave a 6-inch tail.

② Place the pieces together, with the right sides facing each other and the seam edge lined up. Secure the edge stitches by bringing the needle through both thicknesses from back to front at the right edge, 1 stitch down from the bound-off stitches. Do this twice and pull the yarn through.

③ Insert the needle through both thicknesses, from back to front, about 2 stitches to the left, and bring the yarn through.

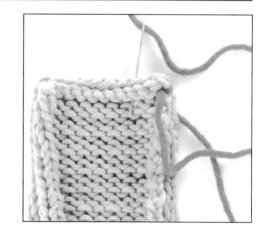

④ Insert the needle from front to back, about 1 stitch in to the right, and pull the yarn through.

⑤ Now bring the needle ahead 2 stitches to the left and insert it from back to front.

⑥ Repeat steps 4 and 5 across the seam until you reach the end, taking care to insert the needle at the same depth each time.

⑦ Weave in the loose ends.

Invisible Vertical Seam

This seam works beautifully for sweater sides and underarm seams. It lays flat and is invisible.

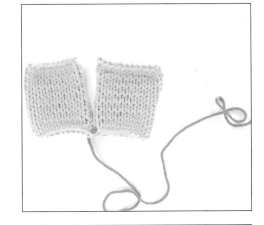

1. Thread a needle with a long enough strand of yarn to sew your seam and leave a 6-inch tail.

2. With the right sides facing up, line up the vertical edges. Sew 1 stitch at the base of the seam to join the pieces: Insert the needle from back to front through the space between the first and second stitches on the lower-right corner of the left piece, pulling yarn through until only about 6 inches remains; insert the needle from front to back between the first and second stitches in the lower-left corner of the right piece; bring needle back through the same spot on the left piece again. Pull the yarn through snugly.

   Now you are ready to work the invisible vertical seam.

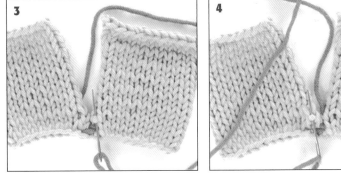

3. Find the horizontal bar of yarn between the first and second stitches. Insert the needle under that horizontal bar, between the first and second stitches, 1 stitch up from the joining stitch, on the right piece. Pull the yarn through.

4. Insert the needle under the horizontal bar between the first and second stitches, 1 stitch up from the joining stitch, on the left piece. Pull the yarn through.

5. Insert the needle under the next horizontal bar up on the right side and then under the corresponding bar on the left side. Continue in this manner, alternating from side to side, to the end of the seam.

6. Weave in the loose ends.

   CONTINUED ON NEXT PAGE

Invisible Vertical-to-Horizontal Seam

This seam is excellent for joining a bound-off edge to a side edge, as in joining a sleeve cap to an armhole.

1 Thread a tapestry needle with a long enough strand of yarn to sew your seam and leave a 6-inch tail.

2 With the right sides facing up, line up the bound-off edge and the side edge.

3 Insert the needle from back to front through the V of the first stitch on the right side of the lower piece, below the bound-off edge, and pull the yarn through until about 6 inches remain.

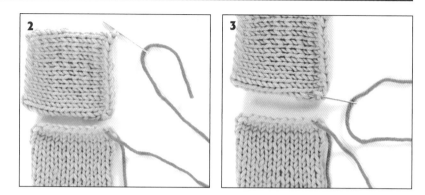

4 Insert the needle on the other side of the join—directly across from the same point on the vertical piece—under one of the bars between the first and second stitches on the horizontal piece. Pull the yarn through.

Note: *Because you are matching rows to stitches in this join, and because there are usually more rows per inch than stitches, you need to pick up two of the bars on the horizontal piece every other stitch or so to keep the seam even.*

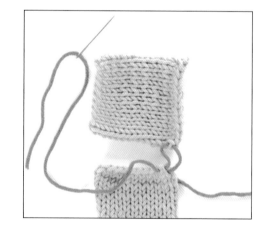

5 Bring the yarn across the join and pick up the loops that make the point of the upside-down V of the next stitch on the vertical piece, pulling the yarn through, trying to imitate the size of each stitch in the knitted piece.

6 Continue alternating between the upper and lower pieces until you finish the seam.

7 Weave in the loose ends.

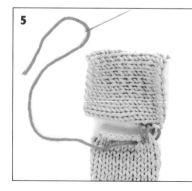

Grafting—which is a good choice for unshaped shoulders, toes of socks, and mitten tips—involves joining an open row of stitches to another open row of stitches or to another edge. The stitches are joined while they're still on the knitting needle, and the final result looks like a row of stockinette stitch.

A contrast color yarn was used here to sew the seams for illustrative purposes. Be sure to sew your seams with the yarn used to knit the pieces.

Three-Needle Bind-off

To prepare to join edges with the three-needle bind-off, you need to put each set of stitches onto a knitting needle and have handy a third knitting needle.

1. Hold the needles parallel, with the right sides of your knitting facing each other, as shown.

2. Insert a third knitting needle into the first stitch on the front needle as if to knit and then into the first stitch on the back needle as if to knit. Wrap the working yarn around the tip of the third needle as you would to knit normally.

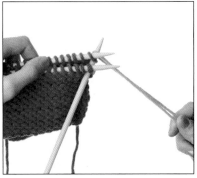

3. Bring the loop through the first stitch on the back needle, as if to knit, and then bring the same loop all the way through to the front of the first stitch on the front needle as well.

4. Slip both old stitches off the parallel needles, as you would to knit them.

   You should now have 1 stitch on the third needle.

5. Repeat steps 2–4. There should now be 2 stitches on the right needle.

6. Pass the first stitch on the right needle over the second to bind off.

7. Continue knitting together the corresponding stitches from each needle and binding off as you go, until only 1 stitch remains on the right needle. Cut the yarn, leaving a 6-inch tail, and pull the tail through the last stitch to secure.

8. Weave in the loose ends.

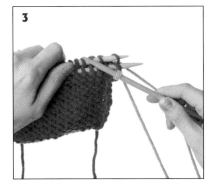

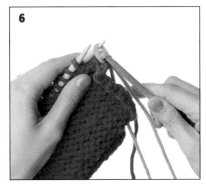

CONTINUED ON NEXT PAGE

Kitchener Stitch

To prepare to join edges with Kitchener stitch, put each set of stitches onto a knitting needle.

1 Using yarn that matches your knitting, thread a tapestry needle with a strand that is roughly twice the length of the seam.

2 Lay both pieces of knitting on a table, with the wrong sides down and the needles running parallel to each other, with the tips pointing to the right.

3 Insert the tapestry needle into the first stitch on the lower needle as if to purl; pull the yarn through until only about 6 inches remain. Leave the stitch on the needle.

4 Insert the tapestry needle into the first stitch on the upper needle as if to knit and pull the yarn through snugly, leaving the stitch on the needle.

5 Insert the tapestry needle into the first stitch on the lower needle again, this time as if to knit (a); then slip this stitch off the needle (b).

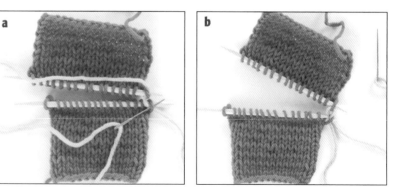

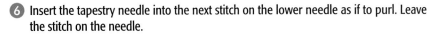

6 Insert the tapestry needle into the next stitch on the lower needle as if to purl. Leave the stitch on the needle.

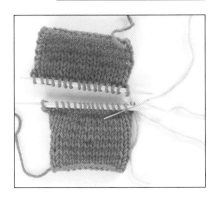

7 Insert the tapestry needle into the first stitch on the upper needle again, this time as if to purl (a); then slip this stitch off the needle (b).

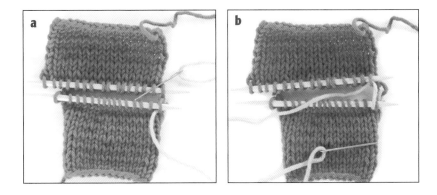

8 Insert the tapestry needle into the next stitch on the upper needle as if to knit. Leave the stitch on the needle.

9 Repeat steps 5–8 until all the stitches have been completed. Remember: On the lower needle, the first insertion is as if to purl, the second insertion is as if to knit, and then the stitch comes off; on the upper needle, the first insertion is as if to knit, the second insertion is as if to purl, and then the stitch comes off.

Making Buttonholes

The buttonholes described here—the eyelet buttonhole and the one-row horizontal buttonhole—should get you through most situations.

EYELET BUTTONHOLE

This is the easiest buttonhole to make. It works very well for children's and babies' clothes, as well as for small buttons.

1 Work to the point where you want the buttonhole to be and then k2tog, yo; continue the row as established.

2 On the next row, work the yo as you would a regular stitch.

You have made a 1-stitch eyelet buttonhole.

ONE-ROW HORIZONTAL BUTTONHOLE

There are several methods for making horizontal buttonholes over two rows; this one-row buttonhole looks tidy and does not need to be reinforced later.

1 On the RS, work to the point where you want the buttonhole to be placed. Bring the yarn to the front, slip the next stitch from the left needle as if to purl and bring the yarn to the back. *Slip the next stitch from the left needle to the right and pass the first slipped stitch over it and off the needle. Repeat from * three times, keeping the yarn at the back the whole time.

You have bound off 4 stitches.

2 Slip the last bound-off stitch back to the left needle.

3 Turn your work so that the wrong side is facing and bring the yarn to the back.

4 Insert the right needle between the first and second stitches on the left needle and wrap the yarn around the right needle as if to knit.

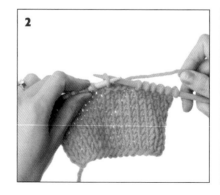
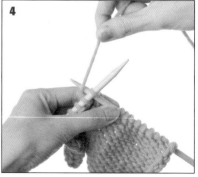

5 Bring the loop through to the front as if to knit, but instead of slipping the old stitch off the left needle, use the right needle to place the new loop onto the left needle.

You have cast on 1 stitch.

6 Repeat steps 4 and 5 four more times and then turn the work back so that the RS is facing.

You have cast on 5 stitches.

7 Bring the yarn to the back and slip the first stitch from the left needle to the right needle; pass the additional cast-on stitch over the slipped stitch to close the buttonhole. Work to the end of the row as usual.

You have made a one-row horizontal buttonhole.

HOW TO FINISH A BUTTONHOLE WITH BUTTONHOLE STITCH

Finishing a buttonhole is easy.

1 Thread a tapestry needle with matching or contrast color yarn.

2 Bring the tapestry needle through from back to front, leaving a 6-inch tail at the back.

3 Working from right to left, insert the tapestry needle from front to back, with the tip of the needle pointing toward the buttonhole, looping the yarn under the needle.

4 End your stitching on the WS. Cut the yarn, leaving a 6-inch tail.

5 Secure yarn ends at the back and weave in the loose ends.

Picking Up Stitches

You need to pick up stitches to add button bands, neckbands, collars, or decorative borders to the already finished edges of your knitting.

HOW TO PICK UP STITCHES ALONG A BOUND-OFF EDGE

Using a needle a size or two smaller than your working needles, pick up stitches, working from right to left.

1 Start at the top-right corner, with the RS facing, and insert the needle into the center of the V of the first stitch, just below the bound-off row.

2 Wrap the working yarn around the needle as you would to knit, holding a 6-inch tail, as shown.

3 Bring the loop of the working yarn to the front, as you would to knit.

You have now picked up 1 stitch.

4 Repeat steps 1–3 across the edge, working from right to left, for each stitch.

Note: *When you are done picking up stitches, be sure to switch back to your working needles.*

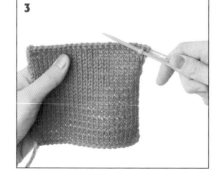

HOW TO PICK UP STITCHES ALONG A CURVED EDGE

You sometimes need to pick up stitches along a curved edge, such as with neck shaping.

1. Starting at the top-right corner, with the RS facing, insert the needle into the center of the V of the first stitch, just below the bound-off edge of the shaping.

2. Wrap the working yarn around the needle, as you would to knit, holding a 6-inch tail, as shown.

3. Pick up all the stitches on the horizontal section of the shaping until you get to the vertical section.

4. Continue picking up stitches, skipping a row every few stitches, if necessary. Be sure not to insert the needle into any large holes caused by the shaping, as doing so will result in a hole in your picked-up edge.

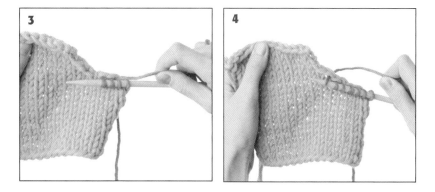

HOW TO PICK UP STITCHES EVENLY

Sometimes it's difficult to pick up stitches evenly over a long stretch of knitting, such as around the fronts and neck of a cardigan. If you don't pick up stitches evenly, your final result will look decidedly off: It will cinch in or look stretched.

1. Place pins, spaced evenly apart, along the edge where the stitches are to be picked up.

   Note: If you prefer, you can tie bits of yarn as markers at even intervals instead of using pins at the edge.

2. Calculate how many stitches should be picked up between markers by dividing the total number of stitches to be picked up by the number of spaces between pins.

3. Pick up the appropriate number of stitches between each pair of markers.

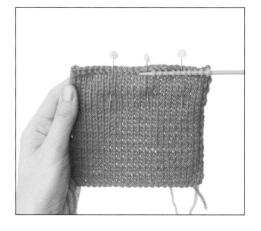

HOW TO ATTACH A PATCH POCKET

Knit and block the pocket you want to sew on. (The sample here is a 4-inch square.) Have ready a tapestry needle, straight pins, and yarn to sew the pocket.

1 Pin the pocket in place exactly where you want it to be and thread a tapestry needle with the appropriate yarn.

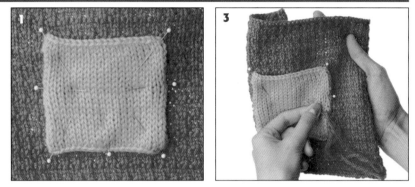

2 Insert the tapestry needle from back to front through both the knitting and the upper-right corner of the pocket. Loop the yarn around from front to back to front once more to reinforce the corner.

3 Sew on the pocket as shown, ending at the upper-left corner. Reinforce the corner as in step 2, ending with the needle on the WS.

4 Weave in the loose ends.

HOW TO PICK UP A PATCH POCKET

To pick up a patch pocket, you need straight pins, a tapestry needle, and yarn and needles to knit the pocket. You also need a knitting needle one or two sizes smaller than the one used to knit the garment; this is for picking up the pocket stitches.

1 Use pins to mark the outline of where you want the pocket to be.

2 Weave the smaller knitting needle under and over horizontally through the row of stitches where the base of the pocket will be.

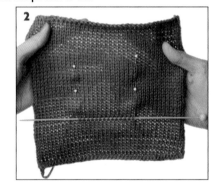

3 Using the yarn you intend to knit the pocket with and the working knitting needle, purl across the picked-up stitches. (The first row is a WS row.)

4 Beginning with a knit row, work from here in stockinette stitch until the pocket is the length you want it to be.

5 Bind off loosely.

6 Pin the pocket sides and stitch them in place as shown.

HOW TO MAKE AN INSET POCKET

Inset pockets have a less noticeable appearance than patch pockets, as the front of the pocket is actually your knit garment. You knit the back of the pocket, or the lining, separately and put it on a stitch holder ahead of time; then you incorporate it when knitting the face of the garment that contains the pocket. You should follow your pattern's instructions for size and placement of an inset pocket. The following steps illustrate how to create an inset pocket.

1 Knit the pocket lining(s) to the size indicated in your pattern's instructions. Instead of binding off the stitches, put them on a stitch holder. Steam the lining to block it.

Note: Pocket linings are usually knit in stockinette stitch so that they lie flat. You can knit a pocket lining in the same color as the overall piece, or, if you prefer, you can knit the lining in an accent color.

2 On the piece of the garment that will hold the pocket, work across the row on the RS to where the pocket will be placed. Bind off the same number of stitches as used to knit your pocket lining and work to the end of the row.

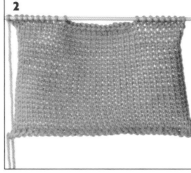

3 On the following row (WS), work across to the bound-off stitches. Hold your pocket lining so that the WS is facing you. (The RS of the lining will be facing the WS of the main garment piece.) Work across the lining stitches from the holder.

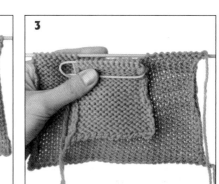

Note: You may have to slip your lining stitches from the holder to a needle if the stitch holder feels awkward or is not facing the right direction for you to work from it.

4 On the next row (RS), work across as usual and continue on that piece of the garment as established.

5 At the finishing stage of your garment, pin the bottom and sides of the pocket lining in place and stitch to attach (see "How to Attach a Patch Pocket" on the previous page).

6 Steam the sewn-in lining to flatten it, taking care not to press, which would bring the outline of the lining to the front of your work.

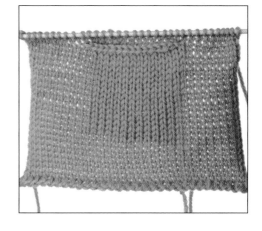

Note: You can also make an inset pocket by putting the stitches where the pocket is to be placed onto a holder after working across them on the RS. Then you continue across the row to the end and place the lining. At the finishing stage, you can then work from the held stitches to create an edging, such as ribbing, seed stitch, or garter stitch.

You work some collars by picking up the stitches around the neck and knitting on a collar directly; you work others as separate pieces that you sew on to the neck later. You can work any collar in a wide variety of stitch patterns; they can even have cables or color work involved. It is best to use a stitch pattern that does not curl, such as ribbing, seed stitch, or garter stitch, or to knit a flat-lying border around the edge of the collar to temper the curling.

SEWN-ON COLLAR

One easy way to make a collar is to knit it as a separate piece and then sew it on. You measure your sweater's neck circumference to determine how long to make the collar. When you have finished knitting it, you sew it on with the RS facing if it will fold down, so that you don't see the seam along the neck edge.

TURTLENECK

For a turtleneck like the one shown, you pick up stitches from the right side and knit in the desired pattern to the desired length. You can work a crewneck or turtleneck like this either back and forth in rows by working the collar when only one shoulder seam has been sewn and then sewing the collar's side seam later. Or you can work this type of collar in the round after both shoulder seams have been sewn.

KNIT-ON COLLAR

You can pick up stitches along the neck to create a collar. When knitting a split-front collar directly onto a sweater, you need to be sure to pick up stitches from the wrong side if the collar is going to fold down.

You can sew a zipper into the front of a cardigan instead of using buttons. A thin but firm edging like garter stitch or single crochet will help it look neat. The following instructions are for sewing a zipper into a sweater, but you can use the same technique to attach a zipper to a knitted bag.

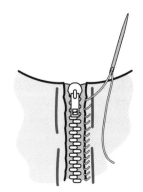

How to Attach a Zipper

Be sure that the edge that the zipper is sewn to is the same length as the zipper, or your garment will be distorted.

1. With the zipper closed and the RS of your garment facing, pin the zipper along and under the front edges so that the edges are almost touching each other and so that they cover the teeth of the zipper.

2. Still working on the RS, use a contrast color thread to baste the zipper to the sweater edges to temporarily hold it in place. Make sure your stitches are close to the zipper teeth for a firm hold.

3. Working on the WS, use thread in a matching color to neatly and evenly whipstitch the outside edges of the zipper to the fronts of the sweater.

4. Turn back to the RS and neatly sew the edges of the sweater to the zipper, right next to the teeth, but not so close as to interfere with the zipper's functioning.

3

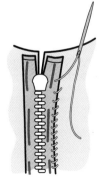

4

Making Pompoms and Tassels

You may want to liven up a scarf, hat, or sweater with one of these decorative additions. For pompoms and tassels, you can use either the same yarn used to knit your item or a contrast color.

HOW TO MAKE A POMPOM

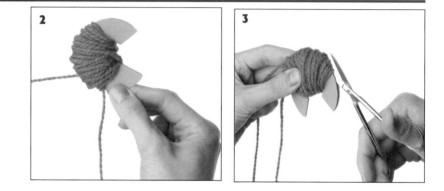

1. Cut two pieces of cardboard into circles the size you want your pompom to be. Cut a pie piece out of each circle and then cut a circle out of the center of each of the circles. The two pieces should be identical.

2. Match up the two cardboard pieces, one on top of the other, and wrap the yarn around them tightly and densely. Cut the yarn end.

   Note: *Use less yarn for a loose pompom and more yarn for a dense pompom.*

3. Insert the scissors between the two circles and under the yarn, as shown. Cut the yarn all the way around the outside of the cardboard pieces.

4. Bring a strand of yarn that is at least 12 inches long between the two cardboard circles and around the center of the cut yarns. Tie it very tightly in a square knot.

5. Remove the cardboard circles and trim the edges of the pompom to make it nice and round.

HOW TO MAKE A TASSEL

1. Cut a piece of cardboard into a rectangle the length you want your tassel to be.

2. Wrap the yarn around the cardboard to the desired thickness.

3. Thread a tapestry needle with a 12-inch strand of the same yarn and insert the needle between the cardboard and the wrapped yarn. Tie the strand's ends in a knot at the top edge of the cardboard.

4. Cut the tassel free along the bottom edge of the cardboard.

5. Wrap a 10-inch strand of yarn around the tassel a few times, about ½ inch down from the tied end and tie the ends tightly in a knot. Conceal the strand's ends by threading them through a tapestry needle, pulling the needle through the tassel top, and trimming.

6. Trim the tassel ends to neaten them.

Fringe can use up a fair amount of yarn, so make sure you have enough before you begin. Fringe made with thick yarn requires fewer strands of yarn than fringe made with thin yarn. Experiment with different thicknesses or amounts of yarn to see what works best for your particular project.

1. Determine how long you want your final fringe to be. Cut yarn to double that length, plus an inch extra for the knot.

2. Hold the strands together, with the ends matched up, creating a loop at the top.

3. Hold your knitting with the right side facing you. Insert a crochet hook from front to back into the corner, just above the cast-on row.

4. Take hold of your loop of folded strands with the crochet hook and use the hook to pull the strands through from back to front.

5. Pull the loop from under the cast-on row and pull the fringe ends through the loop and tighten.

6. Repeat steps 2–5 across the base of your knitting to complete the fringe.

7. When you have finished attaching the fringe, trim it with scissors so that it is even.

Making Knitted Balls

A knitted ball can decorate hats, scarves, shawls, and pillows. You can sew it directly on your knitting or first sew on a knitted cord and then attach it so that it dangles. To make a knitted ball, you need a set of double-pointed needles several sizes smaller than your yarn recommends.

How to Make a Knitted Ball

1. Cast on 8 sts and divide them among 3 double-pointed needles, leaving a 6-inch tail.

2. Join rnd, and using a 4th double-pointed needle, knit into the front and then into the back of every st—16 sts.

3. Knit 3 rnds.

4. Next rnd: K1, m1, *k2, m1; rep from * to last st, k1—24 sts.

5. Knit every rnd without further shaping until ball measures 2 inches from cast-on edge.

6. Next rnd: *K2tog; rep from * to end—12 sts.

7. Rep last rnd once more—6 sts.

8. Cut yarn, leaving a 6-inch tail. Pull tail through rem stitches, cinch tight, and secure.

9. Stuff bits of polyester stuffing into the ball through the hole at the cast-on end until it is firm.

10. Thread tail left from casting on through a tapestry needle and weave it in and out along the cast-on edge. Cinch tight and secure. (You can use this end later to sew the ball to your knitted item.)

11. Weave in the end at the top, pulling it down through the center of the ball and trimming it to neaten up the top.

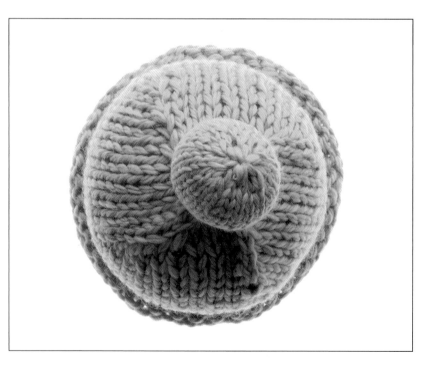

You can use knitted and twisted cords for all kinds of useful details, such as hat ties, bag handles, and mittens cords.

Knitted cords also have all sorts of decorative uses. Try looping and configuring one into a heart or flower decoration for a hat. Or use knitted cords in place of fringe. You can make a twisted cord with two or more colors or yarn types to create a cord with a lot of color or texture.

HOW TO MAKE A KNITTED CORD

Knitting a cord is like knitting in the round on a tiny scale. You need two double-pointed needles suitably sized for your yarn.

1 Cast on 5 or 6 stitches onto a double-pointed needle.

2 Knit across the stitches but do not turn your work.

3 Push the stitches back to the other end of the double-pointed needle, so you're ready to work a RS row again. Insert the second double-pointed needle into the first stitch to knit as usual but firmly pull the working yarn from the end of the row to knit.

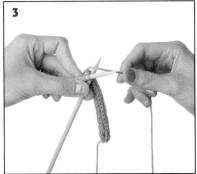

Note: *Beginning the row (round, actually) by pulling the yarn from the opposite end closes the tube.*

4 Repeat steps 2 and 3 until the cord is the desired length. Bind off or cut the yarn and pull it through all the stitches to tighten.

HOW TO MAKE A TWISTED CORD

The thickness of a twisted cord depends on the thickness of the yarn and on the number of strands twisted together. If the cord will be used to bear weight, be sure to make it thick.

1 Determine how long you want your twisted cord to be. Then cut a few strands of yarn three times that length. Knot the strands together at each end.

2 Insert a knitting needle at each knotted end and pull the strands taut. Twist one of the needles in a clockwise motion until the strands are tightly spun together.

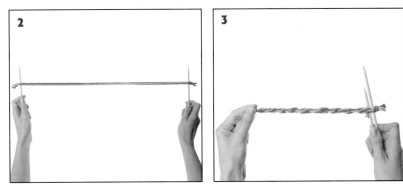

Note: *If your strands are longer than your arm span, anchor one knotted end on a coat hook, a doorknob, or another stationary object.*

3 Maintaining a tight tension on the strands, and taking care not to let them untwist, fold them in half–holding the fold loop firmly in one hand–so that the knotted ends are lined up with each other. Let go of the ends, and the cord twists itself together, forming an elegant rope.

Crocheting

You don't have to be a crochet expert to finish your knitting with simple crocket edgings or chains. A crochet edge can not only neaten and firm up an unstable or curling edge, but it also adds interest and color to a plain-looking piece of knitting. To crochet, you need yarn and a suitably sized crochet hook.

CROCHET CHAIN

Crochet chains work well as hat ties, sewn on as outlines for decorative motifs, or as cords from which to hang pompoms.

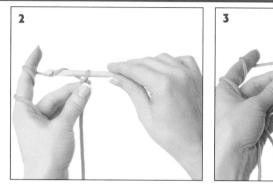
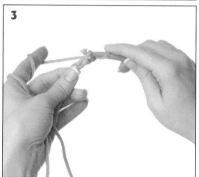

2

3

1 Make a slipknot, leaving a 6-inch tail, and slip it onto a crochet hook.

2 Wrap the working yarn around the hook from back to front (creating a yarn over loop) so that the hook catches the yarn.

3 Holding the working yarn in your left hand and the hook in your right, pull the yarn over loop on the hook from back to front through the slipknot.

You have made 1 loop in a chain.

4 Repeat steps 2 and 3 until the chain is the desired length. Cut the yarn, leaving a 6-inch tail, and pull it snugly through the last loop to finish the chain.

SINGLE CROCHET EDGING

Single crochet provides a neat, firm edge. You work this edging from right to left.

1 Insert a crochet hook that is one or two sizes smaller than the needles used for your knitting into your knitting at the right corner of the edge, with RS facing.

2 Loop the yarn around the hook (yarn over) and pull the loop through.

3 Working from the front, yarn over and pull a new loop through the first loop.

4 Insert the crochet hook into the next stitch to the left on the knitting, yarn over, and pull a new loop through.

You now have 2 loops on the crochet hook.

5 Yarn over the crochet hook again and pull this new loop through both loops already on the hook.

6 Repeat steps 4 and 5 across the edge. When you are done, cut the yarn and pull it through the last loop to finish the edging.

PICOT EDGING

Crocheting a picot edging makes a fancy edge that looks great on feminine sweaters and baby knits.

1 Choose a crochet hook that is one or two sizes smaller than the needles used for your knitting. Insert the hook into your knitting at the right corner of the edge.

2 Work 1 single crochet (see steps 2–5 on the previous page).

3 Chain 3 (or 4, if desired).

4 Insert the crochet hook back into the same stitch, yarn over, and bring up a loop.

5 Yarn over again and pull the loop through both loops on the hook.

6 Single crochet 2 (into the next 2 stitches, moving left).

Note: To create more space between picots, you can single crochet 3 or 4 times.

7 Repeat steps 3–6 across the edge to create picot edging. Cut the yarn and pull it snugly through the last loop to finish the edging.

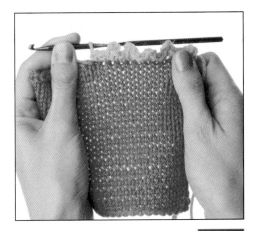

Adding Embroidery

You can decorate your knitting with embroidery stitches, using yarn or embroidery floss, after you have blocked your work. To do any of these embroidery stitches, start by threading a tapestry needle with the yarn you want to embroider with.

BLANKET STITCH

Blanket stitch is just like buttonhole stitch, but you do it on a larger scale to create an edging.

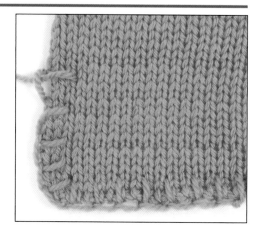

1 Tie a knot in the yarn end about 6 inches up from the bottom. Bring the needle through at the edge of your knitting from back to front, pulling the yarn through until the knot stops it.

2 Moving right to left, insert the needle at the desired depth into the edge and bring it out again to the front, as shown, taking care that the needle tip overlaps the yarn coming out of the starting point.

3 Repeat step 2 along the edge of your knitting to create blanket stitch. When you are done, weave in the yarn end.

DUPLICATE STITCH

This is a fun stitch that duplicates the knit stitch—the V—right on top of it. You can use this stitch to create motifs that look knit in.

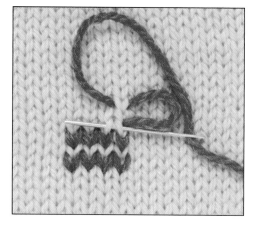

1 Bring the needle through the knitting at the hole just below the V that you want to duplicate. Pull the yarn through, leaving a 6-inch tail.

2 Insert the needle from right to left under both loops of the V above the stitch you want to duplicate; pull the yarn through all the way.

3 Reinsert the needle into the hole below your stitch—the same hole that the needle came through in step 1—and bring it out again below the next stitch to be worked, all in one movement.

4 Repeat steps 2 and 3 to create duplicate stitch. When you are done, weave in the yarn end.

STEM STITCH

Stem stitch is a good outlining stitch, and of course it makes a nice stem for embroidered flowers.

1. Make a ¼-inch straight stitch to start, leaving a 6-inch tail of thread at the back of your work.

2. Bring the needle back through from back to front just next to the center of the stitch you made in step 1.

3. Holding the yarn with your left thumb above the point where it just came through, reinsert the needle about ¼ inch to the right of the first stitch, bringing the needle out at the end point of the first stitch.

4. Repeat step 3 to create stem stitch. When you are done, weave in the yarn end.

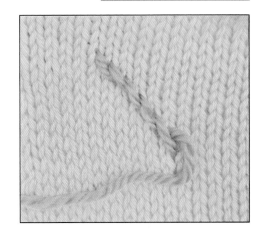

FRENCH KNOT

You can use French knots for infinite purposes: as the centers of lazy daisies, as eyes, or as accents along a line at a border.

1. Tie a knot in the yarn 6 inches up from the end. Bring the needle through the knitting from back to front, pulling through until the knot stops it.

2. Grasp the yarn about 1 inch above the point where it came out and wind the yarn around the tip of the needle three times, moving from the eye of the needle to the tip.

3. Still grasping the wound yarn, reinsert the needle right next to the point where it came out and pull it through all the way to the back to create the knot.

4. Continue making French knots by pulling yarn from back to front and then repeating steps 2 and 3. When you are done, weave in the yarn end.

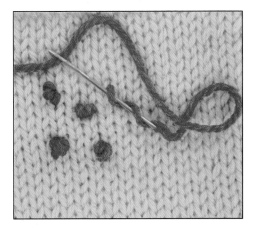

LAZY DAISY STITCH

You can use lazy daisy stitch to embroider flowers onto your knitting. You can use a French knot in the center of each flower.

1. Bring the needle through from back to front, pulling the yarn through and leaving a 6-inch tail at the back.

2. Hold the yarn in a loop and reinsert the needle right next to where it came out in step 1; bring the needle back out over the loop a petal-sized stitch away.

3. Insert the needle just below the loop that is the end of the petal and then bring it back out to the front, above the stitch, as shown, ready to work the next petal.

4. Repeat steps 1–3 in a circle, until you have completed the daisy. When you are done, weave in the yarn end.

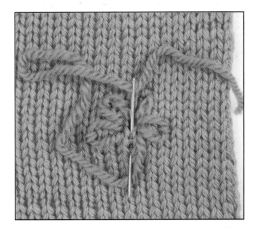

Reference Materials

You can refer to this appendix for knitting abbreviations as well as ideas for how to personalize your knits by working interesting stitch patterns and fancy knit borders into the master patterns or into your own designs. You can choose one of the patterns here or find inspiration in other stitch pattern books. To begin, you need to make a gauge swatch in your chosen stitch pattern. Next, you should compare your gauge to that in a master pattern and choose a size; or you can figure the stitch count required for your own design, based on the gauge swatch.

Abbreviations

The following abbreviations are commonly used in knitting patterns.

KNITTING ABBREVIATIONS

Abbreviation	Meaning	Abbreviation	Meaning
alt	alternate	g; gr	gram(s)
approx	approximately	grp	group
BC	back cross	g st	garter stitch
beg	beginning	hdc	half double crochet
bet	between	htr	half treble (crochet)
BO	bind off	in(s)	inch(es)
C	cable; cross; contrast color	inc(s)	increase(s); increasing
cab	cable	incl	including
CB	cable back	k	knit
CC	contrast color	k1b	knit into back of stitch
CF	cable front	k2tog	knit 2 stitches together
ch	chain; crochet hook	k3tog	knit 3 stitches together
circ	circular	kfb; kf&b	knit into front and back of stitch
cm	centimeter(s)	k tbl	knit through back of loop
cn	cable needle	kwise	knitwise
CO	cast on	l	left
cont	continue(s); continuing	LC	left cross
cr l	cross left	LH	left-hand
cr r	cross right	lp(s)	loop(s)
dbl	double (crochet)	LT	left twist
dc	double cross or double crochet	M	main color
dec(s)	decrease(s); decreasing	m1	make one
diag	diagonal	mb	make bobble
diam	diameter	MC	main color
DK	double knitting	med	medium
dpn(s)	double-pointed needle(s)	mm	millimeter(s)
dtr	double treble (crochet)	ms	make star
epi	ends per inch	mult	multiple
FC	front cross	no	number
foll	follow(s); following	opp	opposite

Abbreviation	Meaning
oz	ounce
p	purl
p1b	purl into back of stitch
p2sso	pass 2 slipped stitches over
p2tog	purl 2 stitches together
p3tog	purl 3 stitches together
pat; patt	pattern
pfb	purl into front and back of stitch
pm	place marker
prev	previous
psso	pass slipped stitch over
p tbl	purl through back of loop
pu	pick up
pwise	purlwise
RC	right cross
rem	remain; remaining
rep(s)	repeat(s)
rev	reverse
rev St st	reverse stockinette stitch
RH	right-hand
rib	ribbing
rnd(s)	round(s)
RS	right side
RT	right twist
sc	single crochet
sel; selv	selvage
sk	skip
skp; skpo	slip 1, knit 1, pass slipped stitch over
sl	slip; slipping
sl st	slip(ped) stitch

Abbreviation	Meaning
sm	small
sp	space
ssk	slip, slip, knit
ssp	slip, slip, purl
st(s)	stitch(es)
St st	stockinette stitch
TB	twist back
tbl	through back of loop(s)
t-ch	turning chain
TF	twist front
tog	together
tr	treble (crochet)
wpi	wraps per inch
WS	wrong side
wyib	with yarn in back
wyif	with yarn in front
yb; ybk	yarn at back
yd(s)	yard(s)
yf; yfwd	yarn forward
yo	yarn over
yo2	yarn over twice
yrn	yarn around needle
*	repeat starting point
**	same as *, but used to separate * instructions from the new instructions
( )	alternate measurements and/or instructions
[ ]	instructions that are to be worked as a group the specified number of times

Stitch Patterns

It's easiest to incorporate a stitch pattern that has a repeat that fits evenly into your stitch count. For example, if your sweater back requires 64 stitches, look for a stitch pattern that is a multiple of 2, 4, 8, or 16. If it doesn't fit in evenly, be sure to center the pattern on the piece and take into account that you will have incomplete repeats at each end.

TEXTURE STITCH (MULT OF 2 STS PLUS 1)

This pattern looks a little like moss stitch but has a tighter feel because of the stitches knit in the row below.

1. Row 1 (WS): K2, *p1, k1; rep from * to last st, k1.
2. Row 2 (RS): K1, *k1 in st below, k1; rep from * to end.
3. Row 3: K1, *p1, k1; rep from * to end.
4. Row 4: K2, *k1 in st below, k1; rep from * to last st, k1.
5. Rep rows 1–4 for texture stitch.

SEED STITCH CHECK (MULT OF 10 STS)

This attractive pattern can look very large and bold when worked in bulky yarns, or it can be delicate and tiny when worked in thinner yarns.

1. Rows 1, 3, and 5 (RS): *P1, k1, p1, k1, p1, k5; rep from * to end.
2. Rows 2, 4, and 6 (WS): *P5, p1, k1, p1, k1, p1; rep from * to end.
3. Rows 7, 9, and 11: *K5, p1, k1, p1, k1, p1; rep from * to end.
4. Rows 8, 10, and 12: *P1, k1, p1, k1, p1, p5: rep from * to end.
5. Rep rows 1–12 for seed stitch check.

ALTERNATING DOTTED RIB (MULT OF 4 STS PLUS 3)

This stitch works well as an allover pattern. It looks like a rib but doesn't pull in as much as a traditional rib.

1. Row 1 (RS): K1, *p1, k3; rep from * to last 2 sts, p1, k1.
2. Rows 2 and 4 (WS): Purl.
3. Row 3: *K3, p1; rep from * to last 3 sts, k3.
4. Rep rows 1–4 for alternating dotted rib.

RICKRACK RIB (MULT OF 3 STS PLUS 1)

This is a very pretty, busy pattern that looks great on vintage-style sweaters.

1. Row 1 (RS): K1 tbl, *yo, k2tog tbl, k1 tbl; rep from * to end.

2. Rows 2 and 4 (WS): P1 tbl, *p2, p1 tbl; rep from * to end.

3. Row 3: K1 tbl, *k2tog, yo, k1 tbl; rep from * to end.

4. Rep rows 1–4 for rickrack rib.

UNDULATING RIB (MULT OF 4 STS PLUS 2)

This pattern is worked like a 2x2 rib, but the addition of twisted stitches and yarn overs gives it a cabled look.

1. Row 1 (WS): K2, *p2, k2; rep from * to end.

2. Row 2 (RS): P2, *[k2tog tbl then knit same 2 sts tog through front loops], p2; rep from * to end.

3. Row 3: K2, *p1, yo, p1, k2; rep from * to end.

4. Row 4: P2, *sl1 wyib, k1, psso, k1, p2; rep from * to end.

5. Rep rows 1–4 for undulating rib.

BELL RIB (MULT OF 5 STS PLUS 2)

This is a beautiful pattern that makes an exciting edging for a women's sweater. It also works well as an allover pattern.

1. Rows 1 and 3 (RS): P2, *k3, p2; rep from * to end.

2. Rows 2, 4, and 6 (WS): K2, *p3, k2; rep from * to end.

3. Row 5: P2, *yo, sl1, k2tog, psso, yo, p2; rep from * to end.

4. Rep rows 1–6 for bell rib.

CONTINUED ON NEXT PAGE

STAR STITCH (MULT OF 4 STS PLUS 1)

This stitch is made up of little knots that look like stars. This pattern includes the following abbreviation:

> ms (make star): p3tog, leaving sts on left needle, then wrap yarn around right needle and purl same 3 sts tog again.

1 Rows 1 and 3 (RS): Knit.

2 Row 2 (WS): P1, *ms, p1; rep from * to end.

3 Row 4: P3, ms, *p1, ms; rep from * to last 3 sts, p3.

4 Rep rows 1–4 for star stitch.

OPENWORK ROWS (MULT OF 2 STS PLUS 1)

This four-row pattern looks almost like a grid of openwork.

1 Row 1 (RS): Purl.

2 Row 2 (WS): *P2tog; rep from * to last st, p1.

3 Row 3: P1, *[purl through the horizontal strand of yarn between last st worked and next st], p1; rep from * to end.

4 Row 4: P1, *yo, p2tog; rep from * to end.

5 Rep rows 1–4 for openwork rows.

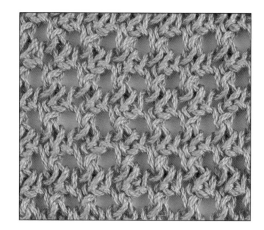

KNOTTED EYELETS (MULT OF 3 STS)

This pattern is easy to work, and the result is a fancy textured stitch that looks great for babies', girls', and women's knits.

1 Row 1 (RS): K2, *yo, [k3, pass the first of these 3 knit sts over last 2 sts just worked]; rep from * to last st, k1.

2 Rows 2 and 4 (WS): Purl.

3 Row 3: K1, *[k3, pass the first of these 3 k sts over last 2 sts just worked], yo; rep from * to last 2 sts, k2.

4 Rep rows 1–4 for knotted eyelets.

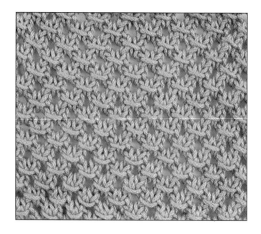

DIAGONAL LACE (MULT OF 6 STS)

This lace pattern is lovely for baby clothes and summer cardigans.

1. Row 1 (RS): *K1, yo, ssk; repeat from * to end.
2. Rows 2, 4, and 6 (WS): Purl.
3. Row 3: *K2, yo, ssk, k2; repeat from * to end.
4. Row 5: *K3, yo, ssk, k1; repeat from * to end.
5. Repeat rows 1–6 for diagonal lace.

FLOWER LACE (MULT OF 8 STS)

This stitch works well as an allover pattern on summer cardigans and shawls.

1. Rows 1 and 9 (RS): Knit.
2. Row 2, 4, 6, 8, 10, 12, 14, and 16: Purl.
3. Rows 3 and 7: K3, *yo, ssk, k6; rep from * to last 3 sts, k3.
4. Row 5: K1, *k2tog, yo, k1, yo, ssk, k3; rep from * to last 2 sts, k2.
5. Rows 11 and 15: K7, *yo, ssk, k6; rep from * to last st, k1.
6. Row 13: K5, *k2tog, yo, k1, yo, ssk, k3; rep from * to last 3 sts, k3.
7. Rep rows 1–16 for flower lace.

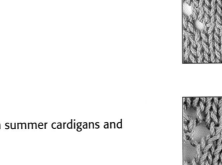

ZIGZAG LACE (MULT OF 6 STS PLUS 1)

Here's a lively openwork pattern that works up over only four rows.

1. Row 1 (RS): K1, *yo, sl1, k1, psso, k1, k2tog, yo, k1; rep from * to end.
2. Rows 2 and 4 (WS): Purl.
3. Row 3: K2, *yo, sl1, k2tog, psso, yo, k3; rep from * to last 5 sts, yo, sl1, k2tog, psso, yo, k2.
4. Rep rows 1–4 for zigzag lace.

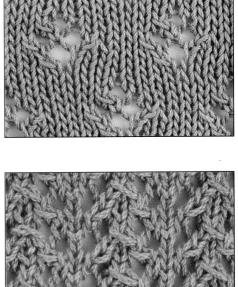

CONTINUED ON NEXT PAGE

WOVEN CABLE STITCH (MULT OF 4 STS)

This pattern, which looks like real basketweave, includes the following abbreviations:

C4F: Slip the next 2 sts to a cable needle (cn) and hold at front, knit the next 2 sts, k2 from cn.

C4B: Slip the next 2 sts to a cn and hold at back, knit the next 2 sts, k2 from cn.

1 Row 1 (RS): *C4F; rep from * to end.

2 Rows 2 and 4 (WS): Purl.

3 Row 3: K2, *C4B; rep from * to last 2 sts, k2.

4 Rep rows 1–4 for woven cable stitch.

HORN CABLE PANEL (16-ST PANEL)

Here's a cable that looks important enough to take center stage but is also simple enough to frame a larger cable. This pattern includes the following abbreviations:

C4F: Slip the next 2 sts to a cable needle (cn) and hold at front, knit the next 2 sts, k2 from cn.

C4B: Slip the next 2 sts to a cn and hold at back, knit the next 2 sts, k2 from cn.

1 Row 1 (RS): K4, C4B, C4F, k4.

2 Rows 2, 4, and 6 (WS): Purl.

3 Row 3: K2, C4B, k4, C4F, k2.

4 Row 5: C4B, k8, C4F.

5 Rep rows 1–6 for horn cable panel.

CLUSTER RIB PANEL (14-ST PANEL)

This pattern uses a cable needle but does not involve actually moving stitches around. The clusters are formed by wrapping at regular intervals the stitches that make up the rib panel.

1 Rows 1, 5, 7, 9, 11, 13, and 15 (RS): P2, *k2, p2; rep from * twice.

2 Row 2, 4, 6, 8, 10, 12, 14, and 16: K2, *p2, k2; rep from * twice.

3 Row 3: P2, k2, *p2, k2; rep from * once; [slip the last 10 sts worked from the right needle onto cn and wrap working yarn around these 10 sts, counterclockwise, three times, then slip the wrapped stitches back to the right needle]; p2.

4 Rep rows 1–16 for cluster rib panel.

BIG CABLE PANEL (12-ST PANEL)

This cable twists to the right, but you can make its mirror image—a big cable that twists to the left—by holding the stitches on the cable needle to the front of the work in row 5. This pattern includes the following abbreviation:

> C12B: Slip the next 6 sts to a cable needle (cn) and hold at back, knit the next 6 sts, k6 from cn.

① Rows 1, 3, and 7 (RS): Knit.

② Rows 2, 4, 6, and 8 (WS): Purl.

③ Row 5: C12B.

④ Rep rows 1–8 for big cable panel.

NAUTICAL CABLE PANEL (24-ST PANEL)

Here's a traditional cable that is perfect for fisherman's knits. This pattern includes the following abbreviations:

> C6B: Slip the next 3 sts to a cable needle (cn) and hold at back, knit the next 3 sts, k3 from cn.
>
> C6F: Slip the next 3 sts to a cn and hold at front, knit the next 3 sts, k3 from cn.
>
> T5B: Slip the next 2 sts to cn and hold at back, knit the next 3 sts, p2 from cn.
>
> T5F: Slip the next 3 sts to cn and hold at front, purl the next 2 sts, k3 from cn.

① Rows 1 and 5 (RS): P2, k3, p4, k6, p4, k3, p2.

② Rows 2, 4, 6, 8, 10, 12, 14, and 16: K the k sts and p the p sts.

③ Row 3: P2, k3, p4, C6F, p4, k3, p2.

④ Row 7: P2, T5F, p2, k6, p2, T5B, p2.

⑤ Row 9: P4, T5F, C6F, T5B, p4.

⑥ Row 11: P6, *C6B; rep from * once, p6.

⑦ Row 13: P4, T5B, C6F, T5F, p4.

⑧ Row 15: P2, T5B, p2, k6, p2, T5F, p2.

⑨ Rep rows 1–16 for nautical cable panel.

Here are a few simple color knitting patterns you can try. Each pattern is illustrated with a stitch pattern chart and a companion color key.

COLOR PATTERN 1:
TWO COLORS

This 6-stitch, 4-row repeat is an easy allover pattern.

COLOR PATTERN 2:
THREE COLORS

This 9-row border pattern works well at the hem or cuff of a Fair Isle sweater.

COLOR PATTERN 3:
THREE COLORS

This 4-stitch, 6-row repeat is a nice allover pattern for sweaters, vests, and mittens.

Sometimes a plain sweater, blanket, or other knitted item needs to be dressed up a little. The borders here can add a special accent to your knitting. If the number of stitches required for your knitting does not work exactly with these numbers, cast on a number that works for the border and that is close to your desired number. Decrease or increase a few stitches evenly across one of the last rows at the end of the border to reach the correct stitch count.

CURLY RUFFLE

This is a fun ruffle that looks great on baby blankets and little girls' sweaters. You need to cast on four times the number of stitches you want to end up with, minus 3. For example, if you want to end up with 60 stitches, you cast on 237 stitches to create a curly ruffle.

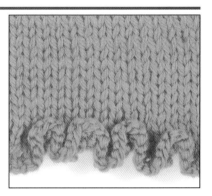

1 Row 1 (RS): K1, *[k2, pass the 1st of these 2 sts over the 2nd and off the needle]; rep from * to end.

2 Row 2 (WS): P1, *p2tog; rep from * to end.

Note: You can work this ruffle on smaller needles if you want the ruffle to be tighter.

BOBBLED BORDER

This border, which is worked over a multiple of 6 stitches plus 5, creates a nice three-dimensional edge. It includes the following stitch:

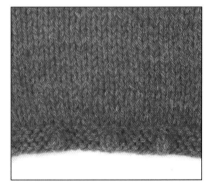

   make bobble (mb): Knit into the front, back, front, back, and front (that's five times) of the next stitch. Without turning work, use the left needle to pick up the 4th stitch and pass it over the 5th and off the needle; pass the 3rd stitch over the 5th and off the needle; pass the 2nd stitch over the 5th and off the needle; and finally, pass the 1st stitch over the 5th and off the needle.

1 Rows 1 and 3–5 (WS): Knit.

2 Row 2 (RS–bobble row): K2, *mb, k5; rep from * to last 3 sts, mb, k2.

MINI SCALLOPS

This is a pretty little edging that is easy to do and adds a delicate touch. You start the edging with a multiple of 5 stitches plus 2 and end with a multiple of 4 stitches plus 1, so plan the body of your garment based on the resulting stitch count.

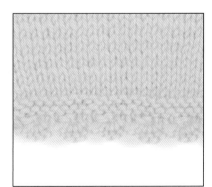

1 Row 1 (RS): K1, yo, *k5, [pass the 2nd, 3rd, 4th, and 5th sts over the 1st st and off], yo; rep from * to last st, k1.

   You now have a multiple of 2 sts plus 3 on your needle.

2 Row 2 (WS): P1, *[p1, yo, k1 tbl] all in next st, p1; rep from * to end.

   You now have a multiple of 4 sts plus 1 on your needle.

3 Row 3: K2, k1 tbl, *k3, k1 tbl; rep from * to last 2 sts, k2.

4 Rows 4–6: Knit.

Index